Finally, an accessible book on the depths of misogyny; its pervasiveness in our relationships, workplace, healthcare, government, churches, and entertainment; and the need for allies, advocates, and interrupters! *For the Love of Women* is a great title because it is truly a book of hope. Dorothy Littell Greco helps us imagine what is possible. She helps us name and identify misogyny, reveals the harm, and provides the antidote. I hope it is widely read!

Aimee Byrd, author of *Recovering from Biblical Manhood and Womanhood* and *Saving Face*

For the Love of Women empowers Christian readers who want to transform the ravages of misogyny because they follow a Jesus who values women. Greco deftly traces the through lines of misogyny throughout history, demonstrating how women have been unfairly blamed for humanity's problems, which has caused harm to women (and men) through medicine, sexualized violence, and sexist theology. An intelligent and utterly timely reframe that reclaims faith-based spaces as safe, *For the Love of Women* offers readers a path forward.

Tia Levings, author of *New York Times* bestseller *A Well-Trained Wife: My Escape from Christian Patriarchy*

For the Love of Women offers an insightful look at the challenges women face in modern life, uncovering the distortions and biases that we too often accept as normal. Greco's journalistic attention to detail pairs with a deep pastoral sensibility that shepherds readers through these difficult conversations and on to the work of envisioning a future of goodness and life—one where women and men flourish together.

Hannah Anderson, author of *All That's Good*

For the Love of Women is a prophetic, pastoral, and grace-filled book. If you are a woman, you will see something of your own experiences in these pages. If you know a woman, you will see something of her experiences here. If you love a woman—any woman, including yourself—I urge you to read this book, which wisely and lovingly exposes a great wrong that is deeply woven into our whole world (including the church)—and then wisely and lovingly points a way forward.

Karen Swallow Prior, author of *You Have a Calling*

The paramount need for a more biblical and thoughtfully Christian view on gender cannot be overstated. This need emerges not only from neglect but also from a diseased imagination and dysfunctional practices around gender that have become the unfortunate norm in many Christian spaces. Neither a screed nor a confession, this now essential text calls for the dismantling of misogyny while also offering a fresh biblical imagination for a better way forward. Greco offers irenic words of pastoral grace without sacrificing a necessary prophetic edge—a helpful antidote to a chronic illness of our times.

Soong-Chan Rah, Robert Boyd Munger Professor of Evangelism and Church Renewal, Fuller Theological Seminary; author of *Prophetic Lament*

It takes a woman of courage and conviction to call out a subject that is difficult yet necessary. I am so proud of Dorothy for doing the hard work that many shy away from. *For the Love of Women* unearths the deeply rooted systems of injustice toward women that have permeated every stream of society. At the same time, Dorothy gives us healthier ways to plant seeds for our benefit and toward coflourishing together. Illuminating, thought-provoking, challenging, and healing, this book is a defining work for our time.

Dorena Williamson, bestselling author, bridge-builder, and pastor

Despite enormous progress achieved in the twenty-first-century battle against ongoing violence, abuse, and injustice against women and girls, this battle will never end until we dismantle it from the roots up. In *For the Love of Women*, Dorothy Greco exposes the cultural, social, and theological forces that continue to hold women down. Only when we understand the depth of the crisis will we be able to find remedies both globally and in our own cultural context. Dorothy has made a significant contribution to our understanding, and I pray her book will be widely read by women and men alike.

Carolyn Custis James, author of *Half the Church* and *Malestrom*

This book is undeniably outstanding. In *For the Love of Women*, Greco skillfully and systematically addresses the ways in which misogyny has shackled women (and men), cultivating a culture of death and destruction. Misogyny hurts everyone. This book is well researched; Greco thoroughly supports her claims. That misogyny exists in all sorts of forms and has ingrained itself into our personal lives, theology, and systems is irrefutable. Greco is clearly brilliant, brave, and bold to write such a book in a Christian context. In doing so, she is doing her part to uproot and upend misogyny within her spheres of influence. I would go so far as to say that this book is mandatory reading for any thoughtful Christian or Christian leader in the United States and throughout the world.

Dr. Marlena Graves, author of *Bearing God* and *The Way Up Is Down*

Dorothy has carefully, clearly, and compassionately helped us understand misogyny—not just "out there" in the world but also "in here" within our churches and organizations. This book is not only a sobering reality check but also a source of hope for a way forward on the path of Spirit-filled harmony and unity. Her research is thorough and honest, and her biblical grounding is firm and edifying. I pray male leaders, as well as skeptics and faithful followers of Jesus, will humbly engage her work. We will all be better for it.

Quina Aragon, author of *Love Has a Story*

Dorothy Littell Greco's courageous effort is not an easy read. But the need for this book is as urgent as ever. It challenges our presuppositions about how we love and respect women. Littell Greco unpacks how misogyny is a form of interpersonal and systemic cruelty that endangers women's lives and the communal flourishing of us all. *For the Love of Women* prompts us to walk the hard road toward repentance. Although it's long overdue, we must take up God's deep love and concern for all women and do right by them.

Sheila Wise Rowe, author of *Healing Racial Trauma*, and Nicholas Rowe, PhD, Hansen Associate Professor of Leadership, Gordon Conwell Theological Seminary; coauthor with Sheila of *Healing Leadership Trauma*

FOR THE LOVE OF WOMEN

Uprooting and Healing Misogyny in America

DOROTHY LITTELL GRECO

ZONDERVAN REFLECTIVE

For the Love of Women

Published by Zondervan, 3950 Sparks Drive SE, Suite 101, Grand Rapids, MI 49546, USA.
Zondervan is a registered trademark of The Zondervan Corporation, L.L.C., a wholly owned subsidiary of HarperCollins Christian Publishing, Inc.

Requests for information should be addressed to customercare@harpercollins.com.

Zondervan titles may be purchased in bulk for educational, business, fundraising, or sales promotional use. For information, please email SpecialMarkets@Zondervan.com.

ISBN 978-0-310-16670-2 (softcover)
ISBN 978-0-310-16672-6 (audio)
ISBN 978-0-310-16671-9 (ebook)

Names and identifying characteristics of some individuals have been changed to preserve their privacy.

Published in association with the literary agency of WordServe Literary Group, Ltd., www.wordserveliterary.com.

HarperCollins Publishers, Macken House, 39/40 Mayor Street Upper,
Dublin 1, D01 C9W8, Ireland (https://www.harpercollins.com)

Cover design: Faceout Studio, Jeff Miller
Cover art: Shutterstock
Interior design: Lori Lynch

Printed in the United States of America

25 26 27 28 29 LBC 5 4 3 2 1

For our granddaughter Pippa.
We wish you could have stayed longer.
We miss you every day.

For Effie.
Thank you for being a tenderhearted truth teller.

And for all the women across the globe who have been or are being harmed by misogyny. You are not invisible, and you are not forgotten.

CONTENTS

Misogyny: A persistent, insidious belief that men's ideas, wants, needs, and experiences are more important than women's and that legal, religious, and social systems, as well as intimate relationships, should uphold this principle. This belief system subsequently influences the laws, policies, practices, and ethos of a given culture.

FOREWORD

Today, bones mark the town of Rothwell in Northamptonshire, England. A rare thirteenth-century ossuary rests under the floor of Holy Trinity Church, containing the mixed-up skeletons of around 2,500 individuals—many of which seem to be the remains of plague victims. The local website recounts the story of an eighteenth-century gravedigger who accidentally discovered the crypt. He reportedly never recovered his mind after falling through several feet of darkness into a pit of bones.[1] It is a grim story.

But it isn't as grim as another story about Rothwell. Several years ago, a PhD student I advised was working on her dissertation. She ran across a letter written in March 1422 by the bishop of Lincoln, Richard Fleming, to an archdeacon and dean in Northamptonshire about a small, poor nunnery in their area: the Rothwell Priory.

This is some of what he wrote:

> Certain henchmen of the wickedness of Satan . . . fell by night and after the fashion of pirates upon a place of religion and set apart to God, to wit the priory of the nuns of Rothwell . . . [and] seized with violence a certain woman of gentle and honest report, by name Joan . . . the while she struggled and made protest according to her strength, and brought her away by force and violence and . . . vilely overcome and violated the same [woman] against her will.[2]

In short, a group of men broke violently into a nunnery, attacked a woman named Joan, dragged her away, and raped her. Then, later in a second attack still targeting Joan, the same men expanded their violence to include physical assault on the nuns and prioress.

> Entering the same priory a second time . . . with naked swords and other sorts of divers weapons of offence, fell . . . upon the same woman, who was then in the presence of the prioress and the nuns in the hall of the same priory—and cudgeled them with cruel strokes, threw them down on the ground and, trampling on them with their feet, mercilessly kicked them and violently dragged off the garment of their habits over their heads, and even as robbers, having caught their prey, carried off the said woman, dragging her with them out of the priory.[3]

Horror permeates Fleming's words. Even six centuries later, his grief for the women and anger against the men responsible comes through his letter loud and clear. The bishop concluded by issuing the harshest sentence in his power, pronouncing excommunication for these "henchmen of satan." He made it clear that the assaulted women were not at fault; only the male aggressors were guilty.

I don't know the outcome of Fleming's letter. I don't know if the perpetrators were caught. I only know that a bishop stood against the violent attack in Rothwell Priory. He protected the female survivors and condemned their male attackers.

As I thought about this, I was reminded of the story of Jennifer Lyell, a survivor of alleged sex abuse by the hand of her seminary professor.[4] She had lost her job at a denominational publishing house after the denominational publishing house portrayed her accusations of sexual assault as a consensual affair. Instead of standing with her, like Bishop Fleming did for the survivors of Rothwell Priory, her faith community stood against her, portraying her as sexually complicit, some even calling her a whore or Jezebel.

The difference between how a medieval bishop stood against violence for women and what I have witnessed from the church's response to abuse survivors today stands out so starkly to me. Likely, the reason Bishop Fleming knew about the attack on Rothwell Prior was because of the survivors. The women told him what happened to them. Perhaps even Joan herself recounted the violence of the assault on her body. He believed the women, and he stood with them. The church today frequently treats the survivors of sexual assault quite differently.[5] Instead of believing their stories and standing with the women, it prioritizes protecting the institution.

Violence against women, rooted in misogyny, is a tale as old as time. It's a story so common it has become unremarkable—we are so accustomed to it that we glaze over the rape and attack of Hagar by Abram and Sarai; we accept our preacher's account of Bathsheba's "complicity" in her "affair" with David. Instead of reflecting the justice and love of God, we have institutionalized hatred and violence against women, even calling it theology.

This is why what Dorothy Greco has written in these pages is so important. The story she tells is like the story of Rothwell Priory. It is hard to hear, brutal in its reality, and convicting to our souls. It doesn't matter if you agree with all her conclusions. I rarely agree with everything I read. What matters is that you listen to her. By writing this foreword, I have chosen to stand with Dorothy Greco against misogyny. It is now your turn, for the love of women, to listen and decide if you will do the same.

Beth Allison Barr
James Vardaman Professor of History, Baylor University
Author of *The Making of Biblical Womanhood*

INTRODUCTION

Over the last twenty-four months, countless friends have asked me, often in a perplexed tone, "Why are you writing a book on misogyny?" I wrote this book because misogyny has been harming American women for almost 250 years and it's time for that to stop.

Back when I was born in 1960, misogyny was shamelessly status quo.

Banks could randomly deny credit applications for married women unless their husbands served as cosigners.[1] Women could be fired at will from certain jobs, like teaching, when they became pregnant.[2]

Only two women served in the Senate and seventeen in the House of Representatives. Legislation addressing women's unique needs—including gender-based discrimination, sexual harassment in the workplace, and a lack of protection from abusive spouses—was still a long way off.

The false beliefs about women's physical strength even limited their recreational opportunities. Women's basketball had six players, three on each side of the half-court line, because men assumed traversing the entire court would be too taxing. The 1960 Olympics offered female athletes twenty-nine events. The male athletes had 121 options.[3] Women couldn't compete in Olympic marathons until 1984, when American Joan Benoit won the gold.

I never had the option of seeing a female doctor or hearing a woman preach until after I graduated college in the early 1980s.

Much has changed since 1960. In 2022, 38 percent of physicians in the US were women, and their numbers continue to grow. As of 2025, twenty-six women serve in the US Senate and 125 in the House of Representatives. Married women can now open their own line of credit without their husband's approval. Women can't be fired from their jobs when they become pregnant (at least not legally). Top female athletes can get paid for winning marathons and playing full-court basketball.

More Americans are now familiar with the concept of misogyny. This is partially attributable to the six million women who courageously typed #MeToo into their social media feeds in 2017, thus drawing attention to the pervasive nature of sexual assault, sexual harassment, and other forms of sexualized misogyny.[4] This was quickly followed by the #ChurchToo movement, which exposed similar abuse in churches and religious organizations.

Based on the increased opportunities and legal protections for women, perhaps we could assume misogyny is no longer an issue. As recently as 2016, a Pew Research Center study revealed that 45 percent of Americans agreed with the statement "the obstacles that once made it harder for women than men to get ahead are now largely gone." And while 41 percent of the men surveyed thought women "still face obstacles that make it harder to get ahead," 56 percent believed "those challenges have mostly been eliminated."[5]

But is this accurate? Are we approaching a post-misogynistic America? Though significant gains have been made, misogyny has not disappeared. A 2023 survey revealed that 45 percent of adult women reported "experiencing gender-based discrimination" at least occasionally.[6] We can't claim misogyny has been eradicated if nearly half of US women continue to experience discrimination—which is only one iteration of misogyny. As I hope to demonstrate throughout this book, misogyny isn't a problem of the past; it's a present-tense, ongoing reality, and it affects every aspect of our culture.

Freedom, justice, safety, and equality do not currently exist for all women in our country. Reaching these goals will require new laws and regulations, top-down changes, a whole lot of repentance, and an unwavering commitment to value, respect, and love women.

One of the main purposes of this book is to help us identify misogyny in all its overt and covert forms. To that end, we'll explore its ancient roots, trace it throughout history, reveal its many adaptations, and learn to recognize how it shows up today.

For the Love of Women examines six spaces in culture where misogyny has influenced laws, policies, structures, expectations, and behaviors: healthcare, the workplace, the government, entertainment and media, sexual relationships, and the church. The final two chapters explore how women and men can heal from the effects of misogyny and partner together to diminish it.

Because it's easy to dismiss misogyny as a problem "over there," I've focused on North America, primarily the United States, though the examples transcend geographic boundaries.

I interviewed dozens of individuals while writing this book. The identities of most of the interviewees have been changed to protect their privacy. This will be notated by an asterisk after the first use of their pseudonym.

I had to make many difficult choices about what to include in this book; it easily could have been twice as long. With this in mind, I've included a list of resources in the appendix.

For the Love of Women is not a memoir, though it is deeply personal. *For the Love of Women* is not an exposé, though some of the content may be distressing. It's not academic, but it contains substantial research. And since I love and respect many men, this book does not promote misandry—the hatred of men.

I'm a journalist with pastoral instincts who writes from a faith-based perspective. My desire to follow Jesus influences all of who I am and how I move through the world. You don't have to agree with my beliefs to appreciate this work. And though you'll see references to Scripture and spiritual concepts, I resist using religious jargon and endeavor to explain anything that might be unfamiliar to those of you who don't share my convictions.

I write as a heterosexual White woman who cares deeply about the intersectionality of misogyny and race. That said, this text will inevitably fail to fully articulate what misogyny looks like from the perspective of Black, Indigenous, Latina, Asian, and other marginalized women.* I'm extremely grateful to all the women who have trusted me with their stories. I've learned a great deal from them and plan to continue doing so.

I wrote this book primarily for women who've had first-person experiences of misogyny. Because misogyny harms, shames, and tries to silence us, I wanted to give voice to and validate our experiences. But this offering isn't only for women. Despite women's courage, resilience, and strength, we won't succeed in eradicating misogyny without men's partnership, which is why I long for men to read this book with curiosity and humility.

It will be important for all of us to hold an awareness of our biases as we progress through the book. Biases—both explicit (conscious) and implicit (unconscious)—function as filters, affecting how we see and understand ourselves and those around us. Biases are shaped by our family of origin, the culture in which we live, and experiences we've had throughout our lives. We see explicit bias and understand at least some of how it affects us. We tend to be unaware of our implicit biases, which means they can be dangerous liabilities.

As you read this book, if you notice yourself feeling defensive, angry, or uncomfortable, try to discern if I might be challenging a bias. Pay attention to those feelings, but please don't let them deter you from engaging with the subject matter. While no one likes to be confronted regarding their beliefs, behaviors, or biases, discomfort in the face of an injustice doesn't have to culminate in shame or self-condemnation.

---

* From this point on, I will use the term *Women of Color* when referring to Black, Hispanic, Asian, Latina, and other Women of Color.

Instead, it can provide the impetus for personal and systemic change, which we need if we hope to diminish misogyny.

The topics and the intensity of this book may trigger complex reactions for some of you. I've tried to avoid graphic details regarding violence, abuse, and sex. Please read slowly and pay attention to what your body may be telling you. Keep a journal if that helps you process. Move your body if you feel dysregulated. Talk to trusted friends or schedule a few sessions with a counselor if you need additional support. If the early chapters feel discouraging, jump ahead to the chapter on healing. If you have a trauma background, you might want to skip the sections on rape culture toward the end of chapter 4, violence in the media in chapter 5, and sexualized violence at the end of chapter 6. The chapter headings will give you advance warnings.

It's long past time for Americans to address the ways misogyny adversely affects us. The #MeToo and #ChurchToo movements raised our collective consciousness, but awareness should never be the end goal when we're talking about injustice. As theologian and author Carolyn Custis James writes in her book *Half the Church*, "One can't simply learn the truth and sit on it. Truth not only changes how we see ourselves, it changes what we do and how we live."[7]

I'm hoping *For the Love of Women* will inspire the type of change that leads to healing, justice, and freedom for all women.

CHAPTER 1

THE AIR WE BREATHE

Misogyny's Persistence and Prevalence

I've spent my entire life gathering research for this book.

By the time I was five, people were referring to me as a "tomboy" because I preferred athletic endeavors and Matchbox cars to dress-up and Barbies. Back then, I didn't understand what stereotypes or rigid gender norms were, but I certainly understood I was being critiqued.

In high school, I experienced the disparities between how girls' and boys' athletic teams were funded and supported. Title IX had become law, but that didn't mean schools and universities obeyed it. The girls' teams were never allowed to practice on "the boys' football field" (the only full-size field our school had) and our athletic director refused to line said field before our home field hockey games. This forced my coaches to purchase enormous bags of flour and line it themselves. The boys enjoyed a new large, bright locker room adjacent to the gym they had first rights to. The girls' locker room was aptly referred to as the dungeon, and we worked around the boys' practice schedules.

While I was on assignment in Central America as a twenty-seven-year-old photojournalist, a policeman pulled me over. He leaned into the car and, upon discovering I was alone, informed me I would need to pay him a bribe or have sex with him. He finally allowed me to drive away after I told him my husband would be very angry to learn this man had dishonored me. I was single at the time but wore a fake wedding ring at the recommendation of other female journalists who had previously navigated this terrain.

Years later, I was walking home from the grocery store when our elderly neighbor approached me to say hello, as was his habit. But on that afternoon, in the middle of the street in metropolitan Boston, he put his hand on my crotch and asked me if I liked sex. I was eight months pregnant and wearing an actual wedding ring.

The chronic health issues that flared up in my forties started in first grade. Symptoms included cramping and frequent diarrhea, anemia, eczema, and annual bouts of bronchitis or pneumonia. I lost count of how many doctors poked, prodded, scoped, and examined me over the next forty years. Because I was functional and didn't exhibit any visible symptoms, most of these healthcare providers discounted my discomfort and told me to "stop worrying so much."

When the pain and fatigue became debilitating after our third son was born, my primary care doctor suggested I see a rheumatologist. After spending ten minutes with me, he informed me depression was the root cause of my health issues and hastily wrote me a prescription. As I walked out of the exam room, I threw the Rx in the biohazard bin and said, "If I'm depressed, it's because no one is listening to me or helping me get well." Two years later, a female naturopath figured out I had celiac disease. I will continue to deal with the ramifications of being misdiagnosed for the remainder of my life.*

In my fifth decade, a West Coast radio personality invited me on his show after reading an article I'd written detailing how my husband and I were raising our three sons to value and respect women. After a few minutes of cordial pleasantries, he dropped this bomb:

---

* As is true for me, undiagnosed, unaddressed celiac disease often leads to autoimmune diseases such as Hashimoto's, fibromyalgia, and a host of other complicated issues that currently have no cure.

> I've noticed that the primary cause of boys hating women starts in the home. Most boys hate their mothers because their mothers have so dominated and controlled them. She imposes her will on them, on their innocence, and the father is not able to stop the mother from doing this because he's been destroyed by his own mother. I guarantee you that unless your boys change, they're gonna be wimpy men. They're gonna go through hell because women hate weak men. They will never get married.

Rather than asking if he wanted to talk about his mother wound, I hung up and promptly burst into tears. (For the record, all our sons have married beautiful, strong women who have voiced appreciation for our parenting choices.)

I was almost sixty when the pastor at the church my family attended asked me to speak on Mother's Day. My husband served as the worship pastor. The week before, as he and the administrator worked out the details for that service, he casually mentioned I would be preaching. A few days later, she clarified I would be sharing, not preaching, because apparently only the (male) pastor could speak from the pulpit with authority. After multiple awkward email exchanges, my husband and I decided it would be best if I backed out. This incident confirmed our suspicion that I would never be fully embraced in this body. We left several months later.

Each of these experiences reveals a different facet of misogyny, including rigid gender roles, biased healthcare, unjust implementation of laws, male entitlement, abuse of power, and the muting of women's voices.

I need not ask female readers to imagine what it's like to endure such scenarios. Nearly all of you have similar stories or others that are far more consequential. In fact, episodes of mistreatment, harassment, and abuse happen so often that most of us cannot imagine life without them. For the men who are reading, chances are not many of you have had experiences like mine. If that's true, you might want to ask yourself why such experiences are axiomatic for women and either unfamiliar or unimaginable for most men.

Despite undeniable progress for women in the twentieth and twenty-first centuries, misogynistic ideologies and the behaviors that flow out of them are so deeply embedded and so widespread that society tends to overlook or excuse them as normative. We laugh off the politician's crude comments. We diminish sexual assault by claiming boys will be boys—or worse, by blaming the innocent woman. We even refer to predatory leaders as misunderstood or victimized visionaries rather than criminals. We accuse the brave women who dare to name their perpetrators of being liars or sluts.

All this excusing and minimizing not only harms women but belies the deeper issue. Misogyny is real. It exists in every culture. It harms everyone. Including men.

Misogyny Is . . .

Before we can pull down the beams that hold up misogyny, we must be able to identify and understand it more fully. The literal meaning of the word *misogyny* is "the hatred of women." But that's not the definitive or even the most helpful definition, because many people who engage in misogynistic behaviors or hold misogynistic beliefs don't hate women. At least not overtly. Linguist Ben Zimmer notes that misogyny "has more to do with ingrained prejudices against women than a pathological hatred of them."[1]

If we define *misogyny* too narrowly, we may be tempted to disregard or deny it. Misogyny encompasses more than specific, tangible acts committed by individuals who admittedly despise women, such as popular, self-proclaimed misogynist Andrew Tate.[2] If we interpret violence or prejudice against women as random and label the Andrew Tates of the world as anomalies, we will fail to see the patterns. If we constrain the definition to include only violent, hateful acts, some men will distance themselves from the conversation and from having any responsibility to change it. We must understand the scope of the issue and expand the definition to fully encompass it.

Misogyny is a persistent, insidious belief that men's ideas, wants, needs, and experiences are more important than women's and that political, religious, and social systems, as well as intimate relationships, should uphold this principle. This belief system subsequently influences the laws, practices, and ethos of a given culture, eventually harming everyone—especially women and children.

Misogyny fuels discrimination, sexism, and other forms of unjust or illegal treatment due to women's biological sex. Misogyny blinds both individuals and entire cultures from seeing women as equal image bearers, fosters androcentric hierarchies, and disdains perceived weakness and vulnerability. According to author and philosopher Kate Manne, "Misogyny ought to be understood as the system that operates within a patriarchal social order to police and enforce women's subordination and to uphold male dominance."[3] It is a man-made construct supported by abuses of power, sustained by the kingdoms of this world, and opposed to God's purposes.

To understand misogyny more fully, we need to recognize all its facets.

Misogyny Is Ancient

Historic manuscripts and artwork reveal that misogynistic ideologies and practices are not new. The myth of Pandora offers a glimpse into how one culture explained the presence of evil while perpetuating misogyny. Most of us would probably recognize the iconic image of Pandora, a beautiful young woman expressing shock as she opens a small box, but the actual story is less well known.

As with many myths, the story of Pandora was first told orally and then written down during the eighth century BCE by the Greek poet Hesiod in *Theogony* and *Works and Days*. According to Greek mythology, many gods contributed to Pandora's character (*pan* meaning "many" and *dora* meaning "gifts"). This first mortal woman was referred to as a "kalon kakon" or "beautiful evil." Zeus sent her to earth as a bride for someone he held a grudge against, along with a mysterious sealed jar she was instructed to never open.[4] Her curiosity (a trait one of the gods had given her) eventually gets the best of her. She opens the jar, releasing evil into the world, and is subsequently blamed for its existence. Certainly, writing or telling the myth did not cause women to be mistreated and abused, but it does help us understand how people at that time associated misfortune and the origin of evil with women.

According to author Jack Holland, "If misogyny has a birthday, it falls sometime in the eighth century BC. If it has a cradle, it lies somewhere in the eastern Mediterranean."[5] The Greeks did not invent misogyny, but they did seem to codify it. They eventually coined the word *misogyny* in the seventeenth century, assumedly because no other word adequately described their past and present attitudes and behaviors toward women and girls. The ways women and girls were treated in Ancient Greece exemplify how individual behavior can simultaneously influence and be influenced by the larger culture. Though Greece was the birthplace of modern democracy, women were excluded from participating in it, not permitted to receive formal education, and seen as men's property. In ancient times, unwanted baby girls could be left on doorsteps or in garbage dumps where they would either die of exposure or be taken home and raised as slaves in Greek households.

Based on historic records, the Greeks weren't the only ones who engaged in misogyny. The ancient Chinese broke and then tightly bound young girls' feet, which prevented their feet from growing and caused lifelong pain. This was thought to increase their marriageability. Girls throughout parts of Africa have been forced to undergo female genital mutilation (FGM) since the sixth century.[6]

Misogyny Is Patriarchal and Hierarchal

Misogynistic beliefs and practices often thrive when patriarchy is normative—and throughout history, many cultures have been patriarchal.[7] In *Gender Roles and the People of God*, theologian Alice Mathews writes, "Whenever we find any arrangement . . . in which one person is 'under' the other person, we have some kind of hierarchy. When that hierarchy has the woman under a man's direction or rule, it's called patriarchy."[8] Historian Judith Bennett describes patriarchy as when male ecclesiastical leaders and male heads of households possess all legal power and when societies promote male authority and female submission.[9] Once a culture or society has codified misogyny (or any other social behavior that injures or discriminates), those on the receiving end of such treatment are viewed as inadequate, flawed, or even expendable.

Patriarchy prefers men and men's narratives. In many ancient cultures, it was a foregone conclusion that men were smarter, more gifted, and of greater value than women. Preferential treatment shows up in many ways, including passing on family properties and businesses to the sons even if the daughters are more inclined or capable. (Patriarchy is based on lineage.) Other iterations include esteeming sons over daughters, which contributed to the abortion and infanticide of girls in China,[10] and blaming women who were raped or sexually assaulted. (More on this in chapter 4.)

Whether we're talking about cultures, institutions, or relationships, patriarchies and hierarchies perpetuate misogyny through control. Control looks like gaslighting, intimidation, punishment, withholding of resources, the silent treatment, and physical and sexual abuse. Control also encompasses micromanaging women's day-to-day lives, including whom they socialize with and how they dress. In some cultures, the latter means concealing every inch of skin from the neck down, and in others, looking "smokin' hot" but never slutty.

Some men exert control by demanding that women relinquish their bodily autonomy (a form of male sexual entitlement), defer to and respect them, and never challenge their one-down positions. Once intimidation or violence has been used effectively against a woman, a man only needs to threaten to achieve the same result. If women comply, the system keeps running. But if women resist and expect or ask for more, they suffer tangible consequences, which we'll talk about throughout the book.

Misogyny Is Pervasive and Adaptable

Misogyny shows up in doctors' offices, courtrooms, boardrooms, and bedrooms. Though misogyny seems to prefer militaristic or dictatorial styles of governance where unbridled power rules, it's adaptable and can flourish in democracies and settings that purport to value gender equality.

Some expressions of misogyny are so blatant that it's impossible to dismiss them. For instance, when militant extremists shot Pakistani schoolgirl Malala Yousafzai in the face for daring to advocate for girls' education,[11] when girls are sold into sex trafficking rings across the globe, or when mainstream media glorifies sexualized violence against women.

It takes a bit more intention to spot the subtler forms. Misogyny is at play when girls are raised and praised to draw the male gaze rather than excel academically and when women's bodies are commodified for the purpose of selling products. When a male boss slowly slides his hand down a female employee's back until it just skims the top of her derrière and continues to talk nonchalantly, that's a form of misogyny. When adults tell boys they shouldn't cry—and shame them if they do—that's also an expression of misogyny. By labeling emotions as feminine, boys and men get the message that such feelings are inappropriate.

Misogyny Is Evil

Finally, if we look at the results of misogyny—hierarchies, blame shifting, division, destruction, physical and emotional harm, and even death—we can see evidence of a force that transcends individual choices. I would call this evil. Perhaps because it's less abstract to blame rogue players than to acknowledge that evil forces are influencing and pulling on us all the time, we often back away from using such binary, modernist terminology. I believe that's a mistake.

Evil is powerful and has the capacity to influence individuals and entire cultures. If we look back at the horrific genocides in Germany, Rwanda, Darfur, and Bosnia, or how Gisèle Pelicot of France was drugged and systematically raped over ten years by more than fifty men—*all recruited by her husband*—such crimes cannot be explained apart from there being some extrinsic force that entices people to behave in a cruel, inhumane fashion.[12]

The apostle Paul explains this concept of good and evil in the New Testament book of Ephesians: "Our struggle is not against flesh and blood, but against the rulers, against the authorities, against the powers of this dark world and against the spiritual forces of evil in the heavenly realms" (6:12 NIV). While acts of misogyny are expressions of evil, they are perpetrated by humans. The presence of evil should never be used to excuse anyone's actions.

In this spiritual framework, misogyny accomplishes several objectives. First and foremost, it seeks to prevent women and girls from flourishing. Second, it denies women the opportunity to have influence or authority. Third, it impedes women and men from partnering together as equals. This final objective is significant, because when women and men forge collaborative partnerships as two equal but distinct image bearers, they reveal God more fully. The enemy of humanity does not want God to be fully or accurately revealed and therefore uses misogyny to thwart this goal.

As we begin to see misogyny through these grids, we can't unsee it.

But Misogyny Is Not Inevitable

Though misogyny is persistent and pervasive, cultures and relationships do not have to be governed by it. We can be assured of this because of how God created the world. (Even if you do not believe in Judaism or Christianity, their ancient texts provide wisdom and insight regarding the human heart.) Before Eve and Adam made the fateful decision to disregard their Creator's boundaries, there is strong evidence of equality and mutuality between them. According to Genesis 1, Eve and Adam were to be co-laborers:

> Then God said, "Let us make human beings in our image, to be like us. They will reign over the fish in the sea, the birds in the sky, the livestock, all the wild animals on the earth, and the small animals that scurry along the ground."
>
> So God created human beings in his own image.
> In the image of God he created them;
> male and female he created them.
>
> Then God blessed them and said, "Be fruitful and multiply. Fill the earth and govern it. Reign over the fish in the sea, the birds in the sky, and all the animals that scurry along the ground." (Genesis 1:26–28 NLT)

Biblical scholar Philip Payne believes "nothing in the creation narrative subordinates woman to man."[13] God issued his commission to Eve and Adam with no indication of Adam being the project manager and Eve being his assistant. The Hebrew word translated as "helper" in Genesis 2, which has diminished connotations in our culture, is *ezer*.[14] Theologian Marg Mowczko explains that *ezer* "is consistently used in the Old Testament in the context of vitally important and powerful acts of rescue and support." She continues, "The word *ezer* is qualified by the word *kenegdo* in both Genesis 2:18 and 20. *Kenegdo*, sometimes translated as 'suitable for him,' gives the meaning that Eve was designed to be a corresponding and equal partner for Adam. There is no sense of subordination stated or implied, or even hinted at . . . in Genesis 2."[15]

When women and men work together to serve and care for God's creation, their differentness is complementary, or additive. If women and men are made in the image of God, then we represent God more accurately when we forge collaborative partnerships. Carolyn Custis James writes, "Adam is one. But the God he represents is plural—a Trinitarian three in one. A solitary image bearer cannot adequately or accurately reveal God in the world, much less fulfill his destiny as a human being."[16] The apostle Paul explains this in 1 Corinthians: "For as woman came from man, so also man is born of woman. But everything comes from God" (11:12 NIV). That kind of essential interdependence assumes equality and fosters harmony.

Prior to the fall, woman and man stood side by side, upright and naked, before their creator. Shame did not exist—because there was nothing to be ashamed of. Post-fall, they each bend away from God, toward their physical source. Men will be tempted, or inclined, to find their identity in work. Women will be tempted, or inclined, to find their identity in men. Both will be tempted to try to control and dominate, rather than live as equal partners who trust each other. Though the story isn't always recounted this way, God never curses Eve and Adam. He curses the snake and then proceeds to explain the consequences of man and woman's choice, including pain in child-birth and toil in work. God is *de*scribing how things will play out, not *pre*scribing. That prefix is incredibly important regarding how one understands male-female relationships, particularly within the church and marriage.

The harmony and unity of pre-fall relationships unravel quickly and the Bible doesn't redact any of it. Harmful misogynistic practices common in ancient cultures included no-fault divorce initiated by men, concubines, rape, the sacrifice of babies and children to idols, and the killing of women caught in adultery. The more God's people turned away from him, the more brokenness and pain they experienced. As patriarchy and gender-based hierarchies became normative, women were increasingly devalued and mistreated. Carolyn Custis James believes misogyny and patriarchy began after the fall: "From that point on, the *ezer-kenegdo* recedes in the biblical narrative. Patriarchy reduces the *ezer-kenegdo* to [a woman's] reproductive powers—specifically measuring a wife's value by the number of sons she bears. She is no longer a full partner in the mission God entrusted to humanity."[17]

Because God never abandons nor forsakes his creations, we can identify a redemptive arc revealing his intentions throughout Scripture. The fifth commandment instructs that fathers *and* mothers are to be honored. Amid a patriarchal and patrilineal culture, Job's daughters receive an inheritance (Job 42:15). Numerous Hebrew women served in significant leadership positions. Scripture tells us that Deborah—a prophet, judge, and the highest leader in Israel—was the answer to the Israelites' prayers for deliverance, not plan B, as some suggest.[18] The prophet Huldah "sparked the greatest revival in the history of Israel."[19] Isaiah prophesied that *all* will be called priests (Isaiah 61:6), and Joel predicted that God's Spirit will be poured out on *all* people, including women (Joel 2:28–29).

During his earthly reign, Jesus ministered to, loved, and valued women in ways that were breathtakingly different from how they were typically treated. He spoke one-on-one with the Samaritan woman at the well, which was taboo. He did not rebuke the woman who had been bleeding for twelve years for touching him, even though according to the custom of that time she should not have touched any man, let alone a rabbi. He offered a pardon and forgiveness for the woman caught in adultery—an offense that could have resulted in death by stoning. He validated Mary's desire to sit at his feet and learn, a spot typically reserved for male rabbinical students. Jesus overturned discriminatory practices against women and opened the way for female believers to participate in God's kingdom. Regardless of whether you believe Jesus is the Son of God or simply a compelling historic figure, his love for women shows us how to dismantle misogyny.

How Misogyny Affects Women

Though the public face of misogyny has certainly adapted over the last ten thousand years, the net results are the same. Women are blamed;

maligned; harmed physically, psychologically, and spiritually; and denied both opportunities and basic human rights.

Misogyny Blames Women

One of the consequences of misogyny is that women get blamed when bad things happen, even if the bad things happen to them. The myth of Pandora and the biblical creation narrative reveal how stories can be interpreted to justify the mistreatment and devaluation of women. (The biblical story differs from the Greco-Roman myths in that God offers the provision of covering for Eve's shame and promises that redemption will come through her offspring.)[20] Pandora did not create or even insert the evil powers into the jar; she naively opened it, thus exposing the world to evil. When the serpent sows doubt about God's goodness and trustworthiness to Eve and Adam, they fall for the lie. The two of them share the forbidden fruit, and as a result, sin, discord, enmity, and death enter the world. Adam was with Eve when this transpired (Genesis 3:6), but as we'll see in chapter 7, some theologians and pastors continue to place the blame squarely on Eve's shoulders even though that's not what the text says. In certain faith traditions, people continue to use this hermeneutic as proof that women are more easily deceived than men.

Though Pandora and Eve bear responsibility for the choices they made, neither of them committed any crimes of atrocity. Compared to men, women seldom do. Why, then, do so many cultures consistently blame women?

One of the reasons women get blamed is that people dislike ambiguity and vulnerability. We believe that if we understand why bad things happen, we can control or even prevent them. But many of the horrible things that happen in our world (like earthquakes, floods, and wildfires) cannot be understood or predicted. This reality may cause us to keep looking over our shoulders and wondering if we might be the next victims, something we want to avoid at all costs. Furthermore, no one wants to believe they have the capacity for evil—even though, as scholar N. T. Wright reminds us, "that fateful line runs down the middle of each of us"—which leaves us with a dilemma.[21]

We sense that evil is real but are unwilling to admit our own potential to harm others, so we conclude that evil must originate outside of us and blame it on individuals and people groups who are different. Because those who hold power also control cultural narratives—and historically in the US, this has been White men—women and other marginalized people groups tend to get blamed. Blaming "the other" absolves those in power and exempts them from any responsibility to change the system. It's important to note that women can be guilty of this behavior too. White women have colluded with misogyny by choosing proximity to power over supporting and protecting their sisters. This was evident during the practice of chattel slavery.

There's another layer worth examining. In Pandora's story, as well as in other ancient myths like Medusa, the female characters are beautiful. Why would men, most of whom are attracted to and appreciative of beauty, be inclined to conflate beauty with evil?

Some men have a complex response to women's beauty and sexuality. They want and need women, but to acknowledge this means they have a gap in their armor—that they are vulnerable. This is rarely acceptable in hyper-masculine, patriarchal cultures. When a man is undone by a woman's beauty, he might seek to subjugate her because he can't predict or control whether she will be dependably available and consistently true to him. It's easier to dominate and control than live as a tender, open-hearted man. By seeing women as temptresses—those who hold the power to seduce—men become the victims and bear less (or no) responsibility for their demeaning, destructive behavior. Of course, men are not victims of women's sexuality. They have agency and are therefore responsible. But misogyny allows them to tell another story.

Misogyny Harms Women's Bodies

Not only are women blamed for men's bad behavior, but they're also often on the receiving end of it. In 2023, 3,849 women and girls were murdered in the United States.[22] More than half of them died at the hands of an intimate partner or close relative. According to the World Health Organization (WHO), approximately one in three women is subject to intimate partner violence—both sexualized and nonsexualized.[23]

Not every argument that escalates to violence originates because of overtly misogynistic attitudes. However, many acts of violence are linked to the demands a man feels he has the right to make on a woman and the kinds of punishment he believes he has the right to impose if she doesn't meet those demands.[24] Whenever men use their greater physical strength against women, it's an expression of misogyny, regardless of the underlying motivation. Those who survive then live with a myriad of visible and invisible scars. The former includes battered bodies; red marks around a neck recently strangled; black eyes; bruises from being grabbed, pinched, or kicked; vaginal/internal damage due to rape or overly aggressive sex; STDs or HIV infections; and bald patches where hair has been pulled out.

Though the psychological and emotional ramifications of misogyny are less visible and therefore frequently minimized by outsiders, they are every bit as damaging. When the message of inadequacy and insufficiency gets drilled into women's heads over and over again, it's akin to psychological warfare. Women internalize the lies and begin to believe the false narrative that they're not as capable or worthy as their male counterparts and therefore don't deserve respect, equitable treatment, or the right to forge collaborative partnerships with men. If the lie goes deep enough, it has the capacity to distort their self-perception and result in depression, low self-esteem, self-hatred, or misandry. It may also lead some women to stay in abusive relationships because they don't believe they deserve better.

Misogyny Marginalizes and Diminishes Women

Women who are raised in, work in, worship in, or marry into a misogynistic reality become adept at intuiting when we're not fully welcomed or when we need to take up less space. On an almost daily basis, we perceive or hear that we're simultaneously too much and not enough. We then may choose to withhold the fullness of who we are because we've either lost track of our true self or concluded that men prefer a smaller, quieter, less powerful version. After I've read a room, it's become common for me to conclude that the least exhausting option is to withhold my opinions and appear less knowledgeable. If this is true for me as a White woman, I can't imagine the mental gymnastics Women of Color regularly go through. Keeping women off-balance and questioning themselves is one of misogyny's goals.

Confident, outspoken women like Joan of Arc, abolitionist Sojourner Truth, and activist Malala Yousafzai who refuse to comply with patriarchal norms threaten the system and pay an exorbitant price for doing so. The pushback that noncooperative women receive is directly related to society's expectations for them. In an interview, Kate Manne explains, "I think most misogynistic behavior is about hostility toward women who violate patriarchal norms and expectations, who aren't serving male interests in the ways they're expected to. There's this sense that women are doing something wrong: that they're morally objectionable or have a bad attitude or they're abrasive or shrill or too pushy. But women only appear that way because we expect them to be otherwise, to be passive."[25] Women who are temperamentally submissive, conflict avoidant, or less vocal might successfully fly under the radar and not attract male ire. As demonstrated by the #MeToo movement and the heroic protests across the globe,[26] women are increasingly less willing to go down without a fight.

Misogyny Traumatizes Women

After women are on the receiving end of emotional abuse or physical violence, trauma often resides in their bodies and has the potential to cause long-term harm. Dr. Nadine Nyhus defines trauma as "an experience that overwhelms a baby, child, or adult with feelings of powerlessness and that results in classic fallout symptoms, including re-experiencing symptoms (through triggering), negative thoughts, negative emotions, and avoidance. . . . It is important to note that even physical or emotional neglect can be traumatic if children feel overwhelmed and powerless as they strive to take care of themselves."[27]

Author and therapist Aundi Kolber defines trauma as "anything that overwhelms a person's nervous system and ability to cope."[28] Trauma was previously limited to acts of violence or threats on one's life, but mental health practitioners now understand trauma includes any events that "confront human beings with the extremities of helplessness and terror, and evoke the responses of catastrophe."[29] Additionally, as research unfolds on epigenetics, mental health experts see how trauma can be passed from generation to generation. Even if we never personally experienced any trauma, our ancestors' trauma might be encoded in our genetic makeup.

Post-traumatic stress disorder (PTSD) symptoms—including nightmares, flashbacks, and aversion to touch—are common for rape or other violent crime survivors and those who have endured ongoing emotional or physical abuse. Trauma survivors can live in a heightened state of alertness and anxiety that gradually wears out their immune system and leaves them more susceptible to long-term illnesses and mental health issues.

The tangible consequences of misogyny are overwhelming. So much so that it can feel challenging for women affected by misogyny to care how it adversely impacts men. But if women hope to find greater healing and help change the system, we will need a deeper understanding of this reality.

How Misogyny Affects Men

As we explore the cause and effect of misogyny throughout the book, it's important to remember that even though men have most of the power, they are also adversely affected by misogeny. Misogynistic beliefs and practices result in many unhealthy, unrealistic expectations about what it means to be a man in American culture, including limiting what emotions are acceptable, encouraging the abuse of power, and fostering male entitlement.

Misogyny Constrains Men's Emotions

American culture esteems strength and independence and equates certain emotions with weakness. Through the generations, American men have been taught to hide vulnerability or evidence of perceived weakness lest they be seen as feminine or less than. Late-night talk show host Jimmy Kimmel became visibly emotional while recounting stories of fellow Californians who'd lost everything in the apocalyptic fires of early 2025 that killed at least twenty-nine individuals and burned more than sixteen thousand homes and structures.[30] Given the devastation, Kimmel's response was appropriate. Joel Berry, managing editor of the *Babylon Bee*, disagreed. Berry eviscerated Kimmel for his vulnerability on the social media platform X, writing, "Good God, man. You're not being paid to cry like a little girl on stage. Your role is to give people a little laugh in a difficult time. If you can't hack it, get off the stage, you low-T narcissist. Disgusting and pathetic."[31]

In a zeitgeist where sadness and tears are unacceptable, anger is the sanctioned male emotion. Because of this, men and boys may become less capable of experiencing and offering all the emotions that are essential in healthy, mutual relationships. Frederick Joseph writes in *Patriarchy Blues*, "If a boy is taught at home or in society that boys don't cry, he will become a man who may not believe in empathy or compassion, maybe even see them as weaknesses. Those weaknesses will be replaced by something deemed more appropriate and aligned, such as anger."[32]

My husband, Christopher, works as a pastor and educator and grew up with an angry, sometimes raging father. He understands the damage that an out-of-control father can inflict on his children and the irony that culture seems to prefer angry men over gentle, tenderhearted ones. He explains, "Men face many contradictions and hypocrisies in contemporary American culture connected to their emotional lives." He acknowledges that male anger is palpable but recognizes that other more complex feelings are under the hood: "In my work as a pastor and counselor, I've opened many meetings by asking men to name one feeling from their day. They disprove the myth that men don't have a broad range of feelings, or if they do, don't know how to express them. Unfortunately, it's rarely beneficial for us to treat the workplace, the athletic field, or the dinner party as a sharing circle. If we reveal our mistakes or besetting limitations, we may be discredited, disrespected, or even punished. In American culture—even American church culture—perceived weakness isn't manly."

Rather than seeing themselves as good gifts with unique offerings, men who don't fit patriarchy's mold (for example, men who are intuitive, articulate about their emotional lives, or prefer activities typically perceived as less manly) can conclude that if they want to be accepted and succeed, their only options are to fake it and conform or opt out. But this may result in debilitating comparisons and self-condemnation. Author and educator bell hooks believes that "no male successfully measures up to patriarchal standards without engaging in an ongoing practice of self-betrayal."[33] In addition to the personal injury caused by trying to conform to rigid patriarchal standards, entire cultures lose out when men fail to develop and express a full range of emotions.

Misogyny Encourages Men to Seek, Prioritize, and Abuse Power

Misogyny emerges out of a hierarchical, patriarchal system that, according to Carolyn Custis James, "advantages and empowers some men and disadvantages and disempowers others."[34] Some men are afforded access to power and authority—or at least the illusion of both—but not all men. Those who succeed in accumulating power and reaching the top of any social-relational pyramid will need to expend a great deal of energy defending their status. This creates social standings that depend on power rather than on character or gifting.

When power is prioritized, certain roles lower down on the social hierarchy become less desirable or acceptable for men. Men who are the primary caregivers for their children or other family members may feel devalued and invisible, especially when they're in the company of surgeons, CEOs, or politicians. This is unfortunate, because what stay-at-home fathers do is every bit as vital as those other high-status roles.

Judging and then rewarding people based on who has the most power is a dangerous practice. When rank and power become the main markers of success, men will be discouraged from admitting their mistakes and serving others because humility and servitude are perceived as weakness. That's part of why Jesus's disciples were so offended when he washed their feet. A man who refuses to serve others or acknowledge his mistakes is not a safe man—in a marriage, a boardroom, a pulpit, or the Oval Office.

Men who live in misogynistic cultures and routinely cauterize their hearts to fit in can grow increasingly numb to the horrors of male violence and injustice. In cultures that idolize power, routinely devalue women, and discourage soft emotions, men and teenage boys become vulnerable to and capable of committing unthinkable atrocities. Recent examples include soldiers raping women in Ukraine and Sudan (the latter has been going on for ten years and includes violating children as young as one).[35] Misogyny "ignites a dark ambition"[36] in the souls of many men, particularly when it happens collectively.

Misogyny Encourages Male Entitlement

Entitlement is one of the dark ambitions that emerges in a misogynistic culture. (We will be returning to this topic throughout the text.) Entitlement includes holding expectations for unconditional respect, unwavering deference, humble submission, and sex on demand from whomever they want. The belief that men deserve these benefits simply because they have both x and y chromosomes infantilizes them. They never have to mature and earn respect. Entitled men unwittingly find themselves on a particular continuum—from "the playground to the boardroom"—that demands ever-increasing displays of power, authority, and competitiveness.[37] The treadmill only increases in speed and has no off switch. One must consciously—and bravely—jump off.

Misogyny is a lose-lose system. No one wins, not even the men who are idolized and supposedly successful. Because I'm the mother of three sons, debunking the fallacy that misogyny doesn't harm men is one of the motivating factors for writing this book.

What's Ahead

An illness can't be healed unless it's accurately diagnosed. Similarly, systemic wrongs cannot be righted unless they are first identified. As it pertains to how women are valued and treated, the source of the illness and the name of the wrong are one and the same: misogyny.

While the #MeToo and #ChurchToo movements succeeded in raising consciousness and initiating important changes connected to misogynistic practices, we still have much work to do. Misogyny is not confined to the director's couch, certain old-boy networks, Hooters restaurants, or ultra-conservative religious sects. As my friend Brian Marchionni explained, it's "an unexamined cultural norm that's buried in subconscious thought"[38] and shows up everywhere. Misogyny is neither morally neutral nor random. It's pernicious and calculated.

Where ignorance enables misogyny, knowledge and truth can be the beginning of freedom. Once we have a clear picture of what misogyny looks like and how it adversely affects us, we should be motivated to dismantle it and create cultures, institutions, and relationships where women and girls have ample opportunity to thrive and men and women collaborate as equal partners.

Such goals are ambitious but by no means unattainable. If God is making all things new, then misogyny will not have the final word.

CHAPTER 2

IT'S ALL IN YOUR HEAD (OR MAYBE YOUR UTERUS)

Misogyny in Healthcare

Women's healthcare has dramatically improved over the past fifty years. More research is being done on issues that affect women. New screening and treatment methods are being developed. More women are becoming doctors. Given these improvements, we might assume bias and discrimination against women are no longer issues in the American healthcare system. Things *are* getting better, but misogyny's influence lingers in ways that sometimes go unrecognized and therefore unchallenged. This is particularly evident connected to diseases and conditions that are female specific.

Eliza* began menstruating when she was eleven. Not long after, she started having severe abdominal pain, nausea, vomiting, diarrhea, and extreme fatigue on an inconsistent but regular basis. According to her mom, Melissa,* "Eliza would miss school and other activities and obviously felt terrible physically. But then she started developing other mental health symptoms that got progressively worse, including major depressive symptoms, irrational thinking, risk-taking behaviors, and suicidal ideation. Other times, she was a completely normal, amazing teenager, which made it confusing to understand what was happening."[1]

Melissa recounts, "Eliza thought she was going crazy. She felt ashamed for the way she was feeling and acting and yet couldn't do anything to help herself. As her mother, I was frightened by the worsening symptoms and unsure of how to help her."

During this time, Eliza saw multiple doctors and mental health experts. She was taking both over-the-counter pain meds and an array of psychiatric medications that either didn't help, made her symptoms worse, or had severe side effects. None of the doctors or specialists ever suggested that the symptoms might be related to her menstrual cycle.

Melissa kept a close watch on her daughter. Years later, a friend recommended tracking Eliza's symptoms with her periods. The overlap quickly became clear. After taking her to see additional doctors and digging into research on her own, Melissa finally figured out Eliza had premenstrual dysphoric disorder (PMDD), a rare and severe form of premenstrual syndrome (PMS) caused by a "cellular genetic malfunction in response to hormone changes."[2] When Melissa brought up the possibility of Eliza having PMDD, her healthcare providers discounted her insight but reluctantly followed her lead. She requested Yaz, a contraceptive drug known to successfully treat this disorder, from her daughter's primary care physician (PCP), who was a woman.[3]

Without communicating what she had done, the doctor ordered a different oral contraceptive.[4] Melissa didn't realize what happened until her daughter became suicidal: "This doctor refused to give me the correct prescription. I also requested a referral to a mental health treatment program to make sure Eliza stabilized, which the doctor also refused." The PCP then accused Melissa of making up and exaggerating her daughter's symptoms, stopped taking her calls, and blocked her from getting Eliza an expedited appointment with an OB/GYN.

PMDD is known to cause many of the extreme symptoms Eliza was experiencing. Because patients with this condition may have an increased risk of suicidality, Melissa was justified in demanding her daughter receive timely help.[5] As she reflects on this experience, Melissa acknowledges, "It was horrible."

This is a challenging chapter to write. It would be disastrous if the world lacked doctors, surgeons, physicians' assistants, nurses, and countless other healthcare professionals. They diagnose our diseases, set our broken bones, vaccinate our children, and reduce our pain. During the 2020–22 pandemic, we witnessed their courage and commitment to serve in real time—some even giving their lives. I believe most healthcare providers tend to be problem solvers who care and genuinely want to help. Increasingly, many doctors are expressing frustration that the system makes their job more difficult.[6]

All told, it took five years for Eliza to be properly diagnosed and get the support she needed. Certainly, Eliza's experience cannot implicate all or even most PCPs. However, many women, me included, who have slogged through complex or long-term health issues will confirm that finding healthcare providers who listen to, believe, and support us is not a given. Often, the onus for piecing things together and finding solutions falls on our shoulders. We have to walk the tightrope of advocating for ourselves while demonstrating respect for our providers lest we be labeled as difficult or hypochondriacs. Be forewarned: Shedding tears or displaying anger can quickly discredit you and get you labeled as a hysteric. We must stay one step ahead of our insurance providers to determine if the blood work or scans will be covered. And after telling our stories ad nauseum, we may still be dismissed or minimized, which is demoralizing.

Navigating healthcare in the United States as a woman is not as easy or linear as it might be. In fact, an industry that's supposed to facilitate healing sometimes fails and even harms women. It's therefore imperative that we learn to recognize and call out any of the ways misogynistic mindsets and practices may be fueling bias, discrimination, and mistreatment in healthcare because women's lives are on the line.

An Abbreviated History of Women's Healthcare

Though women have always served as healers and caregivers, men have tended to shape and control the medical world until the late 1900s, when more women started becoming doctors and teaching in medical schools. Cultural biases against women combined with centuries of discriminatory practices (including blocking their admission to colleges and grad schools) have perpetuated misogyny in healthcare. As Dr. Karen Tang explains in her book *It's Not Hysteria*, "History provides the philosophical framework of modern-day medical systems."[7]

Bias against women stretches way back. Hippocrates, often referred to as the "father of medicine," was born approximately 460 BCE. He initiated case studies and advocated treating all patients equally. Despite his innovative approaches, Hippocrates couldn't escape the cultural prejudices about women, which subsequently influenced how he understood and diagnosed female maladies. Hippocrates and other ancient scholars like Plato and Aristotle perceived females to be "weaker, slower, smaller versions of the male human ideal."[8] Women were relegated to this lesser status in part because of their unique anatomy. Possessing a womb obviously benefited culture by housing all future generations for their first nine months, but instead of being esteemed as a blessing, women's lady parts were often seen as the cause of their illnesses—including psychological ones.

Because some influential voices in early medicine believed women's "sole purpose was . . . to bear and raise children, their health was entirely defined by the uterus."[9] The combination of bias (both explicit and implicit), androcentrism, and a lack of data resulted in curious practices for addressing female health needs. One Egyptian document written in approximately 1800 BCE and credited as "the oldest available medical record of Egyptian civilization" included fumigating and dousing women's vaginas and uteri with plants, minerals, and animal by-products, including donkey urine.[10]

Author Elinor Cleghorn explains, "The idea that all women's diseases were related to their reproductive functions seems, today, like the worst kind of misogynistic conspiracy. But in ancient Greece, where women's entire social existence was defined by their uteruses, it made perfect sense that the disorders and dysfunctions of the bodies and minds would be too."[11] Given their limited knowledge of the human body and that dissection was illegal, their ignorance about anatomy is understandable. What's baffling is how men linked women's unique ability to carry and birth children to unworthiness and weakness. Clearly, none of these men ever endured labor contractions or pushed a baby through a birth canal.

Until late in the Middle Ages, it was commonly believed that the uterus moved, or wandered, within a woman's torso, "influencing every conceivable disorder and dysfunction of her body and mind."[12] If a woman was having trouble breathing, it was because her uterus had moved up and was pushing against her lungs. If she was experiencing seizures (possibly epilepsy), it was probably because she wasn't having enough sex and needed to do so with abandon and fill that womb ASAP. Hippocratic physicians even assumed a woman's uterus would "start causing mischief if it was stifled by virginity."[13] Such prejudices and reductionistic beliefs about women and their bodies contributed to *hysteria* becoming a catchall diagnosis (*hystera*, from the Greek, meaning "uterus"). By claiming a woman was hysterical, doctors (or any man) could simultaneously (mis)diagnose and dismiss them—even when they were in significant pain. This form of malpractice rose to prominence during the Victorian era and persisted through the mid-1900s.

It follows that since men held most of the power in the medical field and assumed women were physically weaker, mentally inferior, and prone to exaggeration, women suffering from mental and physical health issues were vulnerable to further abuse and mistreatment. During this time, psychiatrists, including Sigmund Freud, relied on coercive, sometimes abusive psychiatry and unethical medical practices to regulate women's behavior rather than treat their legitimate needs.* According to historian Carroll Smith-Rosenberg, "They all had very definite ideas about how women ought to behave . . . There were general feelings of what caused abnormal behavior, and usually this was a refusal of traditional gender roles."[14] Normal meant being pregnant, devoting oneself to mothering, submitting to one's husband, and cheerfully completing domestic duties. Abnormal could mean anything from advocating for women's rights, daring to imagine a marriage where they were treated as an equal partner, or simply challenging the status quo. Considering how male practitioners have treated women in need, "it was never about mental acuity or medical treatment; it was about exerting control over women's lives and bodies—all under the guise of medicine."[15]

In *The Woman They Could Not Silence*, author Kate Moore tells the harrowing story of Elizabeth Packard, who, in the mid-1860s, was forcibly committed to the Illinois State Hospital for the Insane by her pastor-husband after communicating that she no longer agreed with his interpretation of Scripture and would henceforth be attending a different church.[16] Once committed to the asylum, she started talking with other female patients and realized that, like her, many were totally sane. At that time, a male spouse or relative could commit female relatives to mental institutions against their will (sometimes via physical coercion) for any variety of reasons, including having a disagreeable temperament or ongoing health issues, such as an "unnatural" period or epilepsy; being overly independent; outing their husband's infidelity; and even reading excessively.

Other firsthand accounts confirm that Packard's story was not an anomaly. Since asylums were privatized and unregulated, no one kept

---

* Incest and child abuse were rampant at this time. Some therapists and social scientists believe that Freud either misunderstood or consciously chose to misdiagnose child abuse as seduction complex, thus blaming women for their health issues. Riya Yadav, "Sigmund Freud and Penis Envy—a Failure of Courage?," British Psychological Society, May 8, 2018, updated June 27, 2024, https://www.bps.org.uk/psychologist/sigmund-freud-and-penis-envy-failure-courage.

track of how many women were institutionalized against their will or how many remained there until their death. Records do show that female patients in both North America and parts of Europe were "shut up" by being placed in straightjackets and left in solitary confinement; given lobotomies, clitoridectomies, and hysterectomies; sterilized; and treated with chloroform—which could be lethal.[17]

The institutionalization of women who were noncompliant or struggling with legitimate mental or physical health issues began to trail off at the beginning of the twentieth century. But the practice of controlling and oppressing women under the auspices of healthcare didn't stop. The tactics simply shifted.

Enforcing Misogyny with Pharmaceuticals

The connection between prescription drug manufacturers (often referred to as Big Pharma) and the mistreatment of women within the healthcare industry is complex. Pharmaceuticals alleviate our migraines, stabilize our moods, and heal our infections. But when capitalistic excesses fuse with men's patriarchal expectations of and biases against women, it creates a landscape that's rife for abuse. If we look at how women have been overmedicated in certain situations, undermedicated in others, or given drugs that have not been ethically tested, it's impossible to ignore the ways pharmaceutical companies have perpetuated misogyny.

Morphine came of age during the Civil War when doctors relied on it to treat injured soldiers. Once they realized how effective it was, they started prescribing it for a host of ailments, including women's menstrual cramps, morning sickness, and nervousness. Morphine and opium powders were available over the counter until the early 1900s, contributing to 1 in 200 Americans being addicted, 60 percent of them White women.[18] (Shockingly, opium was commonly given to babies to soothe them until the early 1900s.)[19]

Barbiturates rose to popularity next. They were "used as sedatives meant to treat nervousness and anxiety, [and] the drugs' common use as a sleeping pill fit nicely with the common 'rest cure' prescribed to women . . . by era physicians."[20] Victorian sensibilities regarding the supposed fragility and delicacy of White women continued to impact how doctors diagnosed and treated this demographic. By the 1940s the evidence was in regarding how addictive and dangerous barbiturates could be, and they fell out of favor. But the perceived need to alleviate anxiety, nervousness, and depression increased during this time due to a variety of factors.

Cultural unrest and upheaval were palpable. Not only did women still lack equal educational and employment opportunities, but after World War II, many of the women who had been recruited to fill roles for men fighting abroad were forced to give up those jobs when soldiers returned to the States.[21] Rosie handed over her riveter and either went home or resumed employment deemed more appropriate for women. White women were caught between the strong cultural expectations of finding fulfillment as housewives and their longings for more freedom and more options. Because Black women had fewer opportunities due to ongoing sexism and racism—including economic discrimination—they were less likely to drop out of the workforce and stay home full-time. These tensions helped fuel the feminist movement.

The 1950s and '60s ratcheted up anxiety levels with multiple assassinations, threats of nuclear annihilation, civil rights unrest, and American participation in the highly controversial wars in Korea and Vietnam. Mainstream America was simultaneously becoming more accepting of and curious about the field of psychiatry. This translated to more people (again, predominately White women) being diagnosed with and treated for psychiatric disorders.[22]

The issue of how to address American dis-*ease* without barbiturates was resolved in 1950, when the minor tranquilizer Miltown was released. It quickly became a cultural phenomenon and was followed by Valium, known as "mother's little helper." There's no doubt that women—and men—were helped by such pharmaceuticals. But Valium and other similar drugs were being prescribed to twice as many American women as men[23] even though evidence was piling up regarding their addictive qualities and possible adverse side effects.

Men in positions of power (including doctors, politicians, and CEOs) seemed to interpret anxiety and prescription drug use through a lens of gender bias. Male-variety anxiety was cast as essential to help get the job done, and men were encouraged to get outside and exercise more. Conversely, some experts viewed women's anxiety as a dangerous by-product of the burgeoning women's rights movement and growing discontent about their limited options. In other words, anxiety could serve to motivate men toward greater productivity, but because the end goal for women—more freedom and more opportunities—was seen as less acceptable, perhaps even threatening, women needed to be subdued.

Major pharmaceutical companies smelled an opportunity and began marketing campaigns promising to help women return to "domestic submissiveness and housewifely service to husband and children."[24] The makers of the tranquilizer Serax created an ad picturing an unhappy woman trapped behind bars made of brooms and mops. The copy read, "You can't set her free. But you can help her feel less anxious."[25] Of course, the tragedy here is that the housewife was "trapped" by rigid gender roles and cultural expectations created and enforced by men who then suggested it would be *better for her* to take mind-altering, addictive prescriptions than to experience true freedom. Even today, antidepression drugs disproportionately target women through direct-to-consumer ads, which are legal only in the US and New Zealand.[26]

Certainly, the pursuit of profit factors into why pharmaceutical companies continued to market potentially harmful, addictive drugs to women and why doctors continued writing prescriptions for them. But there are other less obvious layers here, including lack of female leadership at the executive levels in pharmaceuticals and healthcare,[27] the underrepresentation of women in clinical trials (particularly Women of Color and pregnant and lactating women), the inequality between research done and subsequent dollars spent on women's health needs, and finally, the reluctance to believe women when they're in pain.

The US government started requiring pharmaceutical companies to test their products in clinical trials in 1938. They were not obligated to include women, and most trials didn't.[28] Big Pharma claimed these exclusionary practices functioned as a safeguard to protect pregnant women and their babies, which is true. But when we look at how some drug companies tested and promoted their products (until 1962 when the government put stricter legislation in place[29]), it's difficult to trust their stated concerns given the dissonance between their words and their actions.

Consider what happened with thalidomide. In the 1950s and early 1960s, this new drug was being prescribed to pregnant women in Europe and Australia for morning sickness. It was also given to approximately twenty thousand American women of childbearing age, without clear warnings of the potential side effects, without going through full clinical trials, and without FDA approval.[30] In her first month at the FDA, Dr. Frances Oldham Kelsey refused to give the drug a green light because data pointed to dangerous side effects. (Her efforts were recognized in 1962 when she was given the Distinguished Federal Civilian Service Award by President Kennedy.) Pills were initially dispensed to doctors in envelopes marked only with the code "SK&F #5627."[31] An article in *The New York Times* revealed that some doctors were not advised about the potential side effects, and drug reps discouraged them from following up with patients.[32]

The thalidomide recall started in Europe in 1961 when reports linked it to severe birth defects, including malformed or missing limbs. In late 1962, FDA investigators concluded that American manufacturer "Richardson-Merrell had illegally promoted thalidomide before it had been approved."[33] It's still not clear how many babies born in the US were affected by this drug.

If the pharmaceutical companies were indeed concerned about pregnant women, why did this happen? Overzealous sales reps are partially to blame, but the manufacturers of thalidomide could have immediately ceased production and aggressively issued recalls when the first reports of birth defects started surfacing. They didn't. In fact, in a letter to American doctors who'd been given the drug, Richardson-Merrell claimed, "There is still no positive proof of causal relationship between the use of thalidomide during pregnancy and malformations in the newborn."[34] This tragedy led to stricter protocols for clinical testing and FDA approval.[35]

Thalidomide was not the first—or last—prescription drug dispensed and marketed to women via questionable or unethical practices. While developing what we now refer to as "the Pill," Gregory Pincus and Dr. John Rock tested early versions on unsuspecting patients undergoing fertility treatments, mentally ill women and men confined to an asylum (thus unable to give any type of consent), and soon after, women in Puerto Rico who were given high doses of the drug—named Enovid—but not fully informed about the risks. Adverse side effects reported by the latter group were largely discounted.[36] Three Puerto Rican women died while taking this early version of Enovid, but since autopsies were not performed, it's impossible to know what caused their deaths.[37] Pincus was also deceitful about how many women participated in the trials.[38]

After researchers and the pharmaceutical company G.D. Searle deemed these trials successful, the first oral contraceptive was released for sale in the US in 1960.[39] Because the FDA had concerns about its long-term safety, it was only approved for two-year use. It took several years for doctors and researchers to realize that the original dose was too high and could cause nausea, headaches, mood swings, and blood clots. Again, if G.D. Searle and the US government truly had women's welfare in mind, why didn't they wait to release the birth control pill until after they had conducted larger, ethical trials? How much of the motivation to release the Pill when they did was due to the promise of financial gain? G.D. Searle took in $24 million in net profits from the Pill in 1964.[40]

Though the Pill has provided women with more control regarding pregnancy as well as relief for other health issues, some doctors remain concerned about the potential side effects.[41] As with all pharmaceuticals, women need to evaluate the risks versus the benefits. This is easier said than done given that drugs are often not sufficiently tested on a diverse sample of women.

Women were largely excluded from most drug trials until the National Institutes of Health Revitalization Act of 1993, and the percentage of women included still lags behind. Biological females currently represent approximately 41 percent in phase one to three trials.[42] (New pharmaceuticals must go through three phases before they can be marketed to the public.) Because they're often excluded from trials, pregnant women who need help managing depression, pain, or other health issues are forced to make consequential decisions about the safety of prescription drugs without having sufficient data. This is a proverbial catch-22.

Pharmacokinetics also has not been sufficiently studied in women. This refers to how drugs move through the body. Pharmacokinetics depends on body size, weight, fat stores, and the unique way each person metabolizes chemicals, which varies between sexes. Pregnancy also affects how drugs are absorbed and excreted from the body. What happened with the sleep aid Ambien (active ingredient zolpidem) demonstrates why this type of research matters. Twenty years after Ambien was released, doctors finally realized that because women's bodies synthesize the active ingredients more slowly than men, the dosage was twice what women should take, resulting in morning drowsiness and compromised reaction times.[43] This might seem inconsequential, but consider that in those early morning hours, some women are driving their children to school, performing open-heart surgery, or piloting commercial airplanes. In such situations, morning drowsiness becomes far more consequential.

Bias and discrimination against women also show up via disparities in research and federal funding. In Caroline Criado Perez's book *Invisible Women*, she notes, "One research round-up found five times as many studies on erectile dysfunction than on PMS" even though "PMS affects 90% of women."[44] (Statistics vary between studies, but approximately one quarter of American men may experience ED at some point.)[45] In 2023, the NIH budgeted $305 million to study prostate cancer, which only affects men, and $29 million for endometriosis, which almost exclusively affects biological women.[46] In 2022, only 10 percent of NIH's budget was appropriated for health issues that affect women.[47] At the end of 2024, the Department of Defense announced it was committing $500 million to women's health research.[48] It's not clear if these funds will survive the ongoing budget cuts initiated by DOGE and the Trump administration.

It's All in the Blood: Women's Reproductive Health Needs

Some of the most glaring manifestations of misogyny in healthcare occur in connection with women's reproductive health, including menstruation, menopause, and pregnancy. (We'll talk about abortion in chapter 4.)

A woman's reproductive system is nothing short of miraculous. But this potentiality also makes our lives complicated. In certain cultures—including in sub-Saharan Africa and in the Hupa and Ojibway tribes of North America—girls' menarche or the beginning of the menstrual cycle has been celebrated as a rite of passage. Unfortunately, this perspective has not been widespread. A more common narrative is that the menstrual flow is disgusting and menstruating women are unclean.[49]

Most women navigate hormonal fluctuations every month for

approximately forty years. The bloating, energy dips, changes in libido, headaches, mood swings, and cramping can be both physically and psychologically challenging, but they also make women vulnerable to ridicule, stigmatization, and missed opportunities. Additionally, managing periods is costly, which is problematic for the 21.4 million American women living in poverty.[50] In a 2023 survey, 19 percent of college students "reported that they've felt forced to decide between buying period products and paying for other expenses, such as food or other bills."[51] This is known as period poverty. When viewed through the lens of economics and physical discomfort, menstrual cycles can indeed feel more like a curse than a blessing.

As a woman's fertility starts winding down, complex, confusing symptoms can ramp up, and not all healthcare practitioners know how to help or even take menopausal women and their health concerns seriously.* While on a panel with other famous women, media mogul Oprah Winfrey described how doctors discounted and misdiagnosed her heart palpitations, which are fairly common during menopause.[52]

There is no cure-all prescription for the many challenging issues women face as they move through this season. Various types of Menopausal Hormone Treatment, or MHT (also known as Hormone Replacement Therapy, or HRT), effectively address some symptoms for some women but as with any prescription drug, they carry the risk of possible adverse effects for a small percentage of women.[53] Low doses of antidepressants may alleviate hot flashes, but they can also result in side effects.[54] In centuries past, women going through menopause could be institutionalized, regarded as crazy, or, worse, branded as witches. At least in the twenty-first century, healthcare professionals

* Perimenopause typically begins in the mid- to late forties when the ovaries' egg supply begins to dwindle. A woman officially passes through menopause after not having a period for more than a year. I'm using the term *menopause* to include peri- and postmenopause.

are willing to acknowledge that menopause can cause many inconvenient, often unwelcome symptoms and are working to find viable solutions.

The healthcare industry has also failed to consistently provide high-quality care to all pregnant women and mothers.[55] Based on the Centers for Disease Control and Prevention (CDC) statistics, 1,205 women died of maternal causes in the United States in 2021. That's almost three women per day.[56] Despite boasting some of the best medical schools and hospitals in the world, the US consistently ranks in the top three for maternal deaths among high-income nations—with most deaths resulting from preventable causes like infections, high blood pressure, or blood loss.[57] The percentages are highest for Black and Hispanic women, who are more likely to receive substandard care. According to the CDC, "In 2020, the maternal mortality rate for non-Hispanic Black women was 55.3 deaths per 100,000 live births, 2.9 times the rate for non-Hispanic White women."[58]

Given that 53 percent of maternal deaths occur within the first six months after delivery, it's possible that the lack of paid maternity leave is one of the factors for the United States' high maternal death rate.[59] Without paid leave or the guarantee that their jobs will be waiting for them, many women have little choice but to go back to work regardless of whether their bodies have healed or if they have safe, reliable care for their infants. We'll talk more about this preventable tragedy in the coming chapters.

Our high cesarean section rate in the US should be examined as we consider how to best serve women's reproductive needs. Though the World Health Organization (WHO) recommends only 10 to 15 percent of the total births in a given country be done via this procedure, the US rate is approximately 32 percent for first-time C-sections.[60] According to Dr. Ian Askew, director of WHO's Department of Sexual and Reproductive Health and Research, "Cesarean sections are absolutely critical to save lives in situations where vaginal deliveries would pose risks." He goes on to explain that not all C-sections "are needed for medical reasons. Unnecessary surgical procedures can be detrimental, both for a woman and her baby."[61]

C-sections are more expensive, require a minimum six weeks of recovery, have higher rates of complications for the newborn, and can increase the risk of future complications during childbirth, such as bleeding, uterine rupture, and emergency hysterectomies.[62] Multiple factors contribute to elevated C-section rates, including America's above-average number of high-risk pregnancies (many of which require this procedure) and personal preference. Some women proactively choose C-sections over vaginal birth due to past trauma or pre-existing health issues or because it offers them more control.

Optional C-sections (as well as induction at thirty-nine weeks*) may point to the ways the healthcare industry values convenience and profit over what's best for women. In North America, hospitals receive almost twice as much from insurance companies for a C-section than a vaginal birth. The nationwide average is $13,000 for a vaginal birth versus $23,000 for a C-section. C-sections also diminish the risk of doctors or hospitals being sued if something goes wrong. A vaginal delivery is unpredictable and can take more than a day from start to finish. A C-section is typically done in less than an hour. It's a simple return on investment for hospitals. During an interview with Dr. Holly Powell Kennedy, professor of midwifery at Yale University, one obstetrician summed it up like this: "You're going to pay me more [to do a C-section], I get to worry less, you're not going to sue me, and I'll be done in an hour."[63]

There are viable options that could potentially decrease non-necessary C-sections. Studies support that midwives and doulas play a key role in reducing C-sections as well as maternal and infant deaths.

---

* Induction, which essentially kick-starts labor via certain drugs, increased after a 2019 study suggested induction at thirty-nine weeks minimized adverse outcomes for some pregnancies: Suzan L. Carmichael and Jonathan M. Snowden, "The ARRIVE Trial—Interpretation from an Epidemiologic Perspective," *Journal of Midwifery and Women's Health* 64, no. 5 (July 2, 2019): 657–63, https://pmc.ncbi.nlm.nih.gov/articles/PMC6821557/.

Unfortunately, the United States and Canada have a below-average number of midwives compared to all other high-income countries.[64] Before medicine became professionalized and male doctors started taking over obstetrics in the mid- to late 1800s, approximately half of the babies born in the US were attended by midwives—often Black women—in private homes. As of 2021, the US rate was 12 percent.[65]

Rebecca Ray, a certified nurse midwife, helps to explain one of the key philosophies of the way midwives approach labor and delivery: "Nurse-midwives are trained from a nursing model rather than a medical model, which is more holistic in nature and lends itself to more of a relationship-based way of caring for women. Midwives generally practice what is called 'shared decision-making,' which is a collaborative approach, where the woman's values, preferences, and knowledge of her body (she is an expert in her own body) are an integral part of how medical decisions are made." Ray believes that most midwives operate under the assumption that birth is a natural process, "not an illness that women need to be rescued from." The WHO recommends expanding training for midwives to reduce maternal mortality and unnecessary and potentially harmful interventions. Of note, not all insurance companies fully cover this evidence-based care.[66]

Missing the Mark

Anyone navigating a chronic or sudden serious health issue is bound to feel disempowered, discouraged, and overwhelmed from time to time. There are added layers for women, including being misdiagnosed and mistreated.

David Newman-Toker, a professor of neurology at Johns Hopkins School of Medicine, admits, "Women and racial and ethnic minorities are 20% to 30% more likely than white men to experience a misdiagnosis."[67] Misdiagnosis points to multiple factors, including the complexity of certain diseases, diagnostic error, bias about women and People of Color being credible witnesses, and how difficult it seems to be for some healthcare providers to admit they might not know what to do. In his book *Being Mortal*, Dr. Atul Gawande writes, "For a clinician, nothing is more threatening to who you think you are than a patient with a problem you cannot solve."[68] When doctors cease being curious and humble, patients can end up being treated as if they're the problem. Biological women dealing with female-specific diseases like endometriosis or polycystic ovary syndrome sometimes must deal with all these issues as they seek healing.

One hundred and ninety million women across the globe suffer from endometriosis, sometimes simply referred to as "endo."[69] Endometriosis occurs when endometrial-like tissue migrates and implants in other regions of the body. This causes adhesions that "can abnormally bind pelvic and abdominal organs."[70] Author and endometriosis patient Tracey Lindeman explains, "It's as if a bottle of glue" gets dumped into women's abdomens and "as the glue hardens, organs become stuck together."[71] Symptoms vary but include unusually heavy periods, debilitating cramps, pain during intercourse and when having bowel movements, neuropathy, fatigue, and headaches. Based on a study done at Boston's Brigham and Women's Hospital, women under the age of forty who have endometriosis have a 52 percent increased risk of heart attack.[72]

Endometriosis is an incredibly complicated disease that's difficult to diagnose, in part because the presenting symptoms may overlap with other diseases, such as dysmenorrhea. It can take four to ten years for endo to be accurately diagnosed.[73] Once diagnosed, patients can opt to undergo laser surgery, a laparoscopic excision, an ablation, or a hysterectomy. More than one hundred thousand hysterectomies are performed annually in the US to resolve endo, and the associated healthcare costs of the disease are in the billions.[74] Over-the-counter and prescription pain meds can help some women, but they do not eradicate all the symptoms or address the root cause. Healthcare providers have not been able to create clear protocols for diagnosing and treating an illness that affects one out of every ten women worldwide.[75]

Carolyn* was first diagnosed with endometriosis when she was twenty-nine.[76] She had laparoscopic surgery to remove the endometriosis and the adhesions, which brought relief, but she then had to undergo hormone therapy to keep it from progressing. She opted to receive treatment for six months and then go off for the next six in the hope that she might be able to get pregnant. Carolyn recounts, "After a few years of this, I underwent another laparoscopy because I was experiencing debilitating pain all the time, and it affected every part of my life, from doing household chores to making plans with friends and family." She was then forced to go on short-term disability at work. "It wasn't that I was lazy or that I didn't want to make plans or travel. I couldn't do it while managing the unrelenting pain and fatigue. Most people didn't understand how much endometriosis affected my everyday life." Years later, Carolyn chose to have a partial hysterectomy.

Living with chronic pain is bad enough, but women who deal with invisible diseases with unknown etiologies (like endometriosis and fibromyalgia) may also have to contend with not being believed and having their realities discounted as they seek help. In some branches of medicine, "women's pain is much more likely to be seen as having an emotional or a psychological cause, rather than a bodily or biological one."[77] Studies have shown that ER docs are more likely to attribute women's heart attack symptoms to psychological causes (for example, panic attacks) and require a psychiatric evaluation rather than order the crucial tests that could save their lives.[78] This results in women and People of Color being given fewer pain meds than White men.[79]

Women's physical pain has been minimized for centuries. Since the beginning of recorded history, certain cultures have blamed women for misfortune and the origin of sin and then assumed suffering and illness were due punishment. Within this framework, women's health issues—including the discomfort of menstrual cycles and the pain of childbirth—were their own fault and therefore had to be endured as a form of penance, without complaint or pain relief. In the past, it was relatively frictionless for healthcare providers to dismiss women as hysterical and sinful rather than empathize with them or alleviate their pain. This mindset, compounded by racist beliefs, likely contributed to Dr. James Marion Sims's choice to perform gynecological surgeries on Black women during the 1800s without anesthesia or pain medication.* This is an example of misogynoir—a term coined by author and professor Moya Bailey in 2010 to describe the ways sexism and racism overlap.

Dismissing women's pain can be highly consequential. Kayla,* a thirty-six-year-old mother of two, went to the emergency room with severe abdominal pain not long after she learned she was pregnant.[80] She recounts, "A doctor told me I probably didn't have a ruptured ectopic pregnancy because I wasn't writhing on the floor screaming." Her symptoms were minimized despite blood work indicating hormone levels consistent with pregnancy loss and MRI imaging that showed a ruptured fallopian tube, which can be fatal.

Kayla returned home and resumed normal life, but her symptoms did not abate. She finally had lifesaving emergency surgery two weeks later. She says, "It took me months to recover, and I'm still impacted by the trauma of the experience." (Since *Roe* was overturned in 2022, doctors in some states have been tentative or refused to offer appropriate, lifesaving treatment for women who have complications such as ectopic pregnancies due to fear of being reprimanded.)[81]

Not only is the pain connected to women's menstrual cycles, pregnancies, and female-specific diseases minimized or discounted, but far too often it gets normalized.[82] Teens are often told something along the lines of, "This is what it means to get your period. Deal with it."

---

* Sims, often referred to as the father of gynecology, was seeking to learn how to repair fistulas and solve other gynecological problems but chose to experiment on enslaved Black women with only the consent of their owners. Camila Domonoske, "'Father of Gynecology,' Who Experimented on Slaves, No Longer on Pedestal in NYC," NPR, April 17, 2018, https://www.npr.org/sections/thetwo-way/2018/04/17/603163394/-father-of-gynecology-who-experimented-on-slaves-no-longer-on-pedestal-in-nyc.

In other words, constant pain is supposed to be normative for women. But the pain associated with endometriosis can be so intense it causes women and girls to pass out, curl up in a fetal position for hours, or vomit several days a month. This should not be seen as normal, and no one should have to endure such pain. When endometriosis isn't properly addressed, it can cause central and peripheral sensitization (essentially mind-numbing pain throughout the body) as well as mental health issues such as depression—and delirium.[83]

Reread that last sentence and sit with it for a second. Now connect this to how some doctors have labeled women as hysterics rather than taking them seriously and addressing their pain.

Is it possible that women have been dealing with endometriosis for thousands of years, and for thousands of years they've been dismissed and told some iteration of "It's all in your head. It can't be that bad. You're just imagining it"?

An article in the *Journal of Fertility and Sterility* states there is irrefutable "evidence that hysteria, the now discredited mystery disorder presumed for centuries to be psychological in origin, was most likely endometriosis in the majority of cases. If so, then this would constitute one of the most colossal, mass misdiagnoses in human history, one that over the centuries has subjected women to murder, madhouses, and lives of unremitting physical, social, and psychological pain."[84]

When Hippocrates and other ancient doctors suggested that the womb was the cause of many female maladies, they were onto something. Only it wasn't the actual womb that wandered; it was tissue intimately connected to the womb. Their conclusion and their remedy were both dead wrong.

An Rx for the Future of Women's Health

I've often wondered if the woman "with the issue of blood" whom Jesus healed had endometriosis.[85] The Bible recounts that she had been bleeding constantly for twelve years, had "suffered a great deal from many doctors," and had "spent everything she had to pay them, but she had . . . gotten worse" (Mark 5:26 NLT). The afflicted woman believed healing was possible, knew where to turn, and shamelessly pursued that healing. Jesus commended her faith—which means he also commended her self-advocacy—and compassionately met her. This is an important story both for healers and for those in need of healing.

As this industry becomes more diverse and aware of women's unique health needs, misogyny's influence is diminishing. At least in the US and most of Europe, women can no longer be institutionalized against their will by controlling family members. The days of attributing all of women's diseases to their wombs or believing women are incapable of serving in this field are long gone.[86] In 1849, Elizabeth Blackwell was the first American woman to receive her medical degree and license. Fifteen years later, Rebecca Lee Crumpler became the first Black woman to serve as an official doctor. By 1970, women made up 10 percent of all medical students, and as of 2021, more than half of US medical students were women, with approximately 37 percent going on to practice medicine.[87] (Women of Color remain underrepresented as doctors and surgeons.)[88] Female representation has changed the face of healthcare for the better. Women practitioners tend to be more empathetic, listen better, and interrupt less—all of which are healing in and of themselves.[89]

Pharmaceutical companies now include more women in clinical drug trials, though representation is not yet equal between the sexes.[90] Companies are beginning to harness technology to improve women's health with innovative products such as bras with built-in heart monitors and apps such as Citizen Endo that help women manage endometriosis.[91] Alternative methods of dealing with depression and anxiety are becoming more acceptable, such as eye movement desensitization and reprocessing (or EMDR), mindfulness, and, more recently, social prescriptions. When offering a social prescription, doctors and nurses are encouraged to ask the question *What matters to you?* versus *What's wrong with you?* Depending on the patient's response, they prescribe one or more of the following five types of cures: movement, community, nutrition, arts, and nature.[92] Patients are then connected to organizations and individuals who can help them engage in one of these areas. Such modalities, coupled with a greater willingness to value women's experiences, have helped the number of women taking sedatives and other anti-anxiety medications to drop steadily from the all-time highs of the 1950s and '60s.[93]

Despite these encouraging markers, many areas of healthcare need additional transformation to counteract the ways misogyny has adversely impacted women's health. Individual and systemic biases need to be identified and challenged. Illnesses that primarily afflict women must be prioritized and researched. Free menstrual products should be available in schools, libraries, and other public access areas. There needs to be a groundswell of opposition to healthcare corporations and insurance providers raking in astronomical profits while failing to provide affordable options to women.

Finally, we must move toward educating and caring for all pregnant women, regardless of their race or economic status. This includes more comprehensive prenatal education that empowers women to go into labor and delivery well informed so that they might avoid unnecessary interventions when possible. In 2025 New York's legislature passed their Paid Prenatal Leave law, which provides twenty hours of paid leave so pregnant women can attend healthcare appointments.[94] Every state should offer this type of protection as well as a minimum of two months paid parental leave. (More on this shortly.)

Change often begins in small, measurable ways. For instance, when doctors respond to a female patient by saying, "I don't know what's wrong, but I believe you and I'm going to help you figure this out," they can offer much-needed empathy and create a system where women's mental and physical health needs are valued and prioritized. Such change would be welcome.

CHAPTER 3

UNSEEN, UNAPPRECIATED, AND UNDERPAID

Misogyny in the Workplace

In Caroline Criado Perez's book *Invisible Women*, she contends, "Women have always worked. They have worked unpaid, underpaid, underappreciated, and invisibly, but they have always worked. But the modern workplace does not work for women."[1] How does misogyny factor into this reality?

Misogyny shows up in the obvious, often discussed areas like women facing pay inequalities and being passed over for promotions, but it's also present in subtler ways—like women not getting credit for their ideas or being penalized for having children or not behaving like men.

Throughout the course of her career in education, Ana* has faced numerous types of discrimination and bias even though she earned a Doctor of Education from Harvard University and is the superintendent of a school system that serves more than six thousand students.

Before she rose to her current position, she worked as a principal. In a conversation with me, Ana recalled, "People would come to my building and ask to speak to the principal. I would come out, and then they'd give me a quizzical look and ask, 'Are you the principal?' Even now, as a super, if I go somewhere outside of our organization and take a man who's on my senior leadership team, others always talk to him first. They ask what grade I teach or assume I'm the secretary."[2]

After being passed over for a job that should have been hers, she learned that one of the male board members disqualified her because, in his words, "she didn't look like a superintendent." Ana admitted, "I felt invisible when people overlooked all my expertise and experience. It was discouraging and painful." Parents' and peers' responses to her appearance reflect a common cultural expectation that the person at the top of an organization is, or should be, a man. Preferably a tall, White one.[3] Ana is four foot eleven and Latina.

Judgment about physical appearance is one of many forms of discrimination Ana and other women regularly encounter in the workplace. In some male-dominated fields, women continue to be perceived as less capable, encounter resistance when they attempt to advance, and hold significantly fewer leadership positions.[4]

Ana's experience confirms this. "The glass ceiling is real. Gender discrimination has definitely affected my career trajectory. When I was the assistant super in a large metropolitan school system, I partnered with a White man, and together we oversaw K through 8. We left at the same time. His next career move was to become super while I stayed an assistant. His subsequent jump was Commissioner of Education. And again, I remained an assistant super. His trajectory was a steep incline where mine was more circular and lateral."

In the New England state where Ana works there are 250 superintendents. Four of them are Latina women. Nationwide, approximately 25 percent of superintendents are women, but only a small percent are Women of Color. It's difficult for women like Ana to differentiate between racial and gender discrimination because they work in tandem, and Women of Color must contend with both. Though Ana's experiences are unique to her, they are not unusual for women in supervisory or managerial roles.

Because many American businesses tend to center on men, perpetuate male biases, and prioritize profit over everything—including the well-being of their employees and the natural world—workplaces can range from unfriendly to outright hostile to women. We can see this in four specific ways: goods or services designed for and based on male bodies; pay and opportunity gaps; the devaluation of women's work; and harassment, abuse, and exploitation.

The Hidden Costs of Standardizing Male Bodies

Over the past decade, as more women create and run businesses and more gender-specific data becomes available, we've started to see how male bias shapes much of the decision-making during the design and manufacturing process. Goods designed by men and based primarily on men's bodies and needs can inconvenience or even physically harm women.

The "male-unless-otherwise-indicated"[5] theory of design shows up in many everyday products, forcing women to adapt and compensate. The temperature of most office buildings is based on men's metabolic rate, which is higher than women's. This explains why so many women shiver through their workdays or bundle themselves in blankets.[6] Because the octave range on piano keyboards is 7.4 inches and the average woman's handspan is between seven and eight inches, female pianists are more likely to experience hand and wrist injuries than men.[7] Female guitarists, photographers, and smartphone users face a similar dilemma because the tools are simply too large for average-size female hands. Those who designed grocery carts, washers, and dryers presumably weren't tracking who would be the primary users of the appliances. All three are so deep that it's difficult for most women to comfortably reach inside of them.

Women who work in the armed forces or as firefighters have complained for years about how the shoes, clothing, and equipment issued to them tend to be oversized and poorly designed for their bodies, making it infinitely more difficult to do an already dangerous job. Personal Protective Equipment, often referred to as PPE (for example, the gear worn by doctors and nurses while treating COVID-19 patients), is similarly engineered to fit the average American and European male, even though more than 70 percent of frontline healthcare workers are female.[8]

Being inconvenienced by male-centric design is one thing. Being harmed is quite another. When car manufacturers started safety testing vehicles back in the 1950s, they wisely created crash-test dummies. These dummies took the hits and helped designers determine how to make safer vehicles. Unfortunately, these dummies were modeled after male bodies. Women's bodies don't have the same geometry. They tend to be shorter and have less muscle mass and bone density. More than two decades ago, car manufacturers engineered a crash dummy that supposedly approximated the female physique more closely. In reality, they simply followed the "shrink it and pink it" approach and left it in the dryer too long, because at four feet eleven and 108 pounds, Hybrid III is significantly smaller than the average American woman. The female dummies are also more likely to be placed in the passenger's versus the driver's seat when being tested. By not factoring in these key details, women continue to die at a higher rate and suffer more serious injuries in frontal car accidents than men.[9]

Artificial intelligence offers another example of how lack of diversity in design can adversely affect women. AI is only as smart and capable of serving diverse needs as the input it receives. If the programmers and developers fail to consider the needs of women and People of Color—or don't use accurate, responsible data—algorithmic bias is likely to occur.[10]

Algorithmic Justice League founder Joy Buolamwini discovered if the majority of input images were White males, facial recognition software could accurately detect male faces but not women's—and specifically not Black women's.[11] This has already been consequential for governmental agencies that rely on facial recognition software, like the TSA and law enforcement. In 2023, Porcha Woodruff, a Black woman, was arrested by Detroit police on carjacking charges based solely on facial recognition software. At the time of her arrest, she was eight months pregnant and home with her two young children, making her an unlikely candidate to perpetuate a violent crime. Charges were later dismissed.[12]

AI specialist Timnit Gebru has found the current training data results in "models that encode stereotypical and derogatory associations along gender, race, ethnicity, and disability status."[13] Lack of racial and gender diversity has the potential to embed male bias into everything from voice recognition in cars to employment searches, since most Fortune 500 companies now rely on some form of AI to screen potential employees.

I doubt designers, architects, and manufacturers intentionally or maliciously overlook women's needs while creating spaces and products. The choices they make are probably subconscious and based on standardized parts. (Not to belabor my point, but standards based solely on men's bodies are not truly *standards*.) They simply aren't required or expected to consider women's needs. If leaders in these industries were willing to be more thoughtful about the unique challenges women face and then allocate the necessary resources to create standards that reflect and value both sexes equally, they could improve women's lives and better protect them.

Pay and Opportunity Gaps

When male centrism, male entitlement, and male bias are backed by societal norms and legal precedents, it adversely affects women's job options, earning potential, and even whether their start-ups will receive venture capital.

Women are still trying to catch up in many professions both

because their starting lines were decades or even generations behind men's and because biased gender norms wrongly assumed they were less capable. As mentioned in the introduction, through the 1950s, school boards could either refuse to hire married women for teaching positions or fire them when they got married or became pregnant.[14] The ban on women lawyers was not fully lifted until 1971. Trade jobs, such as electricians and carpenters, are still overwhelmingly held by men, in part because individuals learn these professions through apprenticeships and mentoring, which tend to happen within male networks.[15]

The consequences of these historic discriminatory practices continue to play out. Approximately 90 percent of the coveted corner suites in Fortune 500 companies are occupied by men.[16] Only twelve states are governed by a woman. Thirty years ago, that figure was just four. Despite continued gains, many of the top-paying professions continue to be dominated by men. That list includes industrial design (80% male), architecture (67%), surgical specialties (77%), law (61%), pilots (97%), software engineers (78%), and politicians (70%).[17]

Whether we look at dollar-to-dollar comparisons or annual salaries, there's no denying that women make less than men.[18] Even though the Equal Pay Act of 1963 forbids employers from gender-based pay discrimination, women still take home less than their male counterparts. A 2024 report by the Institute for Women's Policy Research found that "women are paid eighty-four cents for every dollar a man makes" and "a persistent wage gap that spans all professions, even those typically held by women," continues to exist.[19] Nationwide, male elementary and middle school teachers earn approximately $150 more per week than females, and male nurses take home $248 more per week.[20] The gap tends to be more notable in male-dominated fields. Male college professors earn tenure nearly twice as often and get paid more than their female peers.[21] Some women, like Google's director of engineering Ulku Rowe, have sued in protest. Rowe was awarded $1.15 million in 2019.[22]

Women who start their own businesses inarguably face more hurdles than their male counterparts, yet another indicator of how male bias shows up in the workplace. Potential female founders receive less venture capital than men even though many of their ideas are scalable and have the potential to turn a profit.[23] The reasons behind this disparity are multifaceted. Some women may be more inclined to focus their energies on smaller start-ups that are less likely to become the next unicorn, which is what many investors are seeking.[24] Others may be reluctant to hand over control of their companies to male venture capitalists.

But sexism also plays a role. Potential funders ask male founders questions like, *What's your vision?* They ask female founders, *How will you be able to take care of your kids and run the business?* Male founders are likely to have families too, but who cares for their children appears to be less relevant to backers. Though women have consistently demonstrated their ability to innovate and work hard, the business world—and capitalism in general—continues to favor men. We are making progress, but we're not where we need to be.

The Devaluation of Women's Work

It's not simply that capitalism and the American workplace prefer men: They devalue women and the work traditionally done by women. Companies and cultures that esteem profit above the health and welfare of their employees will do whatever it takes to protect that profit. Costs must be minimized so profits can be maximized. If that means refusing to offer parental leave, health insurance, flexible work hours, or childcare, so be it.

An inherent problem with this philosophy is that no country, culture, or company can survive without raising up the next generation or caring for the current one. Every human needs to eat, sleep, receive adequate healthcare, and have a place to live. Children and aging family members must be cared for. All these life-sustaining caregiving activities—disproportionately done by women—are time consuming, un- or underappreciated, and never compensated based on the value they provide.

Admittedly, caregiving work can be somewhat difficult to monetize because there's no product to sell. But that doesn't make it any less essential. Approximately thirty million American women provide some form of care to family members or friends.[25] Typically, they are not paid, even though according to a 2015 study, family caregiving was estimated to be worth $470 billion.[26] Oxfam calculated that if American women "were compensated for their unpaid work with minimum wage, they would have made $1.5 trillion dollars in 2019."[27] All told, women spend 4.5 hours per day doing unpaid work while men spend 2.8 hours.[28] Sociologist Arlie Hochschild referred to this as "second shift" work.[29] Though most women still do disproportionately more caregiving and household work than their male partners, the gap is closing.[30]

Overlooking the importance of caregiving while prioritizing profit might be exacerbated by contemporary capitalistic practices (which have become increasingly dehumanized thanks to automation, AI, and outsourcing), but it's not a twenty-first-century phenomenon. In her provocative book *Who Cooked Adam Smith's Dinner?* Swedish journalist Katrine Marçal explains why male economists concluded that women's work was not worth quantifying back in the 1880s:

> The fruits of male labor could be stacked in piles and measured in money. The results of women's work were intangible. Dust that is swept away collects again. Mouths that have been fed grow hungry. Children who sleep, wake. And after lunch, it's time to do the dishes. And after the dishes comes dinner and more dirty dishes. Homework is cyclical in nature. Therefore, women's work wasn't an "economic activity." What she did was just a logical extension of her fair, loving nature.[31]

By refusing to acknowledge the importance of or place a dollar amount on women's work, economists confirmed the prevailing attitude that women's work carried a diminished value compared to other jobs and roles. By refusing to factor the life-sustaining caregiving work women do into the gross domestic product calculation (GDP), the government made it official.[32] This is one of the many ways economics and misogyny intersect.

Regardless of whether governments, workplaces, or family systems recognize and duly compensate women for their essential work, civilization would come to a grinding halt if women stopped extending their "fair, loving natures." This played out in October 2023, when 90 percent of Iceland's women went on strike to protest gender pay inequality.[33] Schools, libraries, banks, and shops closed for the day. Public transportation suffered delays. Hotel rooms went uncleaned. Little was divulged about whether the strike extended into private homes, and if it did, how men fared.

If women across the globe followed Iceland's example and stopped doing all of their essential, unpaid work—including planning menus, shopping for groceries, prepping for meals, washing dishes and clothes, tending to aging parents, cleaning, and carting dependents to dentists and doctors, by no means an exhaustive list—the male CEOs, heart surgeons, and construction workers of the world would not be able to effortlessly clock their eight to ten hours of paid work that *is* included in the GDP. Again, quoting Marçal, "The work that is traditionally carried out by men is what counts. It defines the economic world view. Women's work is 'the other.' Everything that he doesn't do but that he is dependent on so he can do what he does."[34] As journalist and sociologist Ann Crittenden wryly explained, "Without conscientious mothers, there would be no economic man."[35]

The notion that caring for other human beings is worthless, at least in economic terms, is misguided and illogical. Imagine if we flipped this script and expected a man doing a job traditionally done by men to work for free—for example, a professional football coach.

In season, they impart knowledge, teach essential skills, offer encouragement, resolve petty conflicts, and help players form a functional team. All essential stuff—and when you think about it, the kinds of things mothers do every day. But then on game day, fans aren't paying to watch coaches pace the sidelines or scream at officials. After all, coaches aren't the ones taking bone-shattering hits, making spectacular passes and superhuman catches, and pushing through massive linemen to cross into the end zone. So why should they get paid? Coaches get paid because everyone understands that teams wouldn't succeed without them. They also get paid because Americans value winning sports teams and are willing to spend their money to achieve this goal. As a culture, we apparently do not esteem women who work inestimably longer hours without the benefits of an off-season or adoring (albeit fickle) fans. At least mothers don't have to explain their parenting choices to a room full of reporters asking inane questions every week.

As demonstrated by who makes what in this country, our priorities are a bit skewed. Salaries are not arbitrary: We pay for what we value. And that's why pro football coaches make between $8 and $25 million a year, preschool teachers make approximately $38,000 to $40,000 a year, and stay-at-home moms (and dads) make nothing.[36] These pay inequalities persist even though it's now well documented that early childhood education and a stable, loving home positively affect a child's future. Quoting Crittenden, "If most of our national prosperity reflects the productivity of our human capital, then the people who provide primary care to children are the single most important source of our most valuable economic asset."[37] As a mother, I can certainly say it doesn't feel that way.

Currently, most workplaces do little to nothing to help families raise healthy children. Given that "the minimum wage doesn't cover the costs of childcare by a long shot, families are confronted with an equation that can't be solved."[38] And women are stuck trying to reconcile the math. In two-parent households, since women typically make less money, they tend to decrease their hours to part-time or drop out of work for a season. Female professionals who do this are essentially stepping off the career track and losing out "on economic security, pension contributions and future earnings."[39] This loss of earnings makes it almost impossible for women to achieve economic equality.

Furthermore, when women create boundaries around their paid work so they can care for their children or family members, their commitment may be questioned. They may be excluded from making key decisions. Raises and promotions—generally handed out to those who can work overtime—may pass them by. It's tough to go above and beyond in the office when you're going above and beyond in the home. This scenario is infinitely worse for single mothers. Ann Crittenden contends, "Motherhood is now the single biggest risk factor for poverty in old age."[40] As a nation, we expect women to do much of the essential work that holds families and cultures together, but we do not offer them the financial compensation they deserve.

The Faces of Abuse

The ongoing systemic devaluation and exploitation of women and their work can easily become a precursor to more consequential forms of abuse, such as verbal and sexual harassment and violence.

Sexual harassment happens in huge multinational corporations, small family businesses, and everything in between. Michelle* worked as a project manager in one of the top investment firms in the US. Mid-meeting, as her team attempted to resolve some vexing issues causing delays in a merger, tempers flared—including hers. But she was the only woman in the room. Her boss sent her a message telling her she sounded "super bitchy." None of the men were reprimanded for displaying anger. Michelle reflected, "This incident made me realize that I would only be acceptable if I fit the norm, which included never getting angry."[41]

Female academics in top institutions are also at risk for abuse. Dr. R* was dean of academic affairs at a graduate school. After questioning the school's president about potential misallocation of funds, she recounted that he would "tear me apart in private and humiliate me in staff meetings."[42] He would also give her work with tight deadlines but prevent her from accessing the information she needed and ask her why she hadn't handed in work she'd never been assigned. He repeatedly told Dr. R in front of coworkers, "You've failed, and I'm so disappointed in you." She took her concerns to the board, but they "concretized the abuse," claiming, "We've never seen him treat women this way. You're being too emotional." After two years of this, Dr. R realized the president was making it impossible for her to succeed and resigned. A year later, thanks to pressure from the faculty, staff, and students, the president also left. She later discovered that other female administrators and staff experienced similar treatment. Dr. R has since returned to her role at this institution.

Sexual harassment ratchets up the danger. A 2018 survey done by Harvard Business School revealed that 88 percent of their female alumni had experienced some form of sexual harassment while at work.[43] The most common forms included sexually suggestive remarks, posts, or messages, and inappropriate touching, including attempts to fondle or kiss. Numerous female employees at powerhouse multinational companies such as Google, PayPal, and Uber have reported being propositioned by bosses, receiving pornographic images on interoffice memos, and overhearing demeaning sexist banter. The highest percentage of harassment happened in settings where women made up 15 percent or less of the company's senior leadership.

Sexualized violence in workplace settings (sometimes referred to as Workplace Sexualized Violence, or WSV) may appear in the headlines more frequently than in the past thanks to the #MeToo movement, but it has always existed.* In an article on the history of sexual harassment, professor and author Kimberly Hamlin explains, "Throughout

* Enslavement cannot be considered equivalent with voluntary paid labor but it's important to note that enslaved African women were routinely abused and raped by their White owners.

the 19th century, most women who worked for pay did so as domestic servants, an employment setting in which women regularly endured sexual assault and harassment at the hands of their employers with little to no recourse."[44] Sexual assault and rape were rampant during slavery and the Age of Industry. Though sexual harassment and abuse are illegal under the Civil Rights Act of 1964, men understand that when they hold the power, there are ways around the law.

Immigrant women who work as domestics in wealthy countries like the US, England, and Canada are particularly vulnerable to abuse and exploitation, especially if they're poor or Women of Color.[45] Many of them are enticed with the promise of good pay and regular work by disreputable individuals who later mistreat and abuse them. Wages are often extremely low, hours are long, medical care may not be provided, contact with their families is sometimes cut off, physical and sexual abuse are common, and they may be threatened with deportation if they speak up. When the employers are foreign diplomats, they are protected by diplomatic immunity and are therefore free to abuse at will.[46]

Anyone who hasn't faced this type of abuse might wonder why women don't speak up or go directly to HR and file a claim. Many workers, including nannies and house cleaners, don't have an HR department to go to. And even if they did, women have learned through experience that doing what seems to be the right thing might result in further mistreatment rather than relief or justice. Jane Park, CEO of a company called Julep Beauty, explained that women "have to make a decision: Do you want to ruin your career? Do you want this to be everything that you end up being about? What you really want to happen is that it doesn't happen again."[47] But it does happen again, and whistleblowers can't count on being believed or protected. They may be bullied, receive poor performance reviews, be gaslighted by HR, and be blackballed at other institutions.[48] Michelle, the project manager who was criticized for displaying anger in her team meeting, communicated what happened to her superior, also a woman, who encouraged her to file a sexual harassment claim. After she successfully went through this process with HR, that same superior was given a poor job review and then demoted. Retaliations of this type effectively silence those who are harmed and perpetuate cycles of abuse.

Such retaliatory measures can reveal a great deal about what motivates those in positions of power. If they do not respect or care about their individual employees or the world in which they live, they will have little to no motivation to fix the system because disrupting the status quo may cost them. When greed and entitlement rule, abuse and exploitation will follow. The desire for more personal wealth and more control leads powerful men to take whatever they want—from the earth, from women, and from anyone with less status—without concern for those who are harmed and without any plans to repair or replenish.

This plays out daily for countless women. The nanny who can't afford childcare for her own children. The woman ringing up your groceries at Whole Foods who can't call in sick without fear of losing her job.[49] The single-mom barista at Starbucks who—like so many gig workers—didn't get her schedule until forty-eight hours before her shift, making it impossible to find childcare and attend her college classes.[50] The tech worker who must either overlook her male colleague's unwanted advances or quit. These realities are not simply bad for women; they're bad for business. And they need to change.

Welcome Posture Shifts and Behavioral Changes

Ending misogyny in the workplace and consistently valuing women's contributions will require behavioral and policy changes. For starters, employers will need to prohibit all practices that are demeaning or hostile to women, like hosting "business lunches" at strip clubs. San Francisco's infamous Gold Club has long been the site of many corporate lunches for high-tech employees and venture capitalists. For less than ten dollars, patrons can get a buffet with a strip tease and a side of pole dancing.[51] No employer should force an employee to witness such dehumanizing and degrading activities. Going out for a business lunch at a strip joint reflects selfishness, sexist entitlement, and profound cluelessness. None of which make for good leadership or good business.

One of the reasons this type of behavior happens in Silicon Valley is that the tech industry is overwhelmingly male. Statistics show that companies with more women in their leadership tend to be more successful across many metrics, including innovation, creativity, lower turnover, and higher productivity.[52] A 2016 study found that increased gender diversity in the highest corporate offices led to a 15 percent increase in profits.[53] When the International Monetary Fund conducted a study of more than two million private and public companies, they found that "on average, replacing just one man with one woman in management or on the board led to a 3 to 8 percent increase in profitability."[54] Tech reporter and author Emily Chang believes, "What's good for women is good for men, good for companies, good for their customers, good for the products they produce, good for the economy, and good for our future."[55]

Of course, simply replacing one man with one woman won't automatically bring positive change unless gender bias and discrimination are addressed. Brigit Helms, CEO of the Miller Center for Entrepreneurship, believes that in addition to the more obvious shifts like offering flexible work hours, the option of working from home, and on-site or reimbursed childcare, companies need to realize the importance of cognitive diversity. Helms explains, "We need to value and understand the ways people like to think and that the preferences they have are important. Different doesn't necessarily mean better or worse."[56]

Helms believes fear is the biggest barrier to male-led companies acknowledging this. If there's no trust, it won't be safe to admit you made a mistake or to have conflict. And if there's an absence of safety or no track record for working through conflict, women (or anyone who has less power) will be reluctant to offer another perspective or challenge an existing idea. According to Helms, "If I don't agree with a decision that's being made by the exec team but am afraid to speak up, I'll walk out of that meeting realizing that nothing will change. That affects my commitment to the job and my sense of worth."[57]

Within the for-profit sector, several companies are already proving that ideological and structural change are not only possible but profitable. Slack, a company built to foster internal communication, grew quickly under the leadership of CEO Stewart Butterfield. From the beginning, he prioritized hiring women. In *Brotopia*, Chang writes, "In 2017, Slack reported that 43.5 percent of its employees were women, including 48 percent of managers and almost 30 percent of technical employees—far better numbers than almost any tech company in Silicon Valley."[58] They offer eighteen weeks of paid maternity leave and flexible work schedules. In contrast to many companies, perhaps specifically tech start-ups in Silicon Valley, their core values include curiosity, diligence, and empathy.[59] In 2023, Slack made $1.7 billion dollars in revenue and has a female CEO.[60]

Patagonia, a high-end outdoor clothing company, was started by the wife and husband team of Malinda and Yvon Chouinard back in 1973. Their commitment to their employees and the environment shapes how they do business. Patagonia offers corporate-sponsored on-site childcare at their headquarters (staffed by trained teachers) along with a host of other family-friendly policies and benefits, including paid family leave. Half of Patagonia's senior leadership and managers are women. Rose Marcario, former CEO of the company, believes Patagonia's commitment to families benefits everyone.[61] Almost 100 percent of the women who became moms while working at Patagonia returned to their roles within five years.

In her book *A Woman's Place*, author Katelyn Beaty writes, "We work in order to live into God's purposes for all of us: to reign over all of creation as his image bearers and representatives on earth. . . . We work in order to properly bear the image of God."[62] We cannot fulfill God's creation mandate unless all of us are justly compensated, treated fairly, and recognized for our contributions.

CHAPTER 4

MAKING IT LEGAL

Misogyny in the Government

Liberty, justice, and equality are core principles promised to all Americans. But can the 168 million women living in the US count on them, or are they only guaranteed for a select group of men?[1] American history reveals that every branch and all levels of the government have written, interpreted, and upheld laws that systematically constrain, discriminate against, exclude, and injure women. Occasionally, the public gets to witness this happening in real time.

Law professor Anita F. Hill, JD, planted a seed for the #MeToo movement long before hashtags or social media existed. On October 11, 1991, she did what was unthinkable at the time by speaking truth to men in power.

Hill testified before a Senate subcommittee, chaired by then Senator Joseph Biden and composed of all White men, on Clarence Thomas's nomination to the United States Supreme Court. After sharing some of her personal background and early legal work as Thomas's special assistant, she described his inappropriate and unprofessional advances.

It started with Thomas asking Hill out on a date. Hill testified, "What happened next, and telling the world about it, are the two most difficult experiences of my life. It is only after a great deal of agonized consideration and a great number of sleepless nights, that I am able to talk of these unpleasant matters to anyone but my close friends."[2]

Hill declined Thomas's invitation: "I was uncomfortable with the idea [of socializing with my boss] and told him so." She assumed Thomas would accept her unequivocal no and move on, but he did not. Not long after, he crossed significant professional and relational boundaries by talking about sex while at work. According to Hill, Thomas would initiate conversations on the premise of discussing various work projects but then "turn the conversation to a discussion of sexual matters. His conversations were very vivid" and included the content of pornographic films he had watched. "On several occasions, Thomas told me graphically of his own sexual prowess. . . . Because I was extremely uncomfortable talking about sex with him at all, and particularly in such a graphic way, I told him that I did not want to talk about these subjects."

When Thomas transitioned from the Department of Education to the Equal Employment Opportunity Commission (EEOC), he invited Hill to go with him. At the time of the trial, those who doubted the veracity of Hill's testimony found it suspicious that she accepted his offer. Several factors were surely at play. High-level government jobs were difficult to come by for women at that time, and Thomas, as her boss, would be key in recommending Hill for another position. Given Hill's intelligence and experience, it's highly probable that she knew the risks of working for Thomas and made a calculated choice to advance her career by moving to the EEOC. Additionally, sexual harassment was so pervasive that most women had learned to accept it as normal. After several months in this new job, Thomas again started pressuring her to go out with him and making sexualized comments about her clothing and appearance.

Hill concluded her testimony by saying she felt she had a duty to report this to the Senate and assured them, "I have no vendetta against Clarence Thomas . . . but I had to tell the truth. I could not keep silent."

By making that bold choice, she violated male politicians' sacrosanct rule that women should be silent—or invisible—in the halls of power.

The pushback was swift and cruel. Then Senator Arlen Specter from Pennsylvania said to Hill, "You testified this morning, in response to Senator Biden, that the most embarrassing question involved—and this is not too bad—women's large breasts. That is a word we use all the time."[3] I'm not sure how to read that response other than an admission that Specter and his peers routinely objectified women.

Hill was vilified by the press. Many male pundits accused her of lying even though she voluntarily took—and passed—a polygraph test.[4] Thomas refused to take one. Hill received sexualized phone messages and even bomb and death threats. Thomas was confirmed, and as of 2025, he is the oldest member of the United States Supreme Court.

That the senators tried to impugn Hill's character while giving Thomas a pass was egregious enough, but they also missed the point. Hill was willing to risk her reputation and career because she understood the connection between Thomas's past behavior and the potential for him to abuse the greater power that would be afforded to him as a member of the Supreme Court. Since he had already leveraged his power and sexually harassed at least one female employee, what would stop him from doing it again?* Hill recognized how his male entitlement and disrespect for women might affect how he would interpret laws, specifically those connected to workplace harassment, women's economic rights, and public safety—all of which are under the EEOC's jurisdiction.†

Despite the attacks against her, Hill's choice to come forward had an enormous and lasting impact. Her courage empowered other women

---

* Several other women were willing to corroborate Hill's experience, but Senator Biden never called them to testify.

† Given that the EEOC is "responsible for enforcing federal laws that make it illegal to discriminate against a job applicant or an employee because of the person's race, color, religion, sex . . . national origin, age . . . disability or genetic information," Thomas's actions should have disqualified him from the Court. U.S. Equal Employment Opportunity Commission, https://www.eeoc.gov/overview.

to acknowledge similar harassment and speak up. During a 2019 interview with *The New York Times*' editor Jessica Bennett at the New Rules Summit on Women and Power, Bennett reported, "In the year after your testimony, complaints to the [Equal Employment Opportunity Commission] about sexual harassment went up 73 percent. Some of the working women's groups like *9to5* reported their phone lines ringing off the hook with women—largely women—saying, 'You mean this is illegal? You mean I can do something about this?'"[5]

These proceedings gave the nation a window into some of the ways misogyny manifests in the US government. Though progress has been made since 1991, including more diverse representations and heightened awareness of bias and sexism, misogyny still has an oversize role in creating and upholding laws that prohibit women from consistently experiencing liberty, justice, and equal opportunity.[6]

The Birth of a Nation and the Denial of Women's Rights

When fifty-five men assembled in Philadelphia's Independence Hall to create the US Constitution in 1787, they undoubtedly discussed historic examples of effective governments. Given post-Enlightenment Europe's reverence for the classical elements of the Greco-Roman empire, it was only natural that the Founders incorporated many of the principles that governed Ancient Greece and Rome into the Constitution.

As early as the sixth century BC, the Greeks were developing a democratic system that included elected representatives, a written constitution, and courts of law. Despite these innovations, women were not permitted to vote or serve as representatives, because according to prevailing wisdom, they were not capable of governing themselves, let alone others.[7] They were also not allowed to participate in public debate or own land. If a husband predeceased his wife, she could inherit his wealth only if no sons or brothers were living. Though married women had social and familial influence, they lived under the authority of their husbands and were expected to produce male heirs. Many of these discriminatory practices were carried forward into the English and American governments.[8]

By the time the US Constitution was being written, women had been proving their physical hardiness and intellectual vigor for generations by leading, teaching, and innovating in many disciplines.[9] They also successfully managed households and worked side by side with men in family-owned businesses. Yet when men had the opportunity to acknowledge women's contributions and grant them equal rights, they apparently had misgivings.

Denying women and People of Color the right to vote was one of the most egregious and consequential flaws in the Constitution. It's impossible to fully understand the Founders' logic regarding women's right to vote, but it was likely connected to the commonly accepted lie that women had inferior intellects and fragile bodies. Some men believed if women thought too much or participated in politics, "their ovaries would atrophy."[10] This absurd thinking did not go uncontested. In a letter to her husband, John, Abigail Adams wrote, "In the new Code of Laws which I suppose it will be necessary for you to make I desire you would Remember the Ladies, and be more generous and favourable to them than your ancestors. Do not put such unlimited power into the hands of the Husbands. Remember all Men would be tyrants if they could."[11] Her charge was prescient. The men did forget the women, and they have abused their power.

The Founders were gifted men and they certainly attempted to create a form of governance that could serve and unify a pluralistic nation.[12] The three distinct branches of government, the system of checks and balances, the freedom given to individual states, and other innovations have permitted the US to function as a (mostly) cohesive, (mostly) united country. However, those who created the Constitution did not factor in how men's lust for power and deeply ingrained bias against women and People of Color would prevent the entire nation from fully flourishing for generations to come.

When misogyny is part of any government's DNA, women will face ongoing mistreatment and be judged as less than. For almost 250 years, American women have had to fight for equality and respect. In 1914, popular MIT biology professor William T. Sedgwick expressed a common concern that if women were given the right to vote, there would be "a total destruction of wifehood and the home, a total destruction of all the tender relations and associations that home involves, *but there will never be a relegation of the man to a subservient position*."[13] This perhaps names the unspoken reason some men didn't want women to vote: If women were given greater voice, it had the potential to erode male entitlement and require them to get their hands dirty by scrubbing floors and changing diapers.

Similar draconian sentiments were resurrected leading up to the 2024 US presidential election. A number of pastors, social media influencers, and politicians espoused their belief that the Nineteenth Amendment was a mistake and women's (specifically wives') right to vote should be revoked.[14] Hearing men harken back to an era when women were muted and prohibited from participating in governance was infuriating and chilling. It's impossible to explain such thinking apart from the presence of misogyny.

(Lack of) Equality

Denying women a voice in the government for the first 140 years resulted in multiple, highly consequential disadvantages, including the right to manage their finances, experience equal employment and educational opportunities, and receive fair trials. While these unfair practices may not have been formally written into the laws of the land, the government did little to prohibit them or foster equality.

It wasn't until 1974, when the Equal Credit Opportunity Act was passed, that women's right to open their own bank accounts and apply for credit was protected. In 1980, lawmakers and the courts finally agreed that sexual harassment was a form of discrimination based on the Civil Rights Act of 1964. Harvard University did not accept women into their medical school until 1945 or their law school until 1950. Yale University excluded female undergrads until 1969. The government chose to ignore these obvious forms of discrimination in education until 1972, when they passed Title IX, which addressed gender bias in all educational institutions that received federal funding.[15]

A concept called coverture can help us understand how such blatant sexism could be normalized and systematized. The term comes from a French expression, *feme-coverts*, or covered women. An eighteenth-century English document explains:

> By marriage, the husband and wife are one person in law: that is, the very being or legal existence of the woman is suspended during the marriage, or at least is incorporated and consolidated into that of the husband; under whose wing, protection, and *cover*, she performs everything; and is said to be . . . under the protection and influence of her husband, her *baron*, or lord; and her condition during her marriage is called her *coverture*.[16]

Though the misogynistic concepts reflected in coverture were obviously damaging and misguided, they found their way into American life and government. Various cases brought before the courts upheld the principles behind coverture, thereby making it common law and influencing how the states understood and interpreted the rights of women—specifically wives—for generations.[17]

Coverture had significant implications for spousal relationships. Because the husband subsumes the wife, implying domination, irrevocable sexual consent was given when a woman said, "I do." A wife's body, as well as any children she bore, were owned by her husband. Since wives were effectively incorporated into their husbands, and because it wasn't possible to charge someone for raping or assaulting themselves, husbands could beat or rape their wives with impunity. Such thinking defies logic and reveals how deeply male entitlement affected the interpretation and enforcement of the law. Marital rape was not abolished in all states until 1993.[18]

Wives were incredibly vulnerable under coverture. If they were physically or sexually abused, they had no recourse. If they needed to flee from their own homes due to the possibility of violence, they risked losing their children. The average wife in the average home had no guarantee her husband would not mistreat, dishonor, or abuse her—and get away with it.[19] This remains true today. Statistics from 2024 show that over half of female homicide victims are killed by a current or former intimate male partner.[20]

The underlying premise of coverture contains a kernel of truth. Women do need protection—but mostly from abusive, predatory men. Assuming male coverage is equivalent to or accomplishes the same goals as ensuring women basic human rights is misguided. Individual states began overturning coverture in 1839, but the Supreme Court did not officially rule against these practices until 1980.[21]

Part of the reason it took the courts so long to make such abuses of power illegal can be traced to the misogynistic biases that have affected the judicial branch of the government. The Sixth Amendment, ratified in 1791, promises all citizens a trial by a jury of their peers. Women had been tried in colonial courtrooms long before the Constitution was ratified, but due to men's misgivings about their intellectual aptitude, women were not allowed to serve as jurors in all capacities, including federal cases, until the Civil Rights Act of 1957.[22] (Women are still appointed to far fewer judgeships.)[23] Even today, research shows women are less likely to win in court—as either defendants or plaintiffs—when no women are on the jury.[24]

Considering American history, it's hard not to wonder how many men who harmed women have been exonerated, and conversely, how many women have been placed in harm's way, wrongly incarcerated, and in some cases executed because of this. Perhaps the most well-known example is the Salem witch "trials," whereby, between 1692 and 1693, nineteen women and one man were executed based on anecdotal evidence.

Given the prevailing negative biases against women, it's no surprise that multiple court cases have upheld discriminatory practices. In 1873, Myra Bradwell sued for her right to practice law in the state of Illinois, citing the Privileges or Immunities Clause in the Fourteenth Amendment. The all-male state supreme court disagreed with her in an 8 to 1 vote (*Bradwell v. Illinois*), citing that married women were prohibited from entering into legal agreements. (Recall the discussion of coverture.)

To further understand how some men in power perceived women, ponder Justice Joseph Bradford's concurring opinion: "The natural and proper timidity and delicacy which belongs to the female sex evidently unfits it for many of the occupations of civil life. . . . The paramount destiny and mission of women are to fulfill the noble and benign offices of wife and mother. This is the law of the Creator."[25] No biblical references were cited. This ruling was not completely overturned until 1971.[26]

Though women can now serve as jurors and judges, the type of misogynistic bias that Justice Bradford espoused has not disappeared from the courtroom. A 2020 study by the state of New York backed up a similar study done thirty years earlier, revealing that "pervasive gender bias exists against women litigants, lawyers, and court employees and is manifest in court dispositions dealing with divorce, child support, custody, domestic violence, rape, prostitution, and awarding of damages."[27]

"Pervasive gender bias" may incline judges, lawyers, and jurors to see women as less credible witnesses. In a paper for the University of Pennsylvania Carey Law School, professors Deborah Epstein and Lisa Goodman wrote, "Women find their credibility discounted by the partners who abuse them, by the larger society in which they live, and by the gatekeepers of the justice and social service systems to which they turn for help."[28] This is particularly consequential when we're dealing with sexual assault. State and federal judicial branches have had the power to make discriminatory practices illegal and protect women, but they've been sluggish to do so. Whenever women are prohibited from voting, serving as elected officials and jurors, or working in certain professions, they're being denied rights that should legally be theirs. While it's true that many antiquated laws have been overturned, the systemic injustices and inequalities created by the government continue to adversely impact women in many areas, including their personal safety and well-being.

Rape Culture

Rape and sexualized violence are among the most blatant and heinous manifestations of misogyny. The effects of these crimes are magnified if those who create and uphold the laws aren't outraged enough to stop them from happening. When a society chooses to normalize or condone sexualized violence against women and children, it may lead to what's known as a "rape culture," a term popularized by feminists during the 1970s. Rape cultures minimize the act, regarding it as an unfortunate or inevitable event, rather than a horrific crime.[29] This mentality results in further injury and injustice, such as protecting rapists rather than rape survivors. The following three cases demonstrate this tragic reality.

In 1944, twenty-four-year-old Recy Taylor was going home from church in rural Alabama when she was abducted and gang raped by six White men. Despite strong evidence and one assailant's confession, all six men were found not guilty. Twice. Both times by all-White, all-male juries. Recy Taylor was a Black mother.[30]

Brock Turner, a White, nineteen-year-old Stanford University student-athlete, was caught raping an unconscious coed near a frat party in 2015. Aaron Persky, a Santa Clara County (California) superior court judge, "sentenced Turner to six months in jail, three years of probation, and lifetime sex-offender registration, saying that a longer prison term 'would have a severe impact on him.'"[31] Certainly, a longer prison term would have had an adverse impact on Turner. But Turner's actions would have a severe impact on his victim for inestimably longer than six months. Judge Persky was later recalled from the bench.

In 2023 a New York jury found Donald Trump liable for sexually harassing (the original charge was rape) and defaming columnist E. Jean Carroll in the 1990s. There was sufficient evidence that Trump was liable for "touching, grabbing, groping for his own sexual pleasure against her will," which lines up with his boasts from the *Access Hollywood* tape.[32] Two other women testified that they'd been similarly sexually harassed by Trump. Carroll was awarded $5 million in damages.

As these three cases reveal, women pay the price in a rape culture. Women are always mindful of their vulnerability, often afraid, and constantly adapting their behaviors to prevent men from violating them. The onus of not being attacked falls on us. This helps to explain why, in a 2024 viral TikTok, many women agreed they would rather encounter a bear in the woods than an unknown man. The reasons women offered for their choice were telling: "If a bear attacked me, no one would say it was my fault." "I couldn't be blamed for what I was wearing." "Bears are more predictable." Most of the men who commented on the post either were outraged or tried to explain ursine behavior to the women on the thread.

Rape is about men wielding power with the goal of intimidating and destabilizing women so they know who's boss. Rape perpetuates male hierarchy and female subordination. Rape is never the victim's fault. Never. Regardless of what the victim was wearing, how much alcohol she drank, or how much she may have flirted. Rape means *non-consensual* penetration. Ninety-three percent of rapes are committed by men. Women are victimized 90 percent of the time.[33]

One of the indicators of rape culture is how victims are treated postattack. In patriarchal, hierarchical cultures where women are perceived as less credible, it's not uncommon for men—and occasionally for women who choose to be adjacent to powerful men—to cast aspersions on, malign, or even threaten women who charge men with sexualized violence. (A small percentage of false rape charges do occur, but that reality should not cast doubt on the vast majority of women's experiences.)[34] Rather than being believed and cared for after enduring a violent trauma, a woman may be subject to indifferent or harsh treatment and her character may be discredited.

One friend recounted how she was passed between three different police departments after being sexually assaulted in a public setting. None of the officers she spoke with were willing to take her testimony, and none of them demonstrated the slightest concern or offered to help. Their indifference communicated she wasn't worth their time. (By highlighting such mistreatment, I am not discounting the police officers who do listen to and believe women and routinely put themselves in harm's way to protect those who are vulnerable.)

Meanwhile, when an attack is reported, men often close ranks around each other. After the military's 1991 Tailhook Symposium in Las Vegas, where eighty-three women and seven men (many of whom were civilians) reported being sexually assaulted by members of the armed forces, top military officials downplayed the severity of the allegations.[35] Lt. Paula Coughlin, among those assaulted, was the first to go public and demand accountability. A lengthy investigation followed, but no one was charged or tried for sexual assault. The secretary of the Navy (Henry L. Garrett III) eventually stepped down and accepted responsibility. After blowing the whistle, Coughlin reported being routinely harassed and receiving poor performance reviews. She resigned from the Navy in 1994.

The disrespectful, dismissive way women may be treated postattack is one of the factors that discourages them from reporting acts of sexualized violence. According to the Rape, Abuse & Incest National Network (RAINN), out of every one thousand sexual assaults, 310 are reported to the police and only twenty-five perpetrators will be incarcerated. These statistics are similar in the military.[36] A 2010 article in *The Baltimore Sun* revealed that 40 percent of emergency calls about rape were never investigated: "*Almost half* of reported rapes [in New Orleans] were called something else in the official paperwork," effectively reducing the city's rape statistics—and further endangering countless women.[37]

Police departments can enforce rape culture based on how they process evidence. During the forensic exam, hair, blood, skin, and saliva samples are taken from the victims and placed in a sealed rape kit. Over the past decade, more than two hundred thousand unopened rape kits have been discovered in police warehouses across the United States. In an article for *The Atlantic*, journalist Barbara Bradley Hagerty asked, "How many rapes could have been prevented if the police had believed the first victim, launched a thorough investigation, and caught the rapist? How many women would have been spared a brutal assault?"[38] Even though DNA samples are one of the best ways to apprehend assailants, police literally shelved the painstakingly collected evidence. As a result, rapists keep raping. Quoting Hagerty again, "In 49 out of every 50 rape cases, the alleged assailant goes free . . . to assault again. Which means that rape—more than murder, more than robbery or assault—is by far the easiest violent crime to get away with."[39] The Department of Justice created a national protocol for sexual assault examinations, but processing rape kits—which cost between $1,000 and $1,500 per kit—is up to the discretion of local officers and requires trained personnel.

Given the accuracy of DNA testing and the emotional and economic cost of sexualized attacks (the per-victim lifetime cost of rape is $122,461), prosecuting and jailing men who sexually assault women should become a priority across all levels and branches of government.[40] Failure to do so sends a clear signal to women regarding the government's skewed priorities and general disinterest in women's welfare. Unfortunately, this is not the only high-stakes scenario in which the government should do everything in its power to protect and support women but chooses not to.

Easing Women's "Undue Burden"

Abortion is one of the most polarizing issues of our time, and the ideological walls that divide us seem to be topped with razor wire and glass shards. To engage with this topic is dangerous, but to avoid it would be cowardly. I can't adequately address all the issues connected to abortion and misogyny in such a limited space. But I do want to explore how the US government contributes to the difficulties and hardships that pregnant women and mothers face via legislation, policy, and court rulings.

I'll lay my cards on the table so you don't have to wonder what's in my hand. I am pro-life from womb to tomb and believe all life is worth protecting. Practically speaking, this means I oppose the death penalty and euthanasia, back families who foster, support commonsense gun control, and think the government should tangibly support and protect children until they become adults.* These convictions are based on my faith, my volunteer work in prison, my personal experiences of motherhood, and our granddaughter's very short life. My beliefs do not prevent me from loving, learning from, and respecting those who disagree with me.

Though we tend to categorize beliefs about abortion as either pro-choice or pro-life, such binaries fail to represent the many nuanced beliefs held by individuals and fail to acknowledge the complex situations we find ourselves in. For instance, some who refer to themselves as pro-life would concede that women should be able to secure a safe, legal abortion in the case of rape or incest and would not oppose the procedure if a mother's life was in danger. (Abortion opponents need to understand the procedure is not always elective. According to the American College of Obstetricians and Gynecologists and Physicians

* This includes pre- and postnatal care, ongoing healthcare, and access to nutritious food, safe housing, and education.

for Reproductive Health, in certain situations, women may need an abortion to survive life-threatening complications.)[41] Increasingly, women on both sides of the abortion debate believe the government is not trustworthy to legislate women's reproductive choices because it has not consistently considered women's best interests when creating and enforcing laws. While many pro-choice advocates see the right to an abortion as an essential component of women's healthcare and personal freedom, they also value motherhood and tend to champion legislation that supports families. Holding an awareness of these complexities while being respectful is essential if we hope to address the disparities and injustices pregnant women and mothers face.

Additionally, when a woman's right to choose is pitted against the developing baby's right to life, the differences can seem irreconcilable and may result in an "us versus them" mentality.* This divides women and makes it difficult for us to work together, even when we see eye to eye.

If eradicating misogyny and making the world a safer, more equitable place for women and children is something that all of us can agree on, then perhaps we could lean toward each other and discern specific ways to care for and support women during pregnancy, childbirth, and motherhood. With that possibility in mind, I want to focus on two overarching factors that harm women and contribute to the hardships that abortion purports to alleviate for women facing unplanned or unwanted pregnancies:

1. The government's failure to understand or care about the massive challenges pregnant women and mothers face, as revealed by the language of the Supreme Court's rulings on abortion.

* I am not comfortable using the term *fetus* as that feels clinical and dehumanizing. The potentiality for life is present, which is why *developing baby* feels more accurate to me. I am aware that not everyone will agree.

2. The government's and our culture's refusal to hold men to the same standard of sexual ethics that they hold women to.

The language in many of the rulings on abortion communicates how the US government has come to understand its responsibilities regarding pregnant women and mothers. In the landmark 1973 case *Roe v. Wade*, the Supreme Court interpreted abortion as a private, individual matter, protected under the Fourteenth Amendment. The majority opinion, written by Justice Harry Blackmun, acknowledged that "maternity, or additional offspring, may force upon the woman a distressful life and future. . . . Psychological harm might be imminent. Mental and physical health may be taxed by childcare."[42]

Nineteen years later in *Planned Parenthood v. Casey*, which affirmed *Roe*'s holding of the right to previability abortions, the court stated their belief that women should have the right to make their own choice because pregnancy might result in an "undue burden."[43] Justice Blackmun explained his support for abortion rights by noting, "The State does not compensate women for their services; instead, it is assumed that they owe this duty as a matter of course."[44] *Harris v. McRae* (1980) held that "the state had no duty to help pregnant women implement their choice about procreation, whether they wanted to terminate their pregnancies or continue them."[45] Other rulings and legislative acts affirmed *Roe* but concluded that federal funds could not be used to cover abortion except in the case of rape, incest, or to save a mother's life.[46]

The Supreme Court's decisions have consistently communicated what seems to be an indifference toward pregnant women and mothers. They have also clarified that since they believe the government has "no duty" or responsibility (moral or legal) to aid or support pregnant women and mothers, they cannot expect or demand that women fulfill the role of bearing children. The right to an abortion became their one concession. This was revoked in the 2022 case *Dobbs v. Jackson Women's Health Organization*, which punted the issue of abortion's legality back to the states.

Basing abortion rights on the belief that the beginning stage of life—the bearing part—is a private, individual matter appeared to respect women's autonomy by entrusting them to make this crucial decision. But if we lift the veneer, the government's logic seems tainted by indifference and a rather remarkable shortsightedness. By using privacy and individual rights as the foundation to support the right to an abortion, the government's meta-message reads along the lines of, "You decide and leave us out of it because this matter doesn't concern us." Not only does this speak volumes to a pregnant woman—particularly one who does not feel confident in her ability to support a child—it belies the reality that raising children cannot and must not be seen as an isolated endeavor revolving solely around the mother and child.

If the child is to grow into a healthy, whole, contributing adult, the mother-child dyad must be surrounded and supported by a community, as well as a functional local, state, and national government. A solitary mother and child will never survive or thrive without education, healthcare, and other essential government-funded services and supports. Again, I'm not arguing that women are incapable of making their own reproductive decisions but rather pointing out how court cases reveal the government's profound apathy and cluelessness regarding what women need to mother.

The government not only cuts women loose to bear and raise children without tangible support but also reinforces cultural norms around men's irresponsible sexual behavior and lack of responsibility regarding parenthood. The 2024 election cycle demonstrated unequivocally that sexually coercive and abusive men will be rewarded. Men are not shamed when they impregnate women, even though biologically speaking, every pregnancy points to a man's contribution. They are not fired from their jobs. They are not ostracized in their religious communities—even when their behavior is abusive or criminal as we'll explore in chapter 7. Yet within some religious circles, women who have had abortions are routinely shamed and vilified. Not only are men free to sow their seeds whenever and however they desire, but they are affirmed and celebrated. As a society, we would rather make women accountable for all pregnancies and any subsequent children than put pressure on men to control their sexual impulses or slightly diminish their pleasure by using condoms. These misogynistic norms weigh heavily on women.

Consider how the deck is stacked against pregnant women and mothers. There is a lack of free, high-quality pre- and postnatal care available to all women. Most women do not receive paid maternity leave. The workplace is overtly hostile to pregnant women and mothers, normalizing "the wombless male body."[47] Our government doesn't consistently punish men for harming women (in the case of rape, coercion, or sexual harassment), doesn't consistently hold fathers responsible for their own children,[48] and fails to value pregnant women and mothers. If some lawmakers have their way, certain states may move toward punishing women who seek abortions—which feels akin to handing male adulterers rocks so they can stone the female adulteress.[49] Why are we surprised that women demand this right? It's one of the ways they can experience autonomy in a world where men try to control them. Access to abortion also allows women to have sex without experiencing any unwanted long-term consequences—something men have always had.

While I understand the importance of autonomy and freedom, I'm not convinced they should be our ultimate goals. Pursuing them via the fight for abortion rights *may* take those healthy desires to unhealthy extremes that end up being more aligned with toxic masculinity than flourishing interdependence. Both have the potential to re-entrench rather than eradicate misogyny and lead us away from rather than toward securing supports and protections for pregnant women and mothers.

There are specific initiatives that the government could take to ease the many difficulties that pregnant women and mothers experience and potentially reduce the felt need for abortions in the process.[*] Before I lay out a few ideas, I want to state my personal belief that it's best for everyone—but especially women—if sexual intercourse is confined to covenanted relationships. I also believe heterosexual couples should engage in more honest conversations about whether they want to be parents before having intercourse rather than relying on abortion as a backup plan. I realize that in a pluralistic society where sexual expression is seen as a birthright, expecting others to agree with me or follow these practices is unrealistic.

Perhaps one of the easiest and most cost-efficient measures to prevent unwanted pregnancy would be to provide free condoms in all health clinics, schools and colleges, and venues where men tend to congregate, such as gyms, sporting events, and bars.[50] Condoms cost much less than other forms of birth control and, when used correctly, are highly effective in preventing pregnancies and STDs.[51] Furthermore, when men use condoms, they take responsibility for preventing pregnancy rather than leaving it up to women. Some men dislike and even disapprove of condoms. If women refused to have intercourse unless men agreed to use them, they would get over it.[†]

Advocating for thorough, agenda-free sex education (including abstinence) alongside providing free, prophylactic birth control typically incites a strong reaction among some Christian subcultures.[‡] They fear that if you talk about sex, even in a clinical fashion, it will incentivize sexual behavior, particularly in vulnerable teens. The reality is teens are appropriately curious, live in a sex-saturated world, and need accurate information. It seems much smarter to provide them with facts than to have them turn to social media or

* I acknowledge that this may not be a priority for everyone reading this. I'm looking at it strictly from a practical perspective. Preventing a pregnancy costs less, is not as inconvenient as having an abortion, and is safer for women in the long run.

† I'm referring to consensual sex here. In the case of coercion or rape, women don't have any say.

‡ Though I understand and respect those who feel any form of birth control cannot be supported by Scripture, I disagree with this.

their peers.[52] If one of the goals is to reduce unwanted or unintended pregnancies so that abortion rates drop, providing free male contraception just makes sense.

Certainly, the government can't legislate or enforce male condom use. But it can create and enforce laws that provide financial support for pregnant women and mothers. These should include covering 100 percent of the cost women incur during pregnancy and delivery.* They must also pay for or subsidize childcare for all qualifying families and provide paid maternity leave. Because of what pregnancy and childbirth requires of them, women need at least eight weeks off from work just so their bodies can heal—longer if a C-section is required or there are any complications. If we factor in bonding, which is essential for a baby's development, families would most benefit from one parent having eight to twelve months of paid family leave.† As previously mentioned, there is no federally supported, paid maternity (or paternity) leave in the US except for certain federal employees.[53] Some states and employers offer a version of parental leave, but many do not guarantee full pay, and the length of leave tends to be far too short given how expensive childcare is.[54] By contrast, the European Union mandates a minimum of fourteen weeks paid leave for both parents, and some EU countries offer far more generous leave for one or both parents.

Expecting women to fulfill the duty of parenthood as they simultaneously pay the emotional, physical, and fiscal cost is unreasonable and unfair, particularly for single mothers or those who lack financial

* Though the Affordable Care Act is supposed to cover all costs related to pregnancy and childbirth, it doesn't. Many women who have delivered babies in the last five years have confirmed that they are still paying for services, some in the thousands of dollars.

† After decades of research, it has been proven that a parent and child's ability to bond is essential for a baby's health and well-being. Bonding is based on emotional-physical needs being consistently, lovingly met by a caregiver, especially during the first two to three years. Marshall Klaus, John Kennell, Phyllis Klaus, *Bonding: Building the Foundation of Secure Attachment and Independence* (Boston: Addison & Wesley, 1996).

means. This is partly why some women feel the right to an abortion is so crucial. The estimated price tag for raising a child for eighteen years is upward of $300,000.[55] Currently, the federal tax credit is $2,000 per qualifying child, which barely touches one year of expenses.[56] Any parent knows that the psychological and spiritual cost of caring for and raising a child cannot be quantified. I think most women would agree with me that motherhood is a sacred, beautiful, and deeply transformational experience. That said, we should not expect women to bear and raise children without ongoing tangible support.

I want to paraphrase my definition of misogyny from chapter 1. Misogyny blinds both individuals and entire cultures from seeing women as equal image bearers, fosters cruel hierarchies, disdains weakness and vulnerability (in all forms), and prevents people groups and individuals from fully thriving.

Until every sexually active man commits to using contraceptive measures to prevent unwanted pregnancy, refuses to overpower or take advantage of women, and takes responsibility for any children he sires; and until the government, the culture, and the church tangibly support women during their pregnancy and into motherhood, many women will continue to experience pregnancy and motherhood as an undue burden. That's the bitter fruit of misogyny.

Moving Toward Liberty, Justice, and Equality for All

Despite the many manifestations of misogyny described in this chapter, we are moving toward a more just and equitable society. We're just not there yet, and progress should not be mistaken as victory.

Women have been—and continue to be—key drivers in this slow and steady gain. Soon after the Nineteenth Amendment was enacted in 1919, it became clear how women would influence the laws of the land for the betterment of everyone. In 1921, the legislature approved the Sheppard-Towner Maternity and Infancy Protection Act that provided federal funds to reduce infant mortality by educating and supporting women before and after they gave birth.[57] This act was based on the work done in the previous congressional session by Representative Jeannette Pickering Rankin (the first woman elected to Congress), Julia Lathrop (head of the Children's Bureau), and the Women's Joint Congressional Committee. Lathrop and Rankin received no credit for this innovative bill.

President Franklin Delano Roosevelt appointed social worker Frances Perkins to his cabinet as Secretary of Labor, where she served from 1933 to 1945. Perkins believed that the government should protect women, children, and employees. She had an astonishing career serving under FDR. She capped women's workweek to forty-eight hours, fought for minimum wages, and helped create the Social Security Act. Esther Peterson, who served as Assistant Secretary of Labor under President Kennedy, spearheaded the landmark Equal Pay Act of 1963. An article in *The New York Times* states,

> Women in Congress sponsor and co-sponsor more bills than men do, and bring 9 percent more federal money to their home districts, according to a study in the *American Journal of Political Science.* Those bills are more likely to benefit women and children or address issues like education, health and poverty. In Congress, for instance, it was women who fought for women's health coverage in the Affordable Care Act, sexual harassment rules in the military, the inclusion of women in medical trials, and child care vouchers in welfare overhaul.[58]

Even if we consider these and other similar gains, our government is not yet truly for *all* the people because it doesn't provide liberty, justice, and equality *for all.* (The federal government still has not ratified the Equal Rights Amendment.)[59] We won't get there unless more of us become engaged, however we're able. This will require the kind of sacrifice, intentionality, and courage Anita Hill demonstrated. Toward the end of her book *Speaking Truth to Power*, Hill shares that she is often asked, "Would you do it again?" She responds, "I would do it again, but I could only do it because of the great tangible and intangible support I had throughout."[60]

Like Anita Hill, some of us will be called to tell our stories and speak truth to power. Some will be called to create policy, defend those who are vulnerable, or change policing protocols. And others will step up to encourage and support these individuals. Regardless of our specific calling, if we want to disrupt the many ways misogyny has affected our local, state, and national government, we can't simply sit back and expect the professionals to do the work. It's up to each of us.

CHAPTER 5

BEHIND THE SCREENS

Misogyny in Media and Entertainment

The entertainment and media industries run on stories. Stories of life and hope. Stories of death and despair. Stories that draw us together and stories that polarize us. These stories have the capacity to speak truth and bring healing—which means they also have the power to distort reality and cause harm. The latter is particularly problematic when misogyny is written into the storyline.

Simone Biles is one of the most gifted athletes of all time. She won Olympic gold in four gymnastic events, including the individual all-around, during the 2016 games in Rio and was poised to repeat this achievement in the 2021 Tokyo games.[1]

However, after a mishap on the vault during the team competition, she withdrew from further events due to, in her words, "mental health issues." Simone had developed what gymnasts refer to as "the twisties." When this happens, gymnasts lose their sense of where they are in physical space, which can be both frightening and dangerous when performing aerial moves. Biles knew better than anyone the potential consequences for herself and her teammates if she ignored what her body was trying to tell her.

That didn't make her decision any easier. Though young, she was a seasoned competitor and understood how the public would respond. In an interview with podcaster Alex Cooper, Biles recounted that the first thoughts that flooded her mind after landing that vault were, "America will hate me. The world is going to hate me."[2] While her teammates and coaches supported her decision, a vocal minority expressed their displeasure on sports commentaries, nightly news shows, and of course, social media. *Saturday Night Live* co-head writer and comedian Michael Che mocked her on his Instagram account.[3] Aaron Reitz, a deputy attorney general with no gymnastic experience, took to Twitter and referred to his fellow Texan as a "selfish, childish national embarrassment."[4]

Her mostly male critics were either unaware of or unsympathetic to how many layers of misogyny and racism factored into her choice to withdraw. As a Black athlete in a sport that's predominately White, Biles has faced intense pressure to excel. Additionally, she was one of more than two hundred female athletes, some as young as six, abused by Larry Nassar, the USA Gymnastics team doctor. Between the Rio games and the Tokyo games, many of Biles's teammates came forward with their stories and pressed charges. During Nassar's 2017–2018 trial, it was revealed that though other coaches and administrators in the USA Gymnastics organization were informed about Nassar's criminal activity, they did nothing, thus enabling him to continue violating the female athletes.

Biles chose not to testify at the trial because she wasn't ready to be in the same space with Nassar, but her pain finally had a name. In the Netflix series *Simone Biles Rising*, she admitted that "when everything came out, that was all you could think about because it's like walking around with *survivor* on your forehead. Being . . . an advocate for that, it's so mentally exhausting."[5]

As is often the case with women who are public figures—particularly Black women—critics did not approve of Biles taking care of herself. She was not allowed to be a person with limits and needs. Her pain and suffering didn't seem to matter to her critics. They assumed Biles somehow *owed them* and needed to uphold their beliefs about American triumphalism.

Biles is one of many famous young women who have been maligned and mistreated by the press and on social media, where people are increasingly free to share their worst, unfiltered thoughts without any accountability. Naomi Osaka, Taylor Swift, Serena Williams, Britney Spears, Amy Winehouse, and others have all experienced "the media's power to elevate and destroy young women in the public eye."[6] Kindness and respect get sacrificed on the altar of popularity and profit.

When male entitlement, profit, and power are among the driving forces within a biased, hierarchical system, women and girls will inevitably be used and abused. In this type of cultural milieu, women have no chance of thriving because their value is contingent on ever-shifting, unrealistic standards that objectify and commodify them.

Distorting Normal

When families started putting televisions in their living rooms back in the 1950s and '60s, they were ignorant of how the medium—and all the subsequent iterations—would affect them and the culture. We are no longer ignorant. The stats are in regarding hours watched, advertising dollars spent, young minds influenced (for good and ill), and yes, misogynistic ideals and practices propagated. It's not necessarily that the content has become more misogynistic (sitcoms in the '60s and '70s produced some truly wince-worthy content pertaining to women) but that misogynistic ideals and practices have infiltrated every aspect of the media and entertainment industries.

Both industries have deep pockets and enormous influence.* Since their advent, they have been dominated by men. In 2023, women

* I'm including television, movies, advertising, news, professional athletics, and social media in these two categories. The link being mediums that we turn to for news, information, or entertainment.

comprised 14.7 percent of movie directors, 25 percent of screenplay writers, 13 percent of video game designers, and approximately 10 percent of software engineers.[7] That translates to scripts, video games, apps, algorithms, and more conceived of mostly by men, who may or may not be aware of their gender-based biases or misogynistic leanings. Even if they are aware, the companies they work for and their audiences may prefer androcentric scripts.

Because women have less power and therefore less influence in these industries, they have fewer opportunities to call the shots (literally and figuratively). Not surprisingly, many of the narratives perpetuate a misogynistic worldview where women are taken advantage of, play secondary or stereotypical roles, or are on the receiving end of male animosity.

The Bechdel Test, created by graphic novelist Alison Bechdel in 1985, is a simple way to evaluate how women are portrayed in films and other forms of fiction. To pass the test, there must be at least two named women featured, and they must have a conversation about something other than men. That's a low bar, but a BBC analysis revealed that since 1929, only 50 percent of the movies that have won the Oscar for best picture have been able to pass this criterion.[8] (And even if a movie passes the test, it might portray women unfavorably.) The more we learn about these realities, the more difficult it becomes to ignore misogyny's influence.

The primary goal of most entertainment and media companies is to amuse their audience while making a profit, not dismantle systemic injustices such as misogyny.[9] They're giving the public what the public wants. But at the same time, they're shaping and enforcing societal expectations about everything from how much agency women should have to what their bodies should look like. As a result, a mythologized woman becomes the standard, which can make the remaining 99 percent of us feel inadequate and invisible. Though the same could be said about the discrepancies between the average American man and male actors, women—particularly those in the public eye—face more intense scrutiny. When women fail to measure up, we may be referred to in vicious, pejorative terms such as *horseface*, *dogface*, and *fat pig*. I've never heard such demeaning monikers applied to men.

Female beauty is subjective, and at the same time, highly exclusionary cultural biases exist regarding what type of woman qualifies as beautiful. This is true regardless of which culture we're referring to. Considering the women we see on our screens, those deciding where the spotlight rests must work off the same manual. The average American White woman (age twenty and up) is approximately five foot three and weighs from 160 to 170 pounds. Her waist is thirty-eight inches.[10] A typical female model (regardless of race) is five foot eight to five foot nine, weighs 118 pounds, and has a waist measuring between twenty-two and twenty-six inches.[11] Female television and film actresses have an average height of five foot six and a weight of 117 pounds.[12]

Women with high cheekbones, long hair and legs, full breasts, and small waists tend to be seen as the apex of beauty in White culture. Black, Latina, and Asian cultures have their own criteria that narrow the scope of what qualifies as beautiful. Icons who meet the strict metrics hold tremendous sway over all of us, motivating teens and young women to measure themselves against these impossible standards and homogenize themselves via filters and makeup techniques.

Women who succeed in professional athletics, entertainment, and media but deviate from whatever cultural standard is seen as normative are constantly confronted by the ways their beauty doesn't measure up. Serena Williams is considered by many to be the greatest female tennis player of all time. As with Simone Biles, her athleticism and power dazzle. She is both powerful and beautiful. *But she's not White.* Again, the intersection of racism and misogyny results in cruelty. In 2014, the president of the Russian Tennis Federation, Shamil Tarpischev, publicly described Serena and her sister, Venus, as "brothers" who were "scary" to look at.[13] The Women's Tennis Association banned Tarpischev for a year, fined him $25,000, and forced him to apologize.

Rev. Liz Walker began her long tenure as a news anchor when

women were just beginning to be hired in this field. She recalls, "They didn't know what to do with women on television shows. On some newscasts, female anchors had to wear uniforms, but the female meteorologists had to wear hot pants. The standards for how we were supposed to present ourselves were all over the place. I was constantly trying to change what I looked like because I was not what they thought a woman should be."[14] Walker is a stunning Black woman who happens to be six feet tall.

During her first anchor job in Denver, Colorado, she was told she had to get the gap between her teeth fixed, because "according to management, it was unattractive. So I got my teeth fixed. I bought into the whole thing. I was so naive. This was a new frontier. I was willing to do whatever because I wanted to be part of the industry. It wasn't until much later that I realized the big mistake that I'd made. That gap was considered a beauty mark in some African traditions." As Walker and so many other women have learned, it can be difficult to appreciate cultural beauty standards without being beholden to them.

The standard that's presented is actually a mirage that can lead women and girls to feel deficient. As they attempt to address their perceived deficiencies, they may gravitate toward social media for advice and encouragement. Anyone who's spent more than ten minutes scrolling through TikTok or Instagram will attest that no expertise or legitimate credentials are required to reach thousands or even millions of viewers—even if the content focuses on consequential topics like dieting, nutrition, and mental health. Once a viewer shows interest in losing weight by liking a post or clicking a link, the algorithm feeds them similar videos and posts such as "my weight loss journey," pro-anorexic communities, and prescription weight loss products such as Ozempic. Many dieting and body image influencers are teens and young adults who have figured out how to game the industry and capitalize on others' fears and insecurities. Followers are led to believe that if they mimic these stars, maybe, just maybe, down the road they might become the next "bellwether of cultural beauty standards."[15]

I worry that many of the celebrities and popular influencers are leading an entire generation of girls toward a destructive end goal for the sake of their own profit and popularity. The lifestyle and beauty advice they dispense can have adverse, lifelong ramifications. Approximately 2,500 teen girls aged nineteen and under had breast augmentation surgery in 2022.[16] Physician, author, and policy maker Diana Zuckerman likes to remind us, "There are no epidemiological studies or clinical trials on the safety and long-term risks of these procedures for adolescents."[17] Breast implants tend to last between ten and twenty years. That means a seventeen-year-old will need to repeat the surgery at least four and up to six or seven times over the course of her life. Each surgery increases scar tissue and may interfere with lactation.

One popular twentysomething influencer talked viewers through her breast augmentation as she nonchalantly applied fourteen different makeup products to her face. She confessed that part of why she spent her childhood savings on the procedure was that she wanted people to notice.[18] She also admitted, "I know a lot of younger girls . . . are watching me and I don't want to set any unrealistic standards. . . . This is also not me convincing anyone of getting a boob job. You should love yourself, but if there's something you want to do for yourself, then do it. Don't care what other people think." Of course, she just told us she does care what people think. The first comment under her post reads, "I love how alix [*sic*] is so open and she isn't fake and makes her life seem perfect." That this viewer and many others equate perfection with extensive makeup routines, cosmetic surgery, and endless hours creating and watching TikTok videos is tragic.[19]

As Alix's video confirms, girls and young women are being fed inconsistent, confusing messaging. Supposedly, we live in an age of body and sex positivity. Teens and young adults are told to resist anything that holds them back—including gender stereotypes and their innate biology—so they can live as their "authentic, best selves." At the same time, influencers—who are mostly doing the bidding of corporate America—communicate that young women and girls must conform to unhealthy, sexist stereotypes if they hope to be popular.

Sephora and other beauty lines are actively marketing their goods to tweens, including anti-aging creams and serums, some of which are known to damage the skin of young users.[20] Before a single pimple or wrinkle appears, eight- and nine-year-old girls are conditioned to believe they're inadequate and that aging is unacceptable even as they're being coached to appear older and sexier than is developmentally appropriate. Whose normal are we chasing?

The long-term negative impact of social media and advertising directed at teens is just beginning to come into sharper focus. Repeatedly comparing one's body or life to the distortions presented on our screens can have a direct correlation to viewers' self-esteem, overall mental health, and peer relationships. In her book *Over the Influence*, author Kara Alaimo reports that "seeing idealized women's bodies in ads makes girls feel lower body satisfaction afterwards."[21]

According to Facebook whistleblower Frances Haugen, internal research found that "32% of teen girls admitted that 'when they felt bad about their bodies, Instagram made them feel worse.'"[22] A study done for the National Institutes of Health confirmed that "the widespread use of social media in teenagers and young adults could increase body dissatisfaction as well as their drive for thinness, therefore rendering them more vulnerable to eating disorders."[23] Other research shows how extended social media use can contribute to anxiety, depression, and suicidality in teens, particularly girls.[24] Author Donna Jackson Nakazawa warns that "recent suicide trends also point to a growing epidemic of despair among girls." She continues, "The rate at which preteen and teen girls take their own lives has tripled over the past twenty years, including in girls ages ten to fourteen."[25]

Social media harms both sexes, but girls suffer disproportionately. In *The Anxious Generation*, social psychologist Jonathan Haidt writes, "There is a clear, consistent, and sizable link between heavy social media use and mental illness for girls. . . . The more time a girl spends on social media, the more likely she is to be depressed."[26] This is connected to girls' "greater need for communion,"[27] the reality that girls' social capital is intertwined with their looks (which are relentlessly critiqued on social media), and the fact that they spend more time online than boys. Though more research is needed to prove causation, there seems to be a clear correlation between social media usage and mental health issues for girls. Journalist Marcie Bianco observed, "By turning our lives into a series of images, and attempting to be desired or 'liked' by everyone, we end up in a state of alienation—both from others and from ourselves."[28] Additionally, the quest for popularity and acceptance in a culture that is hostile toward girls and young women can create greater vulnerability toward and tolerance of more pernicious forms of harm.

Objectification and Commodification

Women's bodies were objectified and commodified to sell products and promote certain lifestyles long before social media or the entertainment industries came into existence. (Prostitution is intimately connected to these practices.) Objectification and commodification often work in tandem. The former refers to any ways that individuals are deconstructed into separate parts or objects for others' approval, consumption, or pleasure. Commodification monetizes someone or something that doesn't intrinsically have an economic value. When these practices are applied to women in male-driven ecosystems like entertainment and media, the story they tell is that profit and power matter more than women's well-being. Thus, women and their bodies are a means to an end.

Advertising is particularly adept at using women's bodies and the promise of sexual pleasure to turbocharge sales. It matters little if the product has nothing to do with sex. Ad campaigns for alcohol and cars regularly rely on misogynistic tropes. In 2017 the German car company Audi created an ad that compared buying a car to finding a wife. The ad depicted a wedding ceremony interrupted by the groom's mother, who pinches, prods, and effectively looks under the bride's hood to make sure she's soundly built.[29] A 2012 vodka advertisement showed a man forcibly grabbing a protesting woman from behind, with the copy "Unlike some people, Belvedere always goes down smoothly." Company documents confirmed it was meant as a double entendre referencing oral sex.[30]

Once bodies get divided into parts and separated from an actual human being with a mind and a soul, everything and everyone is fair game—even children. These days, it's not just creepy studio executives who are guilty of perpetuating misogyny via objectification and commodification. Parents are in on the game. As reported by *The New York Times*, certain mothers create accounts for their underage daughters—some as young as five—and post seductive photos of them on various sites.[31] Thanks to Instagram's paid subscription option and OnlyFans,[32] viewers can engage in online chats with the girls, receive exclusive photos, and buy clothing items worn in the photos.

To be clear, these are not proud moms bragging about their pretty daughters. It's a bizarre, lucrative cottage industry based on sexualizing girls. While some moms probably hope to jump-start their daughters' modeling careers or receive free merch, technology and health experts have warned that when underage girls interact with the men, "it opens the door to abuse."[33]

New York Times reporters Jennifer Valentino-DeVries and Michael H. Keller found that "some [viewers] flatter, bully, and blackmail girls and their parents to get racier and racier images. *The* [*New York*] *Times* monitored separate exchanges on Telegram, the messaging app, where men openly fantasize about sexually abusing the children they follow on Instagram and extol the platform for making the images so readily available." According to the article, "Meta, Instagram's parent company, found that 500,000 child Instagram accounts had 'inappropriate' interactions every day."[34] Anonymity, parents' willingness to ignore overtly sexualized comments, and the sheer volume of photos create the perfect environment for pedophiles. One male viewer commented, "It's like a candy store 😍😍😍."[35] These parents seem to be virtually pimping out their daughters with little if any concern about their children's vulnerability, digital footprints, or potential psychological repercussions. And remember, not only are the social media companies aware of this disturbing content, but their algorithms push it. Sexualized adult content can easily be accessed on all popular social media sites, including X, TikTok, Instagram, and Snapchat.*

The objectification and commodification that happen online make it more difficult for adolescents and young adults to treat women with respect and form healthy, in-person relationships. In 2016 it came to light that the Harvard University men's soccer team had been creating highly sexualized "scouting reports" on the women's soccer team. The men also assigned their peers possible sexual positions, such as "She seems relatively simple and probably inexperienced sexually, so I decided missionary would be her preferred position."[36] When reports were confirmed, Harvard University canceled the remainder of the men's soccer season.

Their online harassment had a historic precedent. A decade earlier, a Harvard undergrad created a site that allowed students to compare and vote on female students' "hotness." Once discovered by campus authorities, this student faced charges for "breaching [campus] security, violating copyrights and violating individual privacy."[37] After taking the site down and promising not to repost it, he was allowed to continue attending the university. The site was called Facemash, and the student was Mark Zuckerberg, who dropped out of Harvard after his sophomore year to develop Facebook.

Much of the communication that happens between teens and young adults now tends to focus on body parts and sex, which disadvantages and dehumanizes girls and young women. (Males' social

---

* "Typo-squatting" is another common way children get lured into websites with adult content. Sites are set up that have names similar to sites used by children but are a letter or two off.

status increases when they're sexually active, but the opposite remains true for females.) In journalist Nancy Jo Sales's book *American Girls*, a thirteen-year-old girl from a tony New York City suburb explained, "Dating now is just to hook up and take selfies."[38] Sexting has replaced flirting. Boys regularly send unwanted images of their genitals and demand that girls send "noodz" back to them.[39] Tragically, many girls oblige even though they understand that a sext sent to a specific boy can be forwarded to everyone in their social circles (and beyond), resulting in shaming, bullying, and ostracism. One sixteen-year-old girl from New York City admitted, "Nudes are pretty normal. . . . A lot of girls take them and keep them on My Eyes Only on Snapchat, so they have them at the ready when boys ask for them."[40] (Whether or not they realize it, teens are making their own porn when they sext.) By normalizing what should be seen as sexual harassment, girls surrender to men's rules and participate in their own objectification and commodification.*

Hostility, Hatred, and Violence

The harm that flows downstream from objectification and commodification is far-reaching, pervasive, and dangerous. It takes misogyny to another level. (For those of you who have trauma backgrounds or are sensitive, this next section contains violent and disturbing content.)

When pundits started to discuss whether or not President Biden would pull out of the 2024 presidential race and hand the baton to Vice President Kamala Harris, the misogynistic trolls started coming out of their caves. Harris was subjected to threatening, degrading, misogynistic, and racist attacks on social media and in the news. One guest commentator on Fox Business News referred to her as "the

* It may seem incomprehensible to us as adults that teens would willingly engage in this behavior. We have to remember that their prefrontal cortexes are not fully formed and the desire to be popular clearly impedes their thinking. Additionally, we need to categorize boys' behavior as a form of sexual harassment. If girls refuse to comply, they are ostracized. It's a lose-lose situation for them.

original Hawk Tuah girl. That's the way she got where she is."[41] Hawk Tuah refers to a woman performing oral sex. This addition to the lexicon started with a viral TikTok.

Male comedians can be some of the worst offenders. In the world of comedy, women are regularly referred to as "bitches," and their pain becomes the punch line eliciting laughter rather than outrage or empathy. After making light of sensitive topics like rape or sexual assault, comedians such as Dave Chappelle, Russell Brand, and Louis C.K. dodge accountability by admonishing those who were offended. Comments like "You obviously don't have a sense of humor" and "I was just joking" allow performers to avoid critique. Referencing Chappelle, cultural critic Roxane Gay wrote, "When an entire comedy set is designed as a series of strategic moves to say whatever you want and insulate yourself from valid criticism, I'm not sure you're really making comedy." Gay went on to write, "If we don't like his routine, the message is, we are the problem, not him."[42]

Some comedians' misogynistic behaviors extend well beyond crude, inappropriate comments. After a *New York Times* article was published in which five women accused him of sexual harassment, Louis C.K. admitted that he masturbated, sometimes naked, in front of women, often fellow comedians.[43] He did not always ask for or receive permission.[44] When the article came out, Louis C.K. issued a statement acknowledging that he abused power, but he never apologized or seemed to understand just how reprehensible his actions were.[45] His misbehavior did not adversely affect his career. He took a few months off, then returned to the stage (weaving these incidents into his act), and the following year won a Grammy and sold out Madison Square Garden. Many of C.K.'s male peers rallied around him. Fellow comedian Dave Chappelle defended Louis C.K. and categorized his behavior as "no big deal." Chapelle also folded parts of comedian Abby Schachner's testimony about her experience with C.K. into his routine, mocking her in the process. Schachner revealed that she experienced "a tidal wave of hatred" after Chappelle's show.[46]

In the 2023 documentary *Sorry/Not Sorry*, comedy critic Wesley Morris admitted that "everyone casually knew" of C.K.'s bad behavior. *Parks and Rec* co-creator Michael Schur had heard rumors while filming season four in which C.K. had an occasional role and admitted, "My attitude when I look back on it was that it's not my problem." Later in the documentary, he confesses, "That I thought it wasn't my problem is exactly the problem. Everyone was treating this like it wasn't my problem."[47] Exactly. Schur later apologized for casting C.K. in the NBC sitcom.[48] As with many famous men who abuse their power, C.K. told us who he was. In a 2013 HBO special, he quipped, "There's no greater threat to women than men. . . . We're the worst thing that ever happens to them."[49]

There's no reason for comedians to repent or change their schtick because people continue to pay good money to hear them.[50] Performers are rewarded for their vitriolic tirades, celebrated as truth tellers, and offered immunity from consequences. Men who have power fully understand the immunity and freedom it grants them. Writer Hannah Anderson observed that in this ecosystem, "women exist to laugh at men's jokes and be laughed at. When women tell the jokes, they upset the power dynamic."[51] And power dynamics are sacrosanct in misogyny.

The kind of inappropriate, hostile behavior male comedians cultivate becomes supercharged on social media, where there's less accountability. In ex-Marine Anuradha Bhagwati's book *Unbecoming: A Memoir of Disobedience*, she writes, "Marines United was a male-only Facebook group in which over thirty thousand active and former Marines shared sexually explicit photos of US service women and female civilians without the women's consent. Revenge porn; calls to rape, assault, and harass the women; and racist and homophobic comments saturated the site."[52]

It's not uncommon for men to express outright hatred toward women on sites such as X, Reddit, or 4chan. Women who routinely challenge misogynistic or patriarchal narratives such as politicians

Hillary Clinton and Alexandria Ocasio-Cortez are popular targets. These are not only powerless trolls but fellow politicians and influential men with substantial followings. Some of them shame, bully, and even threaten women with rape and other forms of violence. *Brotopia* author Emily Chang points out, "Young women, particularly those aged eighteen to twenty-four, are three times as likely to be sexually harassed online. As one feminist researcher put it, 'Rape threats have become a sort of lingua franca—the "go-to" response for men who disagree with something a woman says.'"[53]

Despite all their potential, social media companies routinely fail women. They're adept at virtue signaling regarding women's welfare but much less competent at identifying and removing violent imagery and permanently blocking users who cross ethical boundaries. Research done by Amnesty International reported that "the violence and abuse many women experience on Twitter has a detrimental effect on their right to express themselves equally, freely and without fear. Instead of strengthening women's voices, the violence and abuse many women experience on the platform leads women to self-censor what they post, limit their interactions, and even drives women off Twitter completely."[54] Perhaps that's the goal.

While social media platforms have become increasingly unsafe for women, they've proven to be safe harbors for individuals and groups that are unapologetically misogynistic, like Andrew Tate and incels.[55] The former doesn't misbehave virtually; he harms actual women. As of 2025 Tate and his brother are facing criminal charges of rape, sex trafficking, and other crimes in Europe. Tate has ten million followers on X and a cultlike following of adolescent boys and young men.

Incel is short for involuntary celibate, a term that describes men who interact online around their shared lack of sex. The incel movement is equal parts conspiracy theory, aggrieved male entitlement, loneliness, and misogynistic ideologies. Though insubstantial in size, incels represent a disturbing trend that perpetuates hatred and violence against those they perceive to be blocking them from their perceived rights, including the right to sex.

In the past decade, "incels have been responsible for a number of high-profile attacks that have resulted in the deaths of over fifty individuals" including the Toronto van attack that killed eleven people and a shooting in Plymouth, England, that killed six.[56] According to a *New York Times* article, "when extremist groups portray women as the 'them' to men's 'us,' that can become a way to justify violence by framing it as defensive rather than aggressive. . . . She's making me feel 'less than.' So rape is the way I get even with her. . . . She has the power, I'm taking it back."[57]

Not all incels agree with or promote violence against women. At this point, there hasn't been enough research to determine how many of the men who self-identify as incels struggle with mental health issues.[58] What is clear is that they seem incapable of connecting their loneliness and inability to forge romantic connections with their hateful rhetoric and victim mentality.

The anonymity of online interactions coupled with male entitlement and approval enable virtual groups like incels and individuals like Tate to act antagonistically, seemingly without experiencing any negative consequences. This may be one of the factors that embolden other forms of male-on-female violence.

Fictional violence also plays a role. Hugely popular mainstream entertainment offerings such as the streaming series *Game of Thrones* and *Fifty Shades of Grey* depict violent acts against women that are so graphic they leave little room for the imagination. Anastasia, the main female lead in the latter film, is stalked, manipulated, abused, and raped. *Fifty Shades of Grey* was advertised as "a fairy tale love story" and released just in time for Valentine's Day 2015. In *House of the Dragon*, a prequel to *Game of Thrones*, viewers watch an "excruciatingly long, graphic scene of a woman having a child cut out of her pregnant stomach without her knowledge or consent to the procedure, killing her in the process."[59] Violence in *The Handmaid's Tale*, including rape and disfigurement, led one reviewer to refer to it as "torture porn."[60]

Some viewers and critics believe cinematic violence against women functions as a form of catharsis and social commentary that raises awareness of real-life violence. These proponents defend the violence—as well as the strong, resourceful female characters in these shows—as important and empowering. While I don't wish to negate this perspective, I find any graphic depiction of violence against women to be unhelpful and counterproductive.

Cinematic violence profits by disempowering women, stripping them of their agency, and communicating that they are expendable. (There's even a term, "fridging," to explain the plot device that kills off female characters to amplify the male character's heroic journey.[61]) Gratuitous violence also numbs viewers to the shock and horror we should feel at watching someone get beaten, raped, or killed. Multiple studies affirm that witnessing violence can be traumatic and has the capacity to cause deleterious long-term consequences, especially for children and teens. More specifically, when this demographic routinely watches violent shows or plays violent video games, they become less empathetic, more fearful, and more likely to behave aggressively.[62]

The following two crimes reveal what can happen when a culture becomes desensitized to violence and fails to condemn hostility toward women.*

Bianca Devins, a seventeen-year-old aspiring social media influencer from upstate New York, was brutally killed in 2019. The murderer, who was known to Bianca, posted graphic images of her bloody body across social media channels, including Instagram, the gaming site Discord, Snapchat, and 4chan, which were all slow to remove the content. Hundreds of posts on the 4chan's website praised

* This is known as emotional desensitization. Industry leaders repeatedly claim that watching doesn't influence viewers' behavior. But if that's true, then why do they spend billions of advertising dollars to shape our choices?

Devins's attacker for committing "another 4chan murder."[63] As quickly as content moderators removed one post of her body, others appeared: "In the months after Bianca's death, the incel community on sites like 4chan picked up footage of Bianca's murder and amplified it."[64] The gruesome photos of Devins continue to be posted on TikTok and Instagram.

At a 2012 high school party in Steubenville, Ohio, two teen boys raped a sixteen-year-old girl who appeared to be too intoxicated to give consent. Witnesses recorded and posted the assault on various social media sites. *Not one of the partygoers intervened.* When the news came out, the outrage was largely directed at the victim. Some residents of the town "blamed the girl, saying she put the football team in a bad light and put herself in a position to be violated."[65]

A normal, human reaction to Devins's murder and the Steubenville rape should have been sorrow, regret, shame, and outrage. Steubenville police chief William McCafferty admitted, "If you could charge people for not being decent human beings, a lot of people could have been charged that night."[66] When we choose to passively watch violence against women and cease to be angered or grieved by what we see, something has gone terribly wrong in our culture.

Getting the Re-Write Right

Despite the pervasiveness of misogyny in the media and entertainment industries, there are influencers, actors, and industry professionals who currently amplify women's voices and counter bias and discrimination. Director Greta Gerwig's 2019 film *Little Women*, based on the semi-autobiographical novel by Louisa May Alcott, invites us to see and feel the complexities of Jo March's life. Much like Alcott, Jo resists the cultural expectations that limit women and prefers to "paddle [her] own canoe."[67]

Barbie, Gerwig's 2023 film, smashes gendered tropes while exposing misogynistic practices. Gerwig rejects the normal romantic script by having Ken's existence revolve around Barbie rather than vice versa. Actress America Ferrera names the internalized misogyny so many of us carry in the emotional climax of the movie:

> You have to answer for men's bad behavior, which is insane, but if you point that out, you're accused of complaining. You're supposed to stay pretty for men, but not so pretty that you tempt them too much or that you threaten other women because you're supposed to be a part of the sisterhood. . . . But never forget that the system is rigged. So find a way to acknowledge that, but also always be grateful. You have to never get old, never be rude, never show off, never be selfish, never fall down, never fail, never show fear, never get out of line. It's too hard. It's too contradictory. . . . And not only are you doing everything wrong, but also, everything is your fault. I'm just so tired of watching myself and every single other woman tie herself into knots so that people will like us.[68]

Tying ourselves into knots so that others will approve of or like us is an all-too-familiar practice for many women. So much so that it often becomes second nature. This is why Simone Biles's choice to withdraw from the Tokyo Olympics took so much courage and self-knowledge.

Several months after the games, Biles testified with several of her teammates before a US Senate Judiciary Committee hearing. After recounting her pride in representing the country during her athletic career, she struggled to remain composed and added, "I am also a survivor of sexual abuse. And I believe without a doubt, that the circumstances that led to my abuse and allowed it to continue are directly the result of the fact that the organizations created by Congress to oversee and protect me as an athlete, USA Gymnastics, and the United States Olympic & Paralympic Committee, failed to do their jobs. . . . I blame Larry Nassar but I also blame an entire system that enabled and perpetrated his abuse."[69] The Justice Department agreed with Biles and ultimately sided with the 139 claimants, awarding them a cash settlement because of the FBI's mishandling of the investigation.[70]

Proving beyond a doubt that she was not a quitter, Biles took the time she needed to heal and then returned to the Olympics in 2024. She showed the world her resilience by winning four more medals, and she displayed her grace by celebrating her teammates' and her competitors' victories.

Because the world in which we live is saturated and shaped by the media and entertainment industries, all of us will need to raise our voices when the stories they tell distort reality and harm women. Women do not exist to be objectified, commodified, injured, or hated. We're here to create life and beauty. To love. To serve. To tame chaos with truth. To eradicate injustice and usher in peace. These are the stories that need to be told.

CHAPTER 6

IN THE FLESH

Misogyny in Sexual Relationships

The first book of the Bible proclaims that all of creation is good. "All" includes men's *and* women's bodies *and* our sexuality. But because of systemic and individual brokenness—some of which points directly to misogyny—we don't always walk in or live with an awareness of that goodness. At least for women, sometimes our bodies, our sexuality, and our intimate relationships feel more like a burden than a blessing.

Amy and Nick* have experienced their sexuality as a mixed blessing since they got married more than twenty years ago.[1] They started dating when they were in their early twenties. Nick came into the relationship having battled both pornography and drugs as a teen. He did share parts of his history with Amy but admits he was not fully transparent regarding the ongoing nature of his struggle with porn. He also failed to communicate his expectation that marital sex would dismantle this addiction. It's not uncommon for some men to enter marriage holding on to the hope that it will cure their sexual addictions.

Amy and Nick's Christian faith advocated waiting to have sex until marriage, and they mutually embraced this decision, which provided them with clear boundaries. On their honeymoon, Nick assumed boundaries were no longer necessary and that his sexual desires could dictate the frequency of their intimate life. This translated to sex twice a day, even when Amy had her period. She was angry but also conflicted because all the advice they had received about sex indicated she was obligated to say yes.

The unrealistic expectations Nick held and the patterns they established early in their marriage resulted in a great deal of pain, misunderstanding, and disconnection. Amy felt used and disrespected. Nick felt frustrated that she didn't seem to care about how important sex was to him. Two decades after committing their lives to each other, they're still working to untangle the ways misogyny—specifically male sexual entitlement and the devaluation of women—has adversely affected their relationship.

As Nick and Amy's story demonstrates, if we lose sight of God's intentions for human sexuality while living in a cultural milieu where misogyny is not only present but normative, women's bodies can become liabilities, sex can take on inflated importance, and male entitlement can lead to distorted sexual practices. Societal norms and expectations then calcify around the culturally bound lies, resulting in pain, disconnection, and even violence. This is not what God intends for us.

Entitlement and Idolatry

As noted in previous chapters, many iterations of entitlement flow downstream from misogyny, including male sexual entitlement. Because hierarchical, patriarchal norms prop up and protect male entitlement, men may conclude (perhaps subconsciously) that their right to sex is inviolable. Any familial or cultural spaces that empower men to believe their sexual drive is more important than a woman's autonomy—including her right to say no—can lead to the abuse of power and loss of trust.

Several years ago, my husband and I were teaching a workshop on marital intimacy at a Christian marriage conference. Our talk included a beat on the hurt and discord that sexual coercion can cause. Christopher was explaining that on a given night, when a wife says she's too tired to have sex, it's more loving if her husband draws near and finds other means of connecting rather than pressuring her to submit to sex. Before he could elaborate, a young man grabbed his wife's hand, literally pulled her out of her seat, and huffed toward the exit. On the workshop evaluations he communicated how irritated he was by our "so-called advice" and defiantly concluded, "When I want sex, I'm going to get sex." I grieve for his wife and all the women out there whose partners subscribe to this ideology. When one spouse assumes they have a right to their partner's body or believes that the preeminent purpose of marital sex is their pleasure, it's not simply selfish, it's abusive.

Additionally, if men hope for a consistent, fulfilling intimate life, such behavior is counterproductive. During the twenty-five years that I've been offering pastoral care, I've had many brutally honest conversations with women who were uninterested in being sexually intimate with their partners. Some had abuse or trauma backgrounds, and intimate touch triggered them. Others had ongoing health issues like vaginismus or endometriosis that led to pain during intercourse. (Vaginismus is a medical condition wherein the muscles in the vagina involuntarily tighten and tense during sex or even when inserting a tampon. It can result in extreme pain during intercourse.) But most of these women cited a different reason for their lack of interest: Their husbands seemed so focused on having an orgasm that they didn't seem to care what their wives wanted or needed to progress from arousal to satisfaction, a process that is generally slower and less linear for women. This left the women feeling disconnected and, at times, used.

Perhaps part of the disconnect that women experience is because of how the world inflates the importance of sex but then overemphasizes male (versus mutual) pleasure—and in the process misses the deeper potential of sexual intimacy. When marital sex includes the following characteristics, it has the potential to be mutually pleasurable as well as transcendent: bonding, respectful, faithful, vulnerable, and restorative. Couples will not be able to achieve these characteristics if one partner assumes they have the right to sex on demand.

The apostle Paul, an unmarried man, offered insightful advice on marital intimacy that counters entitlement and endures to this day. He wrote, "The husband should fulfill his wife's sexual needs, and the wife should fulfill her husband's needs. The wife gives authority over her body to her husband, and the husband gives authority over his body to his wife. Do not deprive each other of sexual relations, unless you both agree to refrain from sexual intimacy for a limited time so you can give yourselves more completely to prayer" (1 Corinthians 7:3–5 NLT).

Some patriarchal, conservative church communities weaponize this section of Scripture against women by conveniently focusing on the wife's responsibility while overlooking the husband's. Paul was advocating mutuality, not laying the groundwork for coverture or sex on demand. When he wrote this, women—and especially wives—had few rights. Husbands were permitted to demand—or force—their wives, slaves, or mistresses to sleep with them. To suggest that a man should give his wife authority over his body was radical. It countered the prevailing gender norms of Greco-Roman culture and helped couples imagine what marital equality could look like. I believe many women still long for the kind of mutuality Paul promoted. To move in that direction, we need to consider why sexual entitlement is so prevalent in American culture and if idolatry factors in.

It's a bit too easy for us as sophisticated postmoderns to dismiss idolatry as an irrelevant, archaic concept. That's a mistake. Though few of us have shrines in our homes replete with statues of golden calves that we bow down to, we're all vulnerable to idolatry. If we fail to understand this or to resist an idol's pull, we may cause ourselves and the people we care about great harm.

At the risk of being overly simplistic, an idol is something we turn to for comfort, relief, provision, or control. Idols often approximate, point to, or represent a desire or legitimate need. It was commonly understood in ancient cultures that physical idols served deities such as Aphrodite (a fertility goddess) or Mars (the god of war). When you wanted a child or to win a battle, you made an offering to the appropriate idol and the idol would do your bidding.* Idolatry, then, is the practice of believing in and serving (via ritualized behaviors) something other than God in an attempt to influence circumstances that are beyond our control. Pastor and professor Lisa Lamb likens this to "grasping after something tangible when God feels distant or intangible."[2] It's a quid pro quo system that can feel more dependable than putting our trust in God, whom we can't control. As we turn away from God toward the idol, we become more bound by our distorted thinking and malformed habits. In other words, we become attached and addicted to lesser, illusory things.

Examples of idolatry are all around us. The prosperity gospel is built on idolatry. It taps into our need for financial resources—which can often feel out of reach—and promises that if we do X, God will reward us with Y. Or take the man whose mother was emotionally unavailable to him as a child because of her undiagnosed mental illness. His appropriate need for affection and nurture was never met, leaving him anxious, insecure, and emotionally stunted. Without understanding how his developmental deficits contributed to his anxiety and insecurity—or how to get actual relief—he turns to pornography (specifically imagery of women's breasts, which symbolize comfort). The ritual (or act of idolatry) offers temporary relief but can never satisfy his God-given need to be comforted, nurtured, and attached. If he is unable or unwilling to trust God and others to meet

* While there are certainly overlaps between this and bringing a concern to God through prayer, one of the main differences is that when we pray, our attitude should be one of humility and submission rather than pride and entitlement. We should never assume we can control God.

him in his place of vulnerability, he will eventually become enslaved to the idolatrous illusion.

The dark, malevolent forces behind idols woo us with the lie that if we keep returning to them, we'll feel better. But we don't. In fact, we feel worse. "Idols always over promise but underdeliver"[3] because they are counterfeits (see Psalm 135:15–18). They cannot provide what we need. Scripture likens our misguided pursuits to drinking from a broken cistern (Jeremiah 2:13). Anything or anyone can become an idol. Sex is an American idol. It permeates our culture, can dominate our thoughts and influence our behaviors, and promises more than it can deliver. The more we bow down to it, the more we become controlled by it, and the more we feel entitled to it. So to answer my earlier question, yes, male sexual entitlement is an expression of idolatry.

One way to discern whether you have any idols in your life is to pay attention to what you think about when you're not fully engaged and recognize how you respond when access to your idol (addiction) is threatened or denied. For instance, when circumstances prevent you from viewing porn or rechecking social media, how do you feel? How angry or disappointed do you get, and whom do you blame?

We never aspire to be addicts or idolaters, but if we don't examine our hearts and moderate our appetites for sex, or power, or whatever else pulls us away from God and loved ones, any of us can land there. This is particularly true for men raised in cultures that amplify sex (including equating sexual conquests with masculinity) and who eroticize their emotional needs and devalue women. In such spaces, broken sexuality and sexualized violence often follow.

Distorted, Disembodied Sex

Entitlement and idolatry not only twist our understanding of our bodies and sexuality but, as the previous section indicated, also tend to affect our sexual praxis. Examples include pornography, prostitution, and sexualized violence. These are by no means the only manifestations, but because they're so ubiquitous and obviously destructive, they offer cogent and clear case studies of how misogyny shows up in the bedroom.

Pornography use is one of the most damaging and destructive practices of our time. A study by the Barna Group defined pornography as material that is sexually explicit, displays intercourse and other sexual acts, is intended for arousal, and contains full nudity.[4] It's impossible to accurately determine the number of individuals addicted to pornography or the amount of time they spend on sites like PornHub, because most people who watch it generally don't admit it—especially those from religious backgrounds.[5]

The pornography industry has expanded and become more degenerate in the past four decades. This is evident in the content, accessibility, and addiction rates. The photos in print magazines I was exposed to as a child are tame compared to what's currently available. Today, pornography includes women being hit and raped, adults having sex with minors, group sex, and even bestiality. Content is often procured via illegal or unethical means. Sites rely on deep fakes (normal photos of women made into pornographic images via AI[6]), revenge porn,[7] and even selfies made by minors that were originally posted as sexts. Some actresses and actors are compensated, but many are trafficked and forced into the industry.[8] Recent court cases have revealed that some women initially hired to do modeling gigs by PornHub's parent company MindGeek were then sex trafficked.[9] This is why it's so important for anyone who consumes pornography, even so-called "soft porn," to consider how their choices not only affect them but also contribute to a system that profits from disadvantaging others.

Thanks to the internet and handheld devices, viewing habits have become more brazen. Anyone can access pornographic content at any time, without cost, and in total anonymity. Various surveys reveal that more women and minors are now watching and confirm that employees view porn while at work.[10]

As pornography becomes increasingly widespread, individuals and cultures are less likely to see it as problematic or immoral. Certain therapists and so-called sex experts would have us believe that watching or creating pornography has no adverse effect. It's spun as another mode of self-expression—one that can even be self-empowering for girls and women. In an article for *Psychology Today*, a male journalist claimed that "all men" watch porn and "to be male is to watch." He also compared viewing porn to taking a "coffee break."[11] Not all men watch porn, and evidence strongly contradicts that viewing it has no adverse effects.

It's indisputable that viewing pornography has a negative impact on everyone, but especially children and teens. When children are exposed to adult sexuality, it's traumatic.[12] Images get seared into the brain, the child's understanding of sexuality is distorted, and from an early age, they can learn to objectify women and normalize abuse. Of course, children have no idea how dangerous pornography is when they first come across it. Typically, their curiosity about the human body or the mechanics of sex lead them to innocently type a keyword into the search engine. Pornography was never meant to replace formal sex ed, but that's how it functions in our culture: "In a 2021 study, [24.5 percent of] 18–24 year olds said pornography was the most helpful source of information they received about how to have sex."[13] Unfortunately, it's neither reliable nor accurate.

It's also not helpful for adults. Viewing pornography is more likely to corrupt rather than enhance a couple's intimate life. Watching someone else act out sexually does not make anyone a better lover. Sex then becomes performative and mimetic. Furthermore, because regular pornography use rewires the brain's circuitry, arousal gets fused with specific types of imagery, which can lead to sexual dysfunction or disinterest in embodied sex with an imperfect partner. One longitudinal study found regular pornography use doubles a couple's likelihood of divorce.[14]

By design, sex is meant to ease our aloneness, bring both partners pleasure, and generate new life. Most pornography is consumed alone and centers on male desire and male pleasure. Interpersonal connection and mutual pleasure are not the goals. Though women are depicted as enjoying themselves in pornographic movies and photos, they're only acting out male fantasies. Women's bodies serve as vehicles for men to dominate so they can achieve orgasm. Girls and women who watch porn and assume they should mimic and submit to such behavior sublimate their own desires, discount their dignity, and put themselves in danger. Watching porn doesn't make us freer; it makes us captive to someone else's poorly written script.

Nick, whom you met at the beginning of the chapter, was first exposed to pornography when he was eleven. He watched his father going into the bathroom with stacks of *Playboy* and *Penthouse* magazines and wondered why his dad preferred shutting himself in the bathroom to playing with him. Like Pandora, Nick's curiosity compelled him to look at the magazines, and after a few years, he, too, became addicted. He recounts how it affected him and his marriage:

> Porn taught me to expect sex to be about the performance, climax, and self-gratification. As a teenager and young man, I was afraid of actual sex, because I didn't know if I could compare with or perform like the men in the movies. I retreated from moments of intimacy early in life and in my marriage out of fear and insecurity. This left me with a lot of anxiety around sexual intimacy, which I addressed by viewing porn and masturbating. Pornography gave me a false sense of comfort and a dopamine release, but in solitude, which only increased my anxiety and insecurity.

Several years ago, Nick started to understand that his expectations about sex were unrealistic. He now sees that some of his behaviors and attitudes toward Amy were abusive: "Instead of sharing my anxieties, fears, and insecurities with her, I abused her trust and took advantage of her desire to be a good wife." He continues, "I can recognize how pornography fueled my concerns and worries around sex and created expectations for self-centered satisfaction."

Nick believes the combination of being raised by a narcissistic, sex-addicted father coupled with his own addictions and the church's teachings about male headship led him to conclude that not only was he entitled to sex but that entitlement was God ordained. Part of why it took him so long to figure this out is that he was immersed in a patriarchal Christian culture that empowered misogyny. When Nick shared his struggles with someone from church, they suggested reading the book *Every Man's Battle*, which, according to Nick, "fueled my misogynistic view of entitlement by suggesting that my wife's availability would resolve my issues. It also places more responsibility on the woman to be modest and available than it puts on the man to get help and develop self-control. It did not speak of mutuality. I can now see how toxic that book was to a young, addicted man seeking help." Nick currently attends sobriety groups and therapy as he moves deeper into his healing. He was wise to get help when he did. Studies show that the more frequently one watches pornography, the more extreme the visuals need to be to achieve the same results. Like sustained drug use, pornography can become a gateway to other, more harmful behaviors.

Paying for Sex

Paying for sex is both less common and less socially acceptable than viewing porn. This makes it easy for us to categorize prostitution as fringe and turn away. We may never employ a sex worker, but that doesn't mean we should disregard the plight of those who find themselves trapped in this oppressive industry.

When a man pays a woman for sex, it's a hierarchical encounter.[15] He has the power and takes advantage of a woman's need for provision by paying her to subject herself to all manner of degrading, debasing, and dehumanizing behaviors. She becomes a slave to his desires and fantasies. The goal is to ensure men experience pleasure while being in control. That lack of connection with or concern for women leads to further mistreatment, objectification, and indifference.

It also causes physical harm to and psychological disintegration in those in the industry. Sex workers have significantly higher rates of sexually transmitted infections (including HIV) than the average population.[16] Multiple autobiographies written by sex workers recount how cruel and violent their customers often are. To survive such treatment, they learn to split off or dissociate. Feminist scholar and author Sheila Jeffreys writes, "The practice of dissociation which prostituted women employ to protect their sense of self from violation is so similar to the dissociation employed by sexually abused children . . . that it provides good evidence that the two experiences are similarly abusive."[17] Rachel Moran worked as a prostitute in the UK for seven years, starting when she was sixteen years old. In her autobiography, *Paid For*, she refers to prostitution as "paid sexual abuse."[18] Her book not only recounts the degradation she and others endured but also dismantles the myth that women who choose sex work do so willingly:[19]

> Freedom is universally accepted as one of the fundamental necessities of contentment in human life. The myth of the happy hooker does not make logical sense, because the distinguishing feature of any free person is that their body is inviolable, while the distinguishing mark of the prostitute is that her body is not. Therefore, it is only common sense to conclude that a prostitute does not experience either life or her body as a free person does; in fact, quite the opposite. Are we to believe that women are generally "happy" in this circumstance? In the seven years I spent as a prostitute I met innumerable prostitutes and I have had friends in the trade for more than half my lifetime, and I have *never* met a prostitute who didn't wish she were doing something else.[20]

In a broken world like ours, if money is to be made off the bodies of individuals who have little power or influence, those at the bottom will be exploited. This is overwhelmingly women and children.[21] It's impossible to accurately calculate the total number of women and minors involved in pornography and prostitution, but we do know a high percentage are children, some under the age of ten. Poverty and family violence often force children and women into these industries.[22]

Our individualistic, hedonistic culture encourages us to believe that if something brings us pleasure or benefits us, then there's no reason to question or forsake it. But pornography and prostitution are inherently exploitative and debasing, which means they will never lead to human flourishing. They can, however, warp our understanding of sex to the extent that sexual intimacy becomes inherently dangerous for women.

Sexualized Violence

As discussed in the previous chapter, objectification, commodification, and violence in the media and entertainment industries diminish or even numb the outrage and sadness we should feel in response to women being devalued, mistreated, and harmed. Once numb, any anger or grief fades to indifference, which eases the dissonance men should experience when they bring violence into the bedroom.

Cultures where women are routinely dehumanized and male sexual entitlement is protected and celebrated (recall the sections on coverture and rape culture) can lead to intimate sexual violence.

An article by Matthew Birkhold titled "Patriarchy: A Primer for Men" asserts, "Common ways of referring to sex include, 'hit it,' 'kill it,' 'smash,' and/or 'beat it up.'" (The "it" being referred to here is women's genitalia.) The article continues, "All these popular terms for sex involve men inflicting physical injury on women in the name of sexual pleasure. Patriarchy teaches men and women to think that the metaphoric destruction of the female body is the goal of good sex."[23]

And the destruction is certainly not metaphoric. A *New York Times* article linked fictionalized violence portrayed in pornography and video games with actual sexualized violence, including choking.[24] Men squeezing women's necks during sex as a form of eroticized violence has become more widespread even though it sometimes results in death by strangulation.[25]

One research study revealed, "Approximately 10 to 14 percent of married women are raped by their husbands in the United States."[26] In *The Great Sex Rescue*, author Sheila Wray Gregoire states definitively, "Marital rape and sexual assault, whether by physical force or coercive threats, are real and are wrong."[27] The following are examples of coercion and sexual assault: when a husband demands sex (or specific sex acts) from his partner, when agreeing to sex is the only way to prevent or stop verbal or physical abuse, and when sex is rough or painful and requests to stop are ignored.[28]

All nonconsensual sex or any acts of violence during sex should never be tolerated within any culture—particularly one that claims to be Christian. In societies that uphold or celebrate unrestrained male sexuality and sexualized violence, women will never feel safe, because they know at any moment they could be overpowered and harmed. That potential robs women of their peace and makes it difficult to believe and live in the inherent goodness of their bodies and their sexuality. Sex becomes a lethal weapon indiscriminately wielded by irresponsible men. When women offer our bodies to our lovers, we are at our most vulnerable. If this trust then gets betrayed, the wound penetrates to the bone and leaves lasting scars.

The Weights Women Carry

Because I'm now in my sixties, I've had a great deal of time to consider the many ways misogyny has affected my relationship with my body. As a twelve-year-old, I remember feeling absolutely horrified when a friend whispered that my new boyfriend was going to try to get "up my shirt" at her party that night. I had no interest in having him touch my breasts, but I also understood what was expected of me. I strategically blocked him from his goal by making sure we were never alone. He broke up with me soon after.

That summer, I was standing on the swim-team dock, dripping wet, between laps. My toned body was barely covered by a thin layer of blue nylon. The pride I felt in my athleticism was instantly subsumed by self-consciousness and shame as the boys standing on the beach started critiquing my female teammates and me. I wondered if my body passed their scrutiny but also felt furious that they were brazenly deconstructing us.

I remember walking to my high school football game in my drill-team miniskirt, cars slowing down so male drivers could gawk and make crude comments. That was the year I decided to get a pixie haircut and started wearing what's now referred to as "gender-neutral" clothing. I intuitively knew that de-emphasizing my femininity would create a bit of a buffer between my body and male desire. I was strong, but not strong enough to protect myself from a man who felt entitled to my body. The following fall I traded in my drill-team pom poms for a field hockey stick.

These events were more than fifty years ago. Though there are now more laws protecting women and there's more awareness about sexual harassment and abuse, it feels like little has changed regarding male entitlement and broken expressions of sexuality. If anything, it's gotten worse. I can't recall a time when it felt so dangerous to be a woman. Consider some of the ways misogyny manifested in the US between 2016 and 2020.

An overtly misogynistic man who bragged about sexually harassing and abusing women had just been elected president of the United States. Trump was certainly not the first president to engage in sexually inappropriate criminal behavior, but we can track how quickly culture has shifted toward greater acceptance of powerful men mistreating women by comparing the public outcry regarding Bill Clinton's scandal (1998)[29] and public support of Trump.

I was working as a journalist during the 1990s and remember

the collective moral outrage, particularly from White conservatives, regarding Clinton's sexual impropriety. (To be clear, I agree that his actions were reprehensible and predatory due to age and power differentials.) But the same demographic who led the charge for Clinton's impeachment also voted Trump into office. Not only was there a notable lack of outrage regarding Trump's behavior, but men and women seemed to celebrate it. When men at the top of an organization engage in and promote misogyny, it signals to other men that they can get away with it too.

Thanks to *New York Times* reporters Jodi Kantor and Megan Twohey, the world learned one of Hollywood's dirty secrets. Director Harvey Weinstein had sexually assaulted, raped, and threatened more than eighty women, most of whom are now well-known actresses. In April 2024, the New York State Court overturned Weinstein's 2020 conviction based on a technicality. If he is retried, his victims will have to revisit their trauma. This is not justice.

In 2018, the trial against the USA Gymnastics team doctor Larry Nassar came to a dramatic and highly publicized end. Nassar was charged with abusing more than 156 gymnasts; the youngest was six years old.[30] During the final days of the trial, Judge Rosemarie Aquilina allowed the victims to address Nassar. Their courageous and heartbreaking statements invited us to enter their pain and mourn with them. If those who criticized Simone Biles for withdrawing from the Tokyo Olympics had bothered to listen to these testimonies, perhaps they would have been more sympathetic to what she was going through.

Next, Dr. Christine Blasey Ford testified about being sexually assaulted decades earlier by US Supreme Court nominee Brett Kavanaugh. The results of her testimony were similar to Anita Hill's: Ford's integrity was questioned, she was publicly maligned, the nominee denied everything, and he was ultimately confirmed by the Senate.

Then in 2019, the news broke about the long-term systemic abuse within the Southern Baptist Convention, which we will discuss in the next chapter.

And we must not forget the millions of women who were raped and sexually assaulted during that same time span in the United States.[31]

All women walk around with an awareness of our bodily vulnerability. Every. Single. Day. We know we could be overpowered, raped, infected with an STD, and possibly impregnated. We constantly have to evaluate whether our clothing is appropriate, if the place we parked is safe or if we'll need an escort, if the male boss can be trusted when he requests an after-work meeting, if our "no" will be respected. If we're in a relationship, there's a standard of attractiveness we must uphold while not transgressing the invisible line that might "cause" our brothers to stumble. What men want and expect of us can feel impossible to achieve. Honestly, it's exhausting.

When we fail, shame is always waiting in the shadows. Shame about our breasts being too small (or too droopy) and our hips being too big (or too boyish). Shame about the way our bodies smell during our cycles (which is due to the mineral content of the blood and the body's unique biome). Shame about body hair. Most of the critiques we endure aren't because our bodies are flawed but because they don't align with the surgically or digitally sculpted bodies some men now expect thanks to pornography. (The desire to meet men's idolatrous expectations helps to explain why so many women choose to have risky and expensive cosmetic surgeries such as Brazilian butt lifts, breast augmentation, and labiaplasty.)[32]

And there's an additional layer. Women are told—directly and indirectly—that because men's sexual needs are more important than ours, if we want to keep our partners happy and sober, we'll need to sublimate our sexual desires and emotional well-being so that we can please them. Hence faking an orgasm. (I contend that women wouldn't go this route if men were as committed to pleasuring women as they are to achieving their own climax.) As mentioned earlier in the chapter, one of the main problems with husbands viewing their wives as the antidote to their sexual addictions or ongoing anxiety is that women end up feeling diminished and used. Nick's wife, Amy, explains what it's been like for her to reconcile her body and her sexuality with the presence of sexualized misogyny in her marriage:

> Both of us came to marriage with some harmfully shaped sexual expectations. The Christian books I'd read communicated to me that as a wife, when my husband wants sex, I ought to say yes. I wanted so badly to honor God by being a good wife, and I had been taught by mentors whom I admired that "good" meant submitting—saying "yes" to my husband unless what he was asking me to do was sinful. It didn't register that his selfish pursuit of an orgasm was indeed sinful. In the worst moments of exhaustion, it felt like I was being emotionally raped as I lay there waiting for it to be over. Sex in that kind of emotional space eroded my self-worth and broke down the trust in our relationship.

When a woman chooses to ignore or minimize her pain or mistreatment, the dissonance may weaken her confidence and make it more difficult for her to establish healthy boundaries. Reflecting on her experiences, Amy concludes, "I had been groomed to be a subservient wife, taught to gaslight myself when it felt wrong. These experiences with sex, within my own marriage, have fundamentally changed me. Before we got married, I felt optimistic, light-hearted, confident, and fun. I expect untangling the church-ordained misogyny I internalized as a young person will be a lifelong work."

She speaks for many women.

Redeeming Sex

What does it look like for us as broken, needy people to move toward God and each other as sexual beings? How can we raise the bar regarding sex and sexuality and dismantle the false paradigms such as men are always thinking about sex, more sex equals better sex, or women are temptresses? Can we change deeply embedded beliefs and experience redemption in this area? Based on personal experiences and what I've witnessed in my pastoral care work, yes. I agree with pastor and author Jonathan Grant's thoughts here: "Genuine and tangible personal change is not only possible; it is an imperative of the gospel."[33] But only if we start by turning back to our source.

Because our sexuality is so powerful, it can lead us to greater personal integration and toward God, or it can disintegrate us and lead us away from God. The biblical view of sex and sexuality offers a grounded, integrated alternative to cultural narratives. As Grant writes, "God's vision of life is a plan for comprehensive human flourishing in all its fullness."[34] That includes our bodies and sex. A careful reading of Scripture will help untie the misogynistic knots that generations of bad theology and misinterpretation have created. Theologian Amy Peeler writes in her book *Women and the Gender of God*, "Privileging the masculine over the feminine is the way the world has often run but should not and need not continue forever."[35]

There are no easy answers or quick fixes. As Amy and Nick have come to understand the ways that misogynistic ideologies and practices have caused harm in their marriage, they are making slow and steady progress toward healing. According to Amy,

> We've spent the last several years doing a lot of unlearning and processing with therapists. We've found a lifeline in voices and mentors within the church who love Jesus, are filled with the Spirit, and who believe in and embody the goodness of mutuality in relationships. I am learning to see myself, and my husband is learning to see me and all women, as full persons to be valued, listened to, and respected, without feeling threatened by us. I no longer feel like a body to be consumed. There is an inner strength and peace, a courageous quiet confidence in knowing I stand with my husband on equal footing. We now both understand that sex is meant to be a continuation of emotional intimacy with an unconditional

requirement of mutually felt safety and trust; there is no room for misogyny in this marriage bed.

As it pertains to the ways misogyny affects relationships, much work still needs to be done and much healing needs to happen so women can flourish consistently. Before we turn our attention to that topic, we need to explore how the church has contributed to misogyny.

CHAPTER 7

BAPTIZING SIN

Misogyny in the Church

The temptation to accumulate and abuse power is common to humankind. Jesus himself had to resist this during his forty-day fast. Power is not inherently bad. But when it's used to manipulate, control, subjugate, silence, harass, deceive, or violate others, it becomes a manifestation of evil. Some of Jesus's harshest words were directed to men who abused power. His rebukes are every bit as applicable and necessary today as they were two thousand years ago.

Emma* and her husband joined Mars Hill in the early aughts.[1] At that time, it was a dynamic, theologically conservative church in downtown Seattle. Emma loved the music and was drawn to lead pastor Mark Driscoll's preaching. The elders soon recognized her gifts and invited her to minister to women.

Though she enjoyed serving and can recount multiple times when Mark and his wife, Grace, cared for and supported her family, Emma and her husband began having some concerns about how Mark viewed and treated women—specifically, women in leadership.

Driscoll has unabashedly shared his opinions about women (and sex) from the pulpit and in his writing. He seems to believe that Adam deferred leadership to Eve, and ever since then, women's desire has been to take control of men and usurp their authority. He refers to this as a Jezebel spirit. He fleshed this out during a 2023 conference:

> [Eve] takes control. She's the boss. She takes the reins. She has the argument with Satan. She gets confused. She sins. . . . She's the leader. He's the follower. And the truth is, men hear me in this, if you don't lead your family, Satan will. . . . What happens then is God comes to Eve, and he says, as part of her curse, she will want to do what with her husband? Rule, control, dominate, be the boss. That's the beginning of the Jezebel and Ahab pattern.[2]

If I'm understanding Driscoll correctly, he assumes that, starting with Eve, women are motivated by a desire for control and are prone to confusion. This hermeneutic provides the backdrop for his concerns regarding weak men and domineering women. Emma came to understand, "In his mind, women in the feminist movement weren't fighting for equal rights, equal pay, or against spousal abuse. They wanted to take over." She admits, "I bought into it. I knew women who were angry and manipulative growing up and I didn't want to be like them. I loved God and I didn't want to control my husband or any other man."

Driscoll's teaching combined with the church's philosophy on women's role in marriage and leadership had a negative effect on Emma: "At times, I feared speaking out when something felt off because of this common criticism and the shame of being possibly labeled a gossip or, worse, a contentious woman." Rather than trusting her discernment, she began to doubt her insights and became increasingly unable to voice concerns or stand up for herself. As is often the case in these situations, her inner knowing proved prescient.

Things began to go sideways at Mars Hill years before Driscoll resigned in 2014. According to eyewitness reports, he fostered a culture of fear and became increasingly domineering and controlling.[3] When Emma and her husband decided it was time to leave, they asked to meet with him. Emma knew she had to let her husband do the talking or face accusations and criticism from Driscoll. Her husband laid out the issues and then turned to her to ask if she wanted to add anything. She declined. Months later, Emma learned Driscoll had made a disparaging remark about her in a meeting with leaders of the Acts 29 network (the umbrella organization Mars Hill was under), implying that she wasn't being submissive in her marriage and couldn't be trusted.[4]

Emma's career had been flourishing in this season, but after Driscoll maligned her, that changed: "No one in the Christian circles I operated in invited me to contribute anymore. Mark's comment was like a scarlet letter." Driscoll's actions affected Emma professionally and personally: "I continued to doubt my voice for years. I felt confident speaking boldly to women, but not to men, and not even to my husband."

Driscoll is one of several highly visible Christian pastors and religious leaders who have weaponized Scripture and abused their positions of authority, particularly against women. This type of behavior isn't limited by denomination, geography, or church size. And regardless of the setting, the net results are the same.

When misogyny is practiced and upheld in the church, it can be more consequential and psychologically damaging than when it shows up in other settings. That's because most other spaces aren't claiming to speak for God or serve as the ultimate authority. Misogynistic ideologies and practices don't simply corrupt the nature of the church, they go against the very reason the church exists: to overcome brokenness and injustice by reconciling all things. This is why misogyny must be identified and uprooted from any churches or religious organizations that claim to be following Jesus.

The Church in Reverse

It's incontrovertible that in the early years of the Christian church, women functioned and served alongside men. They were deacons

(Phoebe, Romans 16:1), prophets (the four daughters of Philip, Acts 21:9), house church leaders (Priscilla, Romans 16:3–5), patrons (Lydia, Acts 16:13–15), evangelists (the Samaritan woman in John 4), and even an apostle (Junia, Romans 16:7).[5] The apostle Paul thanked twenty-nine exceptional leaders in the early churches. Ten of them were women.[6]

And then came what Christians refer to as the miracle of Pentecost. God's Spirit powerfully fell on and filled both women and men, fulfilling Joel's prophecy and ushering in what could have and should have been a permanent transformation between men and women—at least in the church and within believing families. God's Spirit also empowered and inspired Christians to upend cruel, inhumane practices. Church members rescued babies (often girls) who had been abandoned to the elements. They cared for lepers. They fed the hungry and provided for widows. Thanks to the women and men who took Jesus's mandates seriously, that little corner of the world experienced God's kingdom breaking in.

As I referenced in chapter 1, Jesus's life and teachings revealed the purposes of God's kingdom and demonstrated how power should be used to accomplish those purposes. This included bringing justice for all and overturning misogynistic practices toward women. Though the early church made bold advances toward valuing and esteeming women, it didn't take long for Christians to revert to pre-Pentecost practices. Many factors conspired to erode the transformative ways the early church affirmed and blessed women to live and serve as equals.

Apparently, some of the most influential church fathers and early theologians weren't won over by Jesus's radical inclusion and acceptance of women. They continued to view women as flawed, inadequate, ignorant, and, in some cases, evil. Tertullian (AD 155–220), a Christian convert and influential apologist, wrote regarding women, "You are the devil's gateway: you are the unsealer of that (forbidden) tree: you are the first deserter of the divine law: you are she who persuaded him whom the devil was not valiant enough to attack. You destroyed so easily God's image, man. On account of your desert—that is, death—even the Son of God had to die."[7]

A few hundred years later, Augustine, Bishop of Hippo, affirmed Tertullian's beliefs in his commentary on Genesis: "I don't see what sort of help woman was created to provide man with, if one excludes procreation. If woman is not given to man for help in bearing children, for what help could she be? To till the earth together? If help were needed for that, man would have been a better help for man. The same goes for comfort in solitude. How much more pleasure is it for life and conversation when two friends live together than when a man and a woman cohabitate?"[8]

In Augustine's cosmology, it seems women's main, or perhaps only, contribution is in bearing children. His perspective creates a bit of cognitive dissonance given that he—and other influential male church leaders who have shared this view—exegeted, taught, and wrote about Christian theology in ways that have helped believers understand the Bible more fully. These contradictions cannot be reconciled. Augustine and other early biblical scholars loved God and provided future generations with helpful insights. But at the same time, they perpetuated misogynistic beliefs that were subsequently woven into the tapestry of the Christian faith.

The institutionalization of Christianity was another one of the driving forces behind the rapid reversal of treating women as equals and encouraging their full participation. Under Emperor Constantine (AD 306–337), the church effectively became state-led and lost some of its countercultural characteristics. In *Reckoning with Power*, author David Fitch explains, "Christianity became aligned with Rome, and godly power became assimilated with the worldly power of Rome," effectively blurring the two.[9] This may have been the first iteration of Christian nationalism.

Being a member of the church was no longer a radical, potentially dangerous choice but a mandate that if not obeyed could lead to persecution and death. Leadership roles were filled according to civic rules and one's status rather than maturity or spiritual gifting. Since public governance excluded women, their opportunities to lead within the church began to diminish.

During this same time period, church meetings transitioned from private homes, where women were free to exercise their gifts and authority, to grand basilicas and cathedrals often built by and for male rulers.[10] The radical idea of believers' bodies being inhabited by God and then serving as the temple (versus when God's presence dwelt in a physical structure) was subverted, and the church looked back to the time when male priests ruled within a temple built by human hands. Theologian Sandra Glahn explains, "With a shift from the believer's body to a physical structure as the temple of God came a return to some physical-temple regulations that affected females, such as barring menstruating women from worship"—and most leadership roles.[11]

Misogynistic philosophies and doctrines encroached upon the church, and gender-based hierarchies and restrictions on women in positions of leadership became normative. Eventually, Christianity was no longer "a priesthood of all believers" but rather a priesthood of male believers where women were relegated, for the most part, to diminished, subordinate roles.

We can trace such philosophies and practices all the way through the Middle Ages, the Reformation, and the Great Awakening (in Europe and the American colonies) to the work of contemporary theologians and church leaders. Despite men's efforts to silence or exclude them, many women (including Catherine of Alexandria, Syncletia, Milburga, Hildegard von Bingen, Joan of Arc, and Saint Térèsa de Lisieux[12]) demonstrated an undeniable witness to the power of God that no person or institution could silence. That doesn't mean they didn't try.

Through the generations, countless denominations and parachurch organizations have created dogmas and rules that restrict—or attempt to restrict—the roles and voices of women. A more recent example happened in the late 1980s when a small group of religious leaders and scholars who called themselves the Council on Biblical Manhood and Womanhood (CBMW) joined together and wrote the Danvers Statement.[13] This document articulates CBMW's core beliefs regarding God's purposes for creation and church structures, including specific masculine and feminine roles and the belief that most key leadership positions should be restricted to men.

What the signers of the Danvers Statement set out to accomplish and what they actually accomplished are two different things. They believed they were protecting the integrity of the church and culture by countering second-wave feminism and the sexual revolution of the 1960s.[14] In reality, the signers simply aggregated power, doubled down on their beliefs regarding gender-based roles, and popularized the terms *complementarian* and *egalitarian*.[15]

There's a wide spectrum of beliefs and practices regarding these two categories. Complementarians tend to believe that men and women are equal by design but have different, God-ordained roles, specifically as it pertains to authority. In an email exchange with me, Kelley Mathews, coauthor of *40 Questions About Women in Ministry*, helpfully clarifies, "While all complementarians believe in gender-based hierarchy, they differ on how to apply that belief to the restrictions on women assuming roles that place them in authority above men."[16]

By contrast, egalitarians affirm the differences between men and women and believe that leadership opportunities should depend on gifting and maturity. In their attempt to level the playing field, egalitarians sometimes flatten the differences. Author Aimee Byrd believes women in egalitarian churches can "feel just as undervalued" because "the work hasn't been done to acknowledge the enrichment that distinct feminine and masculine contributions bring to the church."[17]

It's important to make several distinctions here. A marriage, Christian institution, or church that ascribes to complementarian theology is not automatically misogynistic. For instance, a wife and husband may jointly decide to adhere to male headship and specific gender-based roles while lovingly, generously, and sacrificially supporting each other. Likewise, marriages, churches, and institutions that claim to be egalitarian are capable of being misogynistic. It's not so much what a person or church believes theologically, but how they live out that theology—the praxis—and how they understand the following topic.

Power

Many kinds of power exist in the world. There's the tangible, physical power from moving water that gets converted into electricity and runs along grids into our homes. Touching a live wire can result in electrocution or even death. There's the power that comes from tornadoes and floods, which both possess the capacity to wipe out entire communities. In *Reckoning with Power*, David Fitch differentiates two other types of power: "There is worldly power, which is exerted over persons, and there is godly power, which works relationally with and among persons." According to Fitch, "Worldly power is coercive. A person or organization takes control of things with worldly power. Worldly power is enforced. It is prone to abuse. God's power, on the other hand, is never coercive."[18] The main distinctions here seem to be the source of the power (where did it originate?) and how it's deployed (what is the end result?).

Worldly power makes most of the headlines. Russian president Vladimir Putin leveraged his greater worldly power by invading Ukraine in 2022. Hollywood executive Harvey Weinstein leaned into worldly power by sexually abusing actresses and staffers. Southern Baptist leaders employed worldly power first by committing abuse and then by covering it up.[19] By contrast, Jesus relied on godly power when he healed people and performed miracles.

While it's easy to recognize and fault the more flagrant examples I've just listed, we all have access to some worldly power—in varying degrees—and therefore we all have the potential to use and abuse it.

Fear, greed, and entitlement can lead to the abuse of worldly power. Few of us want to give up our proverbial piece of the pie, especially if we believe we earned it or are owed it. If we sense that someone is reaching for our portion, we'll use whatever power we have to box them out. The pie could be privilege, reputation, income, status, or sex.

One seasoned female pastor reflected, "Many excuse their abuses of power because they may not seem as 'flagrant' as other abuses. And yet, their words or actions might still cause great harm. A person can be 'socialized' into abuses of power, when they spend too much time in a toxic environment and lose perspective. One must be ever vigilant to listen deeply to critique and validate the impact of one's actions on others, whether intended or not." It's imperative for those who hold positions of authority in Christian settings to understand and be aware of this reality.

Abusing Power in God's Name

Every day, men—and women—who claim to be serving God abuse the power they've been entrusted with. This is a form of spiritualized abuse, which psychologist Diane Langberg describes as "God's people us[ing] God's words to sanction things God hates."[20]

Spiritualized abuse has many iterations ranging from subtle (such as shame) to overt (such as rape). Michael Kruger, president of Reformed Theological Seminary, Charlotte, defines this type of abuse as "when a spiritual leader—such as a pastor, elder, or head of a Christian organization—wields his position of spiritual authority in such a way that he manipulates, domineers, bullies, and intimidates those under him as a means of maintaining his own power and control."[21] (While Kruger doesn't explicitly include clergy sexual abuse in his definition, it would still apply to sexual abuse because the perpetrator is in a position of spiritual authority.)

Spiritualized abuse is more likely to happen when churches or organizations systematically exclude women and People of Color from top leadership positions or devalue their input. Miriam* experienced this firsthand. After several years of teaching Bible studies to women at a megachurch in the Midwest, Miriam was offered a job as director of women's ministry. She quickly discovered the environment wasn't as healthy as it appeared on Sunday mornings. Miriam believes the ministry veiled its true posture toward women: "Women were onstage leading worship. The pastors communicated they cared about women. But once I was on staff, I began to see how much was hidden from public view."[22] Miriam realized that she and the other female pastors were excluded from key events: "Every year I was there, they had a staff retreat and the women leaders were never invited. There were other important meetings that we were not invited to. The microaggressions were a mile a minute."

Miriam wasn't the only one being marginalized or noticing that something was amiss. After a leadership conflict that resulted in some elders stepping down and others circling the wagons around the lead pastor, Miriam shot her campus pastor an email. "He refused to meet with me. I'm on staff and he wouldn't meet with me. He told me, 'There's going to be a town hall meeting, and you can come to that.' That's when I knew it was time to leave. After I handed in my resignation, there was an NDA on my desk that they expected me to sign. I refused. My only regret is that I didn't leave sooner."

A few years later, the lead pastor was fired.

Like most sins, the choice to abuse power starts as a thought and inches toward incarnation. I don't believe a pastor wakes up on Saturday morning and randomly decides, *I'm going to stop by the church around the time the worship team finishes practicing and corner the hot lead vocalist in my office.*[23] Temptations and fantasies are nurtured rather than confessed. Entitlement to another's body is rationalized. Opportunities are devised. And finally, trust is betrayed. The apostle James explains sin's progression: "Temptation comes from our own desires, which entice us and drag us away. These desires give birth to sinful actions. And when sin is allowed to grow, it gives birth to death" (James 1:14–15 NLT).

One of the reasons women are vulnerable—both bodily and emotionally—in hierarchical, male-led religious spaces is because it's an ecosystem that requires us to trust men. In fact, the mandate to trust and submit can make it infinitely more difficult for women to create healthy boundaries in both ministry and personal relationships, including marriage.

Carolyn Custis James encourages us to ask, "Are we creating and cultivating vulnerability when we teach women and girls that the Bible's watchwords for them are 'silence' and 'submission'? Or are we equipping females to give a firm 'No!' when *anyone* crosses the line with her?"[24]

Women who minister or lead in spaces governed by patriarchal norms can experience tremendous internal tension and cognitive dissonance. They may be called and equipped by God but simultaneously be marginalized, criticized, or undercut by their male peers. And woe to them if they speak up.

The Christian faith is not categorically opposed to power or authority, but neither does it advocate misusing power or authority to create hierarchies that enable control or abuse. Yet far too often, that's exactly what happens, particularly to women. Either the power for our mics is never turned on or the volume is never set to the same level as men's. We are told in so many ways that our insights, our wisdom, our perspectives, and even our bodies are of lesser importance. Heather Matthews writes in *Confronting Sexism in the Church*, "When power is distorted, as it is with sexism, it causes a diminishing of human dignity, rather than flourishing."[25]

The abuse of power and the subsequent diminishing happens in both private and public spaces. When Christian men abuse power to control their intimate partners, it's particularly damaging. Control exists on a continuum. It includes limiting a wife's input on key decisions, refusing to contribute to household chores, berating and threatening her, demanding sex, or committing physical and sexual abuse. Christian Domestic Discipline offers an extreme example of how some men can abuse their partners in God's name. In CDD, men act as the self-appointed leaders of the home and are encouraged to discipline their wives through corporal punishment (including spanking with a belt), loss of privileges (such as using the family vehicle or credit cards), and social isolation.

Author Tia Levings details what this looked like in her chilling memoir, *A Well-Trained Wife*. She recounts how her husband requested that she call him "lord," spanked her when she was "rebellious" (which could mean something as innocuous as having her own opinion), restricted her creative pursuits, and controlled her friendships. When she shared what was going on to a church-based counselor, she was told to "honor your husband more. Do what he asks. . . . You need to ask yourself what you are doing that's driven your husband to this point, and you need to submit to him."[26] Telling battered or abused wives they need to stay and submit rather than helping them to move to safety is incompetent and dangerous.

Popular author and Bible teacher Beth Moore has been on the receiving end of broken power dynamics in church settings for decades. In 2018 she published a letter on her ministry's website that detailed some of her experiences:

> As a woman leader in the conservative Evangelical world, I learned early to show constant pronounced deference . . . to male leaders and, when placed in situations to serve alongside them, to do so apologetically. I issued disclaimers ad nauseam. I wore flats instead of heels when I knew I'd be serving alongside a man of shorter stature. . . . I've ridden elevators in hotels packed with fellow leaders who were serving at the same event and not been spoken to and, even more awkwardly, in the same vehicles where I was never acknowledged. I've been in team meetings where I was either ignored or made fun of, the latter of which I was expected to understand was all in good fun. I am a laugher. I can take jokes and make jokes. I know good fun when I'm having it and I also know when I'm being dismissed and ridiculed.[27]

The following year, a prominent Southern Baptist pastor shamelessly mocked Moore during the Truth Matters Conference at John MacArthur's Grace Community Church. MacArthur was asked to respond to a word association by panel host Todd Friel. The prompt was "Beth Moore." His response: "Go home." Others on the platform and many in the audience laughed, cheered, and applauded. Elder Phil Johnson, who was on the stage with MacArthur, added, "Narcissistic. . . . This is what it looks like to preach yourself rather than Christ." MacArthur then chimed in, "Feminists want power, not equality. This is the highest location they can ascend to that power in the evangelical church and overturn what is clearly scriptural."[28]

Perhaps such leaders are projecting their own understanding of power onto Moore. Perhaps they fear sharing "their" power with women because the power they exercise is worldly and finite. They are simply protecting their piece of the pie.

Moore left the SBC in 2021.

Treating women in these ways often coincides with—and sometimes predicts—more widespread and consequential abuses of power that may affect anyone lower in the organization's hierarchy. In most religious, government, and workplace settings, this tends to be women. Men can also be on the receiving end of abusive power in spiritual settings, but it takes on another dimension for women because we never know if other more consequential lines will be crossed in the future.

Once men have repeatedly tested boundaries and assessed how far they can go without being challenged or stopped, it becomes relatively frictionless for them to sexually harass or abuse women and children both in their own families and within wider circles. Tragically, this type of abuse is perpetrated within every type of church and religious organization—including Christian colleges and seminaries—particularly where power is concentrated at the top of the hierarchy and dissenting voices are muted or silenced.

During the 1980s, reports of priests abusing children began to appear in the news. Catholic leaders repeatedly assured parishioners these were isolated incidents. But they weren't. Over the course of the next ten to twenty years, it became clear that systemic and widespread abuse had gone on for decades and was continuing to happen.[29] A report by Massachusetts Attorney General Thomas F. Reilly reads, "According to the Archdiocese's own files, 789 victims have complained of sexual abuse by members of the clergy; the actual number of victims is no doubt higher. The evidence to date also reveals that 250 priests and church workers stand accused of acts of rape or sexual assault of children."[30] Priest John J. Geoghan apparently abused more than 130 victims over thirty years.[31] Reassignment was a common method of "dealing with" known abusers and pedophiles.

For decades, Protestants tried to make this a Catholic issue. We now know it's far more pervasive. Revelations of sexual abuse within various Protestant churches and organizations abound. One of the most recent—and most damning—happened within the Southern Baptist Convention. In 2019, the *Houston Chronicle* reported that more than seven hundred women, girls, and some boys and young men were sexually abused by SBC pastors, deacons, Sunday school teachers, youth pastors, and volunteers.[32] *Chronicle* reporters wrote, "Many of the victims were adolescents who were molested, sent explicit photos or texts, exposed to pornography, photographed nude, or repeatedly raped by youth pastors. Some victims as young as 3 were molested or raped inside pastors' studies and Sunday school classrooms."[33] One teen was impregnated by a pastor and then forced to "stand in front of the congregation and ask for forgiveness without saying who had fathered the child."[34] Such heinous abuses of power should make us weep.

Similar to the situation in the Catholic Church, higher-ups knew. In 2007 a secret list of accused abusers within SBC-affiliated churches was started, eventually growing to more than seven hundred names.[35] At their annual convention in 2008, SBC officials rejected a proposal to create a database of sexual abuse allegations and offenders, saying such a database would not be possible.[36] More than ten years later, the organization continued to claim it didn't "have the power to force churches to report abuses to a central registry, or to consult a registry when doing hiring decisions," ostensibly because the 47,000-plus churches operate autonomously.[37] Per the leadership's point, the SBC lacks a clear organizational structure and carefully monitoring that many churches would be a daunting task. Yet during this same time, they were able to keep track of churches where women were serving as pastors and kick them out of the organization.[38] They clearly weren't inept at compiling data and following through on administrative tasks.

In an interview, *Christianity Today*'s news editor Kate Shellnutt explained, "It's not just that there was negligence or lack of response but that there was active resistance to the response and a demonization of the victims who were coming forward and trying to help."[39] According to Christa Brown, a survivor of clergy abuse and outspoken advocate for church reform, former SBC president Paige Patterson referred to her and other child rape victims who were part of SNAP (Survivors Network of those Abused by Priests) "as reprehensible as sex criminals."[40] Equating sexual abuse survivors with sex criminals is an egregious abuse of power.

Fourteen years after the list of abusers was initially created (which *is* a type of database), the SBC finally agreed to commission an investigation by a third-party organization. After Guideposts completed the report that validated the abuses, one high-ranking SBC official said, in reference to victims' allegations, "The whole thing should be seen for what it is. [It is] a satanic scheme to completely distract us from evangelism."[41] Why was his outrage focused on the victims and not the perpetrators? And why did these men fail to understand that any type of abuse—let alone sexual abuse of women and children—would seriously undermine their Christian witness?

It's reprehensible enough that sexual abuse was happening in God's house by God's "anointed," but what makes it particularly evil was that those in positions of authority who could have done something to stop it, didn't. Instead, they lied, protected the abusers, and ignored or vilified the victims.

Broken Systems

Abuse doesn't happen in a vacuum. A diminished view of women, the unrestrained pursuit of power, and sloppy organizational structures conspire to foster and perpetuate abuse within churches and religious settings. Churches across the United States are overwhelmingly pastored by men.[42] Many of these churches prohibit women from having influence regarding church polity or vision and don't allow them to preach or to teach men. In such closed systems, if men believe they alone can hear from God and feel threatened by the presence of women—particularly those who are strong, gifted leaders—they may be inclined to overlook or minimize dysfunction and disregard reports of harm.

In retrospect, this is what happened when Emma and her husband expressed concerns to Mark Driscoll about how he treated women and fellow staff members, when John MacArthur responded about Beth Moore, and when Miriam's pastor refused to meet with her, and this is how countless pastors and leaders within the SBC reacted when survivors and the parents of survivors came to them with details of abuse.

Restricting or silencing marginalized voices becomes even more consequential when there are no clear criteria for reporting abuse and organizations and churches rely on nondisclosure or nondisparagement agreements. Regarding the former, Liberty University in Virginia, one of the largest Christian colleges in the US, was hit with a $14 million fine for failing to disclose information about campus crime and safety, failing to maintain accurate records of assault and harassment crimes, and fostering a climate of fear for victims of assault.[43] Such practices create barriers for survivors to come forward and receive care. They also needlessly endanger others who might have been protected if the abusers had been stopped.

Some businesses argue that nondisclosure agreements (NDAs) are essential to protect trade secrets and allow HR to graciously let go of unqualified employees. But because they are frequently abused or used inappropriately—even by Christian institutions—they are currently being reevaluated. When an employee has been harassed, mistreated, or abused and then coerced to sign an NDA (perhaps given the ultimatum that if they refuse to sign, they won't receive their severance), it effectively protects the status quo.

Some former pastors at Mars Hill, families with children abused by Catholic priests, and SBC abuse survivors were pressured to sign NDAs. This wasn't about protecting trade secrets; it was about protecting secret sins, toxic systems, and abusive leaders. NDAs in these situations silence survivors and prevent them from pursuing justice. (In 2022, Congress passed the Speak Out Act that prevents employers from prohibiting employees from speaking out about sexual assault or sexual harassment even if they previously signed an NDA.)[44] Churches and Christian organizations requiring new employees to sign NDAs may be telegraphing their inclination to protect the organization rather than vulnerable individuals. Should you ever find yourself in this situation, proceed with caution.

Rebuilding the Foundation

If the church is to bring healing, reconciliation, justice, and peace to every corner of the earth, it has to be unrelenting in purging sin from its ranks. This includes examining all practices and teachings to discern if they truly represent Jesus's heart for women—or if they perpetuate misogyny.

For starters, we have to be willing to acknowledge that complementarian theology provides, and sometime fosters, an environment for abuse. Again, that doesn't mean all churches or all individuals ascribing to complementarian practices and theology will be blind to or tolerate abuse. However, complementarianism seems to deny the reality that we live in a broken world. The belief that all men will faithfully protect women and consistently create spaces (whether familial or institutional) for women to be safe and flourish is noble. But it's an ideal that doesn't consistently work as intended, because misogyny is so endemic and the pull to worldly power is so strong.

Author and theologian Hannah Anderson believes, "Complementarians who minimize the dangers that women actually face—whether in the church, in a marriage, or in the world—will find themselves unable to protect women against these dangers. You can't protect against a threat that you don't see as real."[45] Women are invited into a system supposedly created and sanctioned by a God who loves and wants the best for them. This system encourages women to trust and submit and then promises to keep them safe. It says, *We care about you. We've got your back. There's no need to worry or be afraid. Trust us.* Or, in Mark Driscoll's words, *You don't need to be a Jezebel.*

But when that lone wolf (or in some cases, pack of wolves) starts preying on the flock and women call for help, some of the same men who encouraged them to submit and promised to protect them either become strangely silent or blame and discredit the women. Those most proximate to the abusers—those who have the most to lose—twist theology, which baptizes the sins that should be confronted. Anderson continues, "If you place a sword (meaning Scripture) in abusers' hands, they will use it violently."

One obvious problem is that not enough men are holding those who abuse power accountable. If we hope to diminish misogyny, there can be no more rallying around the abuser. Men must stop all abusive behavior and make sure their brothers face the consequences of their sin, including removal from their positions of authority and possible incarceration. Because this isn't consistently happening, women are left trying to reconcile church-based harm with an all-good, all-powerful God who seemingly allowed evil to happen in his house. This is impossible, because it doesn't make sense. Ever. In *Redeeming Power*, Diane Langberg reminds us, "Anything done in the name of

God that does not bear his character through and through is not of him at all."[46]

The question we should be asking here is not *Why didn't God stop them?* but *Why didn't other men stop them?* USA Gymnastics officials, SBC officials, and Louis C.K.'s peers all knew and chose to protect their proximity to power over women and children's welfare. Abuse of power can happen in any culture that doesn't check it. The male leaders mentioned in this chapter—and many, many others who were not named—are not simply bad apples. They reveal a diseased tree. In these situations, the people of God are dividing the house, making it difficult for God's kingdom to break in. The church, which should be actively, aggressively fighting against misogyny, is seemingly fighting for the enemy. This cannot continue.

Far too much harm has been done to women in church and religious settings. But because God is a God of redemption and compassion, he never forgets about those of us who have been wounded. He has not forgotten about Emma or her need for healing after what happened at Mars Hill. Since she left the Seattle megachurch, her new pastors have gone out of their way to affirm her and validate her voice.

For years, Emma "waited for the other shoe to drop." She assumed these new pastors would also suspect her motivations, criticize her, or try to shut her down. That has not happened. Instead, "Each one of them has looked at me and essentially said, 'You have obvious gifts and our church needs those gifts.' I haven't had to convince them of anything. In fact, they've made the case for me to be involved. They've invited me to speak up."

Emma will probably never receive an apology from Driscoll, but she has forgiven him and moved on. That doesn't mean the journey has been effortless or quick. It took her twelve years to get over her fear of speaking out and trusting her voice. Twelve years is a long time to doubt yourself. "I have no problem speaking up now," she says. "There's no suspicion, so my pastor and I can approach each other with mutual respect, even if we disagree. I know the elders have my back, and this has empowered me to walk in my gifts again." She concludes, "I never wanted to control my pastor or my church. My desire is simply to serve."

Emma's willingness to forgive and continue to engage with the church is quite remarkable. It reveals her maturity, humility, and desire to become increasingly Christ-like. Jesus invites all of us who have been wounded or sidelined by misogyny to forgive those who have wounded us, just as he invites all who have perpetuated misogyny within the church to both repent and restore the church to its full potential.

Heather Matthews writes in *Confronting Sexism in the Church*, "The path to restoration, then, is to continue to advocate for women in the church, to give voice to women, to allow women to fully exercise their gifts within the home, church, and in leadership, and to name and condemn persistent sexism and patriarchy upheld by the church. In this way, the church can use power as an agent of justice and for the flourishing of all people, the church, and the kingdom of God."[47]

May it be so.

CHAPTER 8

NAMING OUR NEEDS AND BROKEN PLACES

Healing Misogyny's Wounds

Though we all need healing from the ways misogyny has harmed us, acknowledging this can be intimidating. It takes tremendous courage to admit our failures and share our vulnerabilities in an individualistic, success-driven culture like ours. The pursuit of healing might lead to being misunderstood, rejected, or shamed. However, if we submit to these fears and resist transformation, we won't be able to fully thrive or help eradicate misogyny from our families and our culture.

Thankfully, men are increasingly willing to take this risk.

Andrew Bauman grew up in North Carolina with a father who pastored a conservative church while concealing his sexual addictions and substance abuse. His dad's hidden life was exposed when Andrew was eight, and his parents soon divorced. Five years later, Andrew began using pornography to self-medicate. He admits that "mixing porn with my oppressive theological upbringing was a toxic combination. It led me to have a low view of women and to objectify and degrade them."[1]

In his early twenties, when Bauman was serving as a pastor, he began experiencing deep shame and cognitive dissonance connected to his pornography addiction. Rather than run away from the pain, he ran toward it: "I had to dive into my own story and my own sin. I faced my deepest shame and deepest fears." He remembers feeling like a fraud, and for a season, he entertained thoughts of suicide.

As Bauman learned, if we want to heal, we must recognize and address our shame. Shame can convince us that we're hopelessly broken, worthless, and unlovable—essentially sucking us into a vortex of self-hatred, anger, and isolation. Or it can convict us of our mistakes and propel us toward maturity and wholeness.

Inviting a trustworthy person into this process can be a game changer. Over the next few years, Bauman worked with a therapist and learned how to recognize his shame spirals and make better choices when shame tried to pull him under. He explains, "My father lived in shame and self-hatred. I wanted to live differently. I wanted to be a giver of life and an advocate, not an abuser." By allowing himself to feel shame and use it "as an agent of grief,"[2] he was able to experience genuine sorrow, take responsibility for his poor choices, and begin the process of healing.

Bauman realized he had to "unlearn so many damaging things and face the fear of disappointing God and not living into what God called me to be. I had to distill what pleased God and what was a man-made construct that I had been spoon-fed from insecure men." Bauman's willingness to wrestle with the inconsistencies of his story and admit his wrongs changed the direction of his life. After gaining sobriety from his addiction, he increasingly realized that "violence against women, pornography, etc., are men's issues because we're the ones who seek them out." He also knew that men "are capable of emotional intelligence and deep intimacy but we can't walk in this if we continue to participate in a system of patriarchy and misogyny. Men must heal so that we are no longer bystanders and can become advocates for women."

Andrew pursued a master's degree in counseling and eventually opened a practice with his wife, Christy. He now supports women and helps his brothers become "good and safe men." By that he means men who are "kind, humble, self-aware, understand how to be angry without being dangerous, and use their anger to fight against injustice."

Misogyny is so deeply entrenched and so powerful that it can sometimes feel like it has us in a death grip. But as Bauman's narrative reveals, that's not true. We can break free and find healing—whether we have perpetrated misogyny or been harmed by it. Or both.

Trauma

Because no two wounds are the same, no two healing journeys will be identical. What is universally true is that there are no quick fixes, particularly for anyone who has experienced trauma. It's beyond the scope of *For the Love of Women* to thoroughly address this topic. However, because failing to recognize and process trauma can become a significant obstacle to healing, it's important to touch on it.*

As discussed in the first chapter, one of the hallmarks of trauma is that the events and memories continue to affect us long after the incident has passed. What registers as trauma varies from person to person, but many of the examples of misogyny mentioned throughout this book qualify, including abuse, coercive sex within marriage, and sexualized violence.† Ongoing, non-life-threatening misogynistic acts that happen in families, intimate relationships, or institutions can also be traumatic.[3] According to expert Dr. Judith Herman, "Not until the women's liberation movement of the 1970s was it recognized that the

* Please check the appendix for resources on how to better understand and heal from trauma.

† Some individuals can experience specific events and emerge relatively unscathed while others are deeply traumatized. Responses depend on the personality of the individual, how old the person was at the time of the experience, the number of traumatic experiences, and perhaps most importantly, whether they had good support.

most common post-traumatic disorders are those not of men in war but of women in civilian life."[4]

The physiological effects of trauma—including the complex ways that the brain processes and stores threatening, adverse experiences—present unique challenges in our healing journeys. According to therapist Aundi Kolber, because trauma is so damaging and outside the realm of what humans should encounter, "the body is unable to metabolize the stress or event and the disturbing experience becomes 'stuck' in the person's nervous system." Kolber continues, "One hallmark of both big T and little t trauma is that the memory of the event isn't normal. Instead of recalling something as though it had happened in the past . . . we experience it as though it were happening in the present."[5]

Mindy* was a nineteen-year-old college freshman when she was abducted and raped. More than forty years later, the trauma still lingers. She admits, "Even when I know my husband or someone else is in the house, I can startle and scream when they walk into the room. It's an uncontrollable reaction."[6] For twenty years, Mindy had a recurring nightmare where a man was standing next to her bed: "I always woke in terror, hearing the words, 'This isn't a dream.' It was so realistic that it felt like I was experiencing an actual trauma. When my husband travels now, I won't sleep despite locking all the doors and windows, turning on every light inside and outside, and putting a lock-bar on the kitchen door."

As Mindy's story illustrates, trauma survivors often live with a heightened autonomic nervous system and can quickly and inexplicably transition into one of the four common reactions to a triggering stimulus: fight, flight, freeze, or fawn (the latter meaning to be compliant). Unexpected sounds, surprises (even positive ones), unfamiliar settings, or proximity to strangers can cause them to be on high alert, making it difficult to relax or be at peace. Trauma can also cause survivors to mistrust others, which complicates the healing process because we can't fully heal in isolation. As Andrew Bauman discovered, once we acknowledge our need for healing and begin to identify our broken places, we will need to talk about our histories with trusted others.

Naming Our Needs, Brokenness, and Anger

Inviting others into our messy places is not easy. America's media-driven culture coaches us to spackle over our cracks, hide our pain, and convince others we're good—fine, actually. From a human vantage point, this is understandable. People aren't always trustworthy and sometimes prey on vulnerability, so why should we give them more opportunities to hurt us?

Furthermore, because misogyny disdains perceived weakness and can't function without hierarchies and power-over, it amplifies any misgivings about being honest regarding our limitations or failures, particularly for men.[7] When men admit need and brokenness (including ways they've been abused by power), it can feel shameful and cause them to lose status and respect. Men who don't fit the Western stereotype of masculinity are told ad nauseam that they're less than and understand all too well how vulnerability can lead directly to mockery and exclusion.

Andrew Bauman notes that some of "the worst curses a boy can endure are being told they're gay because they don't adhere to stereotypical masculinity or something along the lines of 'you throw like a girl.'"[8] While I stood along the sidelines photographing football games, it wasn't uncommon to hear coaches call their players derogatory names—often slang for female genitalia—if they asked to come out after taking a hard hit. This helps explain why so many players stay in the game when concussed. For many men, it's more socially acceptable to go through life wounded than to admit their pain and pull themselves out of the game so they can heal.

The aversion to being compared to or associated with the feminine runs deep in misogynistic cultures. Americans have been so concerned about society—and specifically boys—being feminized that misogyny has even seeped into parenting philosophies. Prior to the late 1980s, many pediatricians and developmental experts discouraged parents from nurturing their babies and toddlers. Mothers were told not to breastfeed. Parents were warned not to cuddle or emotionally attach to their children for fear of spoiling them and making them too needy. This led to generations of children suffering from emotional neglect and going through life hungry for nurture, affection, and acceptance.[9]

If men judge and condemn themselves for exhibiting traits that are considered feminine (and therefore not culturally acceptable), they run the risk of losing touch with their hearts and cutting off a vital connection to themselves, others, and God. This kind of detachment may also contribute to unwelcome health issues.[10]

Women encounter many of the same cultural barriers pertaining to acknowledging need and brokenness, with several additional ones thrown in, including fear. Fear that if we stop playing by misogyny's cultural rules, we'll be rejected or abandoned or lose whatever small portion of influence we hold. Fear that vulnerability and trust will lead to being re-violated or re-wounded. Fear that if we dare ask for anything, we'll be told we're too needy, too emotional, too hormonal. In other words, too much. That accusation is relational death.

While women are judged for being overly emotional, we're simultaneously expected to carry the emotional load in romantic relationships, parenting, and even the workplace. By relegating emotional work to women, men diminish its relevance, miss out on developing in this area, and continue to subordinate women. In a bizarre twist, when women admit brokenness, we're often blamed—as if our wounds were self-inflicted. We also face the likelihood of having our pain mansplained and being seen as projects that need to be fixed rather than vulnerable human beings seeking compassion and companionship, which feels humiliating.[11]

Because fear of being wounded, harmed, or rejected has such a strong presence in women's lives, it's infinitely more difficult for us to acknowledge and voice our anger. Where anger is perhaps *the* approved emotion for men, it's off-limits for women, particularly in faith-based settings. Starting in childhood, boys are shamed or punished for crying and girls are scolded or punished for being angry. We are told to smile more. Smiling might make other people feel better, but it does nothing to address the legitimate reasons girls and women are angry. The prohibition against anger encourages girls to sublimate their indignation and pain and rely on manipulation to get their needs met or effect change. By the time we hit adulthood, most of us have internalized these gendered expectations.

Anger is complicated in part because it rarely has one origin story. It might be masking unhealed wounds that we aren't ready to process. It could be a form of protection to prevent us from further injury. Anger could also be a God-given response to injustice that we must not ignore or shut down.

I reached out to author and speaker Kathy Khang, whose work has helped me better understand the importance of women recognizing and accepting their anger.[12] Khang explained, "I often think about the words of novelist Madeleine L'Engle in *A Wrinkle in Time*: 'Stay angry, little Meg,' Mrs. Whatsit whispered. 'You will need all your anger now.'" Rather than seeing anger as a flaw that needs to be "healed," a sin that needs to be confessed, or an emotion that needs to be sublimated so we don't make others uncomfortable, women need to understand the role it plays in our healing as well as in our calling.

Anger is a messenger that wants to tell us something. As a teen and young adult, whenever I walked past mall kiosks that sold glass tchotchkes, I felt an impulse to smash them. I thought this was strange, but because I had become so proficient at shutting down my anger, I didn't realize the destructive fantasy was really anger trying to get my attention. This troublesome whim disappeared once I started giving myself permission to feel and express my anger productively.

Khang believes "we have been conditioned to ignore the power of our anger because our anger is connected to our recognition of injustice." If we hope to disrupt misogyny or other forms of injustice, we need righteous anger. She continued, "Anger recognizes when an equally qualified woman, or worse an over-qualified woman, is shut down simply because the cultural norms favor men. Anger is one part of the healing and the fuel that keeps me banging the drum for equity for *all* my sisters."

Because she's a Woman of Color, Khang's anger has multiple layers connected to the intersection of racism and misogyny:

> I stay angry because white feminism and white feminists, even in the various iterations of the church, are still committed to the idea of "trickle down feminism": meaning if white women get there first, the others will benefit. For example, the women's suffrage movement did not address the Jim Crow South shutting Black women out of voting for decades or the government denying citizenship for Indigenous or Asian American women. Trickle down didn't happen automatically. I think we women hide and hold back our anger because we have seen others pay the price or we have been told there are consequences. And there are. Especially for Black and other women of color.

The consequences for expressing anger are indeed real for women, but obedience to misogynistic norms also costs us. Denying or shutting down anger causes interpersonal conflict and mistrust as well as internal disintegration (similar to when men suppress their tender feelings). Additionally, women who can't accept and integrate their more powerful emotions may end up being more vulnerable to future exploitation, mistreatment, and abuse.*

As much as we might long for a work-around, if we've been harmed by misogyny and want to heal, we can't deny our brokenness and need. We can't pretend we're good when, in reality, we're little more than dry bones rattling around in a barren desert. Aundi Kolber explains,

* If you are currently in an abusive relationship, expressing anger to your abuser might not be wise. Please seek safety and get professional help.

"From a psychological and physiological perspective, the more disconnected we are from our lived experience, the more overwhelmed or numb to our lives we'll be."[13] Going through life overwhelmed or numb is the opposite of thriving. Deceiving ourselves and others about the true state of our souls also leads us to create and prop up a false, curated version of ourselves that prohibits us from being fully known and fully loved.

Getting well will require us to part company with these deeply embedded habits that prevent us from maturing. Being honest about our limitations and our pain is not antithetical to following Jesus; it's an essential component. Jesus did not turn away from those who acknowledged their brokenness and need.[14] When the sick, troubled, or oppressed came to him, he embraced them with compassion and love. In the Sermon on the Mount, he made the audacious claim that those who are meek, poor in spirit, and pressed down will be blessed. Furthermore, Jesus manifested his greatest power in the midst of what would seem to be his greatest defeat: death. Therein lies the paradox of strength in weakness (2 Corinthians 12:9).

If your default has been denying or minimizing your wounds, or if you've been immersed in a family system or culture that discourages or disapproves of being honest and vulnerable, it may not be apparent how to identify the areas of brokenness and need connected to misogyny. Answering the following questions may offer some insight:

For Women

- How would I describe my relationships with the opposite sex?
- Where have I lost hope or regularly feel a sense of despair about men or relationships with men?
- Do I feel ashamed or self-conscious when I need something from a man? If so, where did that feeling come from? Can I

directly ask for what I need from a man I'm in a relationship with? If not, why?

- Do I ever feel that being accepted by men is contingent upon how I look? How have my experiences reinforced this belief?
- Am I completely and consistently comfortable in my own body, especially in the company of men? If not, what causes my discomfort?
- When I'm in the company of men, do I mute myself? If so, what power dynamics might be at play, and what does this cost me?
- Where or when do I present a false self by dodging or massaging the truth about my fears, hurts, vulnerabilities, or weaknesses? What stories do I *not* tell, particularly when men are present?
- How often and in what circumstances do I feel on high alert? Is this more common when men are present?
- Do I tend to assume or conclude it's my fault when men mistreat or harm me? When and where did I learn this?
- Am I able to feel and express anger to men, particularly in real time? If not, what holds me back? How much anger am I carrying in my body, and how does that affect me?
- How often do I engage in negative self-talk? (For example, rehearsing mistakes or calling myself stupid if I fall short of my expectations.)
- During my childhood, did a parent or authority figure ever or repeatedly tell me I was deficient simply because I was a girl? If so, how did/does this affect me?
- Were both of my parents available when I was a child? Did they consistently, lovingly care for, nurture, value, and protect me? If not, what message did I internalize about being honest with others about my needs and vulnerabilities?
- What traumatic events have I witnessed or personally experienced, and how do they continue to affect me?

For Men

- How would I describe my relationships with the opposite sex? Do I routinely sexualize women or feel aroused by their mere presence? Can I see an attractive woman and not sexualize or objectify her?
- Where and when do I routinely experience conflict with women? Do I allow myself to be truly vulnerable with them, or do I feel pressure to be strong and independent?
- Do I feel ashamed or angry when I'm in need, particularly if I need something from a woman? When and where did I learn it is not acceptable to need?
- When someone of the opposite sex tries to teach me or offer a corrective, am I open and curious or defensive? If the latter, what does that cost me and how does it affect the relationship?
- What's it like to humbly admit when I've made a mistake that has hurt or disappointed a woman I'm in relationship with?
- Am I fully myself and fully free with other men? How about with women? If not, where or how am I disintegrated?
- When was I shamed because I expressed emotions or liked activities that weren't considered socially acceptable for a boy or man? How does that continue to affect me?
- How often do I feel angry? Am I in touch with the source of my anger? Do I ever lose control when I'm angry, and if so, can I discern any patterns? How do I feel after this happens, and what do my outbursts cost those closest to me? How do I feel when women are angry with me?
- Where or when do I tend to dodge or massage the truth about my fears, pain, or weaknesses? What stories do I *not* tell? Where does my false self show up?
- Did I grow up in a household where pornography was used or where women and girls were regularly demeaned or abused? If so, how does that continue to affect me?

- Were both of my parents available when I was a child? Did they consistently, lovingly care for and nurture me? If not, how has this affected me?
- If I've ever been part of an organization that normalized the denigration and devaluation of women, how did that affect my understanding of women?
- What traumatic events have I witnessed or personally experienced, and how do they continue to affect me?

As you answer these questions, linger over your discoveries. Note any feelings of agitation, sadness, cynicism, disgust, contempt, or resignation. If you're not already doing so, talk about what you discover with safe, empathetic witnesses.[15] An empathetic witness will listen attentively, validate your experiences, offer you comfort, and when appropriate, gently point out any distorted thinking. This could be your best friend, your spouse, or a professional therapist.

Paths to Healing

Our upbringings, our personalities, the consistency and quality of support around us, and historic trauma all influence how misogyny affects us and how we repair. While formulas rarely work for anyone seeking healing, certain practices such as addressing trauma, grieving and lamenting, confessing, and forgiving can be helpful.

Addressing Trauma

Tremendous advances in brain science, neurology, psychology, and psychiatry have occurred over the past few decades and have helped clinicians develop innovative, integrated therapy modalities and somatic practices that help trauma survivors heal. These include EMDR (eye movement desensitization and reprocessing), regulation of the vagus nerve, progressive muscle relaxation, and writing (by hand). Today, mental health practitioners also better understand that in therapeutic or group settings, survivors need a sense of safety, empowerment, and a trustworthy practitioner or leader.

Sheila Wise Rowe, therapist and author of *Healing Racial Trauma* and *Healing Leadership Trauma*, encourages those seeking to repair from trauma to understand that "therapy is not an exact science and not everyone will find healing in the same way."[16] In her thirty-plus years of clinical experience, she's learned that some people benefit most from one-on-one counseling while others thrive in group settings. Wise Rowe believes that "whatever works, works." She also emphasizes the importance of "exercising self-compassion, guarding against comparison, and finding empathetic witnesses."

Signs of healing from trauma include being able to remember what happened but be fully present in the moment, play in an uninhibited fashion, imagine positive outcomes, experience internal homeostasis or peace, and bond with safe others. As women, these markers aren't easy to reach because we live in an environment that continues to be hostile.

While we can, and in some cases should, remove ourselves from spaces or relationships that retraumatize us, we can't isolate or barricade ourselves off from the world if we hope to grow. As survivors learn to discern who is safe, they will be increasingly able to give and receive love from trustworthy individuals. Churchgoers are often encouraged to talk to their pastors about difficult or painful topics, but few pastors have the necessary training to serve trauma survivors. Because trauma is complex and has the potential to affect every aspect of our lives, survivors should seek professional help.

Grief and Lament

Despite how common it is to be wounded by misogyny in American culture, we tend not to grieve, and we rarely ever lament with others. We circumvent, deny, minimize, self-medicate, or even normalize our pain. We also vent on social media, perhaps hoping this will satisfy the need for a witness. Except for the #MeToo phenomenon in 2017, such venting rarely achieves that goal. All these responses keep suffering at bay temporarily but end up delaying the healing process. Like trauma, suffering and loss need to be acknowledged and integrated. Grieving and lamenting help us move in that direction.

When we grieve, we give ourselves permission to feel and name our pain, even if the losses happened decades ago. Grief tends to be primal and messy. If we want to grieve fully, we must let go of our fears about what others will think of us. As Andrew Bauman began to understand the ramifications of his pornography addiction and how his mistreatment of women harmed them, he allowed himself to feel the full intensity of his sin. Andrew admits it was terrifying and explains why: "Men are socialized to be strong and tough. We don't want to suffer or feel pain, and we don't want to ask for help. The invitation to us is *Will we die? Will we enter into the pain that's necessary to taste new life?*" The fear of pain and the unknowns of suffering can be so overwhelming that we cordon pain off and try to avoid it. Though such impulses are completely understandable, we can't avoid pain if we hope to heal.

Fear of pain and suffering isn't the only barrier to grieving and lamenting. The American church prioritizes happiness and assumes grief can't coexist with faith. This is a costly mistake. In the middle of writing this book, our granddaughter died. As we talked with her medical team in the hospital hallway and the inevitability of her passing closed in, I wept so hard I could barely breathe. Our family grieved hard for months. This grief did not cancel out our faith. It was an appropriate response based on the magnitude of losing our long-awaited granddaughter.

My husband and I noticed a marked difference in how we processed our grief. My pain was on the surface and immediately accessible. Grief shape-shifted to anger and anxiety for him, and he had to learn to recognize and then express those subtler feelings.

Grieving helps us recognize our finitude and leads us to surrender our feeble efforts to control. If we refuse to grieve, we run the risk of having a shallow faith that will not survive when the floodwaters rage. And they will rage. Furthermore, we can't neatly deny one feeling without muting all the others. Based on his professional and personal experience, Dr. Bauman believes that "grief and joy are on a continuum, and if we deny grief, we also deny joy."

In lament, we voice our grief and all the accompanying feelings to God in the company of others. According to seminary professor and author Soong-Chan Rah, lament "is an act of protest" in which the lamenter "express[es] indignation and even outrage about the experience of suffering."[17] Pastor Brenda Salter McNeil refers to lament as "a cry for help in times of trouble or suffering" and "a form of truth-telling."[18] As we verbalize our pain, witnesses need not explain, fix, or blame the pain on us, as Job's friends did. Instead, they need to patiently, lovingly hold space with us. By doing so, they participate in our healing.

Lament contains the seemingly unbearable present-tense pain yet somehow clings to the hope that ultimately, God, in collaboration with his people, will make it right. Looking forward is part of what differentiates lamenting from venting. Aubrey Sampson writes in *The Louder Song*, "Lament minds the gap between current hopelessness and coming hope. Lament anticipates new creation but also acknowledges the painful reality of now."[19] When we honestly express our pain and anger with others who know and love us—without cursing or blaming God—it helps us move through suffering toward healing, hope, and freedom. We can speak, write, sing, weep, or pray our lament. If words fail us, reading the book of Lamentations or the lament psalms out loud can satisfy the need to express our reality in the company of those who know and love us.[20]

Confession

If we want to be whole and help create a safe culture where women can consistently thrive, we can't hide or deny sin. This is tricky, in part because sin is an unpopular concept. Our postmodern culture tends to resist binary thinking, including right and wrong, and increasingly cancels anyone who makes a mistake. This makes it infinitely more difficult for us to admit when we fail or hurt someone. As I wrote in *Making Marriage Beautiful*, "If we routinely dismiss or minimize our sin—for any reason—we have no impetus to change."[21] It will always be someone else's fault or outside our purview. This will not help us to stop sinning or to reduce misogyny.

Regular confession helps us develop the habit of examining our thoughts and actions in light of the call toward Christ-likeness. Quoting Soong-Chan Rah, "Confession acknowledges the need for God and opens the door for God's intervention."[22] If the goal is to heal from and eradicate misogyny, we will need God's help.

Based on our working definition of *misogyny*[*] and the many examples throughout the book, sins of misogyny that could be confessed include maligning, marginalizing, silencing, objectifying, and demeaning women; demanding sex; and committing any form of violence against women or children. In addition to these specific sins, whenever we witness women being harmed and choose to do nothing, we have something to confess. Women also commit sins of misogyny that need to be confessed. When we judge other women as stupid, shame them because their bodies don't meet the approved cultural ideal (e.g., fat shaming), or criticize them for perceived shortcomings—particularly on social media—we are colluding with misogyny. Since White men occupy many of the top positions of power, when White women take advantage of our proximity to these men, we can disadvantage Women of Color by failing to make space or advocate for them.

Acknowledging any of these sins to oneself is imperative, but they should also be named out loud—sometimes to those who have been directly wounded—and an apology should be offered. Pastor and

* Misogyny is a persistent, insidious belief that men's wants, needs, and experiences are more important than women's and that political, religious, and social systems, as well as intimate relationships, should uphold this principle. This belief system subsequently influences the laws, politics, practices, and ethos of a given culture.

author Thabiti Anyabwile read Beth Moore's 2018 letter quoted in the previous chapter. He had previously dismissed Moore's ministry, making it frictionless for him to overlook how others' treatment affected her. Her nondefensive accounts of her pain allowed him to see this from a different vantage point and brought conviction. In response, he wrote a letter of apology published on The Gospel Coalition's website. Pastor Anyabwile starts the letter by admitting, "I am brokenhearted . . ." and then continues,

> Dear Beth, if you read this, I need to confess and ask your forgiveness. . . . I can't recall saying anything about you as a person. But with a raised eye brow, a shrugged shoulder, a "hmmm" before a redirecting sentence, I passed along what was in my heart, the sinful attitude rooted in the very misogyny and chauvinism you describe in your post. If we communicate most in non-verbal ways, then I'm afraid I've "said" a lot about you, and I have slandered you.[23]

Thabiti's apology is a textbook example of how to apologize well. He did not blame Moore in any way. His post went on to say, "I want to accept responsibility for my action and inaction without qualification. There are no 'if,' 'and,' or 'but' statements to justify or excuse my wrong."

When we confess our sin, how we do it matters. A lot. Far too often, blame or defensiveness gets embedded in the pseudo confession: "Yes, I objectified you, but it's because of what you were wearing." Or "Yes, I spoke disrespectfully to you in the staff meeting, but that's because you didn't agree with me." A confession should simply state the wrong with full ownership, followed by an apology: "I hurt you, and I'm sorry." The backstory can come later—if the person who was wronged wants to hear it.

Public confession is crucial for systemic sins like misogyny that affect entire groups of people. The week #MeToo swept across the internet, Bay Area pastor Brad Wong led the men in his congregation to kneel during the Sunday morning service and audibly confess any of the ways they had dishonored or disrespected women. According to a parishioner who was present, it was a holy moment for both men and women. Regarding public confession, Soong-Chan Rah explains, "American society tends toward a hyperindividualistic narrative. . . . But a hyperindividualistic ethos results in a disengagement with the reality of corporate sin. Social injustice is dismissed to focus solely on individual expressions of sin."[24]

A single person confessing a specific act of misogyny against one woman is imperative for both parties to heal and reconcile, but it's not enough to turn the tide of systemic injustice. We need a movement; a groundswell of people who decide misogynistic behaviors must stop. Corporate and public confession help others see sins like misogyny for what they truly are and cut a path for others to follow.

Forgiveness

Grieving, lamenting, and confessing all have the capacity to move us toward forgiveness because they help us to be tenderhearted truth tellers who live in reality. "When we drop the charges against those who have sinned against us, we are not excusing their actions, minimizing the damages, or opening ourselves up to further mistreatment."[25] Saying "I forgive you" acknowledges that a wrong was done but then cancels the debt and frees us to love more fully.

Forgiveness is an intentional, nonlinear process. Along the way, we face multiple decisions. Psychologist Dr. Everett Worthington helpfully identifies two prongs of forgiveness: decisional and emotional.[26] In the former, we cognitively decide to move toward forgiveness. Emma had to choose to forgive Mark Driscoll. Nick and Amy have repeatedly forgiven each other. To get the full benefit of forgiveness, we then need to actively jettison any residue of unforgiveness, such as malice, bitterness, revenge fantasies, or judgment. This is particularly difficult when those who harmed us continue to sin against us or refuse to acknowledge—let alone apologize for—what they've done.

We may repeatedly cycle through grief, lament, confession, and forgiveness. I think that's what Jesus was referring to when he talked about forgiving seventy times seven. The idea of forgiveness having a cyclical component has been helpful for me. More than a decade ago, friends who were ministry partners made a series of decisions that altered the trajectory of our family's life and caused us profound pain. I worked hard to let go of my hurt, but it was in absence of an apology or honest dialogue. Ten years after this happened, someone approached me at a party wanting to share a Christmas photo he'd received from "mutual friends." He pulled out his phone and scrolled to a photo of this couple. Anger immediately flooded my body. I felt sixty seconds away from a panic attack. After making a socially appropriate response, I quickly excused myself. My visceral reaction surprised me because I truly thought I had forgiven them. Because we had not seen each other since our fallout, I'd mistaken distance for forgiveness. I could have berated myself for what that moment revealed. Instead, I went home and told my husband, "I have more forgiveness work to do—*and* I need help processing how that trauma continues to affect me."

Because forgiving someone is vulnerable and requires us to revisit the painful events, survivors may feel reluctant to forgive. If this is true for you, consider talking with a spiritual mentor or mature friend. Sometimes we're stubborn and resist what we know we should do, but other times we can be genuinely stuck and need another's objectivity and insight to find our way through. And if you have caused any woman harm, please remember that offering a sincere, specific apology will help them to process the pain. Do not apologize expecting to be forgiven. It may be best to do this in a letter versus in person.

Those wounded by acts of misogyny need to set both the pace and the terms of forgiveness. Authority figures tend to rush victims to forgive (this sometimes even happens in cases of rape and domestic abuse), but "victims must have agency to process their trauma and respond to the perpetrator when they are ready. Otherwise, they may be retraumatized."[27] Though all followers of Christ are called to forgive, survivors (specifically survivors of violent or traumatic events) should never be pressured to occupy the same physical space or reconcile with someone who harmed them unless they feel ready and have the necessary support in place. Higher, less permeable boundaries will probably also need to be established.

Healing Metrics

Because healing is such a slow and internal journey, it can be difficult to recognize and track our forward movement. We can gain encouragement and comfort along the way if we know how to identify certain signposts. These include experiencing reconciliation, having access to a full range of emotions, growing in empathy, having agency, and being able to love others extravagantly.

Scripture tells us Jesus came to reconcile all things and that anyone who follows him is called to be a reconciler, to the extent that they are able. Reconciliation is needed wherever we're estranged from others, from God and his creation, or from ourselves. Misogyny not only estranges men from women (external estrangement) but leaves men and women estranged from themselves and their bodies (internal estrangement). Both were true for Natalie, who is a wife, mother, and spiritual director. Over the course of the last twenty years, she has pursued healing from self-hatred that flowed downstream from familial misogyny.

Natalie admits to being cut off from certain aspects of her body and femininity as she was going into marriage. She explains, "I felt neutered for the first forty years of my life."[28] She even told her fiancé, "I will never have children, and you cannot make me." Eight years into marriage, she was the mother of three but struggled to bond with them. When she attended a healing conference, the speaker gave two talks that addressed her deficit: the first on what it looks like to have a sense of well-being and the second on misogyny.

Natalie stood in an arena full of people but had a very intimate experience with Jesus that felt dialogical.* She sensed him ask her a question: "'Natalie, what came out of my side when I was hanging on the cross and they pierced me with a sword?' And I said, 'Water and blood.' And then he asked, 'What comes out of a woman's womb when she's giving birth?' And I responded, 'Water and blood.' He responded, 'Natalie, do you see the correlation? Life pours out of a woman's suffering as she gives birth. Life poured out of me in my death. I am speaking life over you. There's no longer any need to hate how I created you.'"

In regard to that moment, Natalie said, "I understood for the first time why I felt the way that I did about not wanting to have children. It was related to my own mother and how she was unable to connect and bond with me." As Natalie was growing up, her mom was cold and distant with her while warm and attached to Natalie's brothers.

Natalie continued, "During the conference, the Holy Spirit basically said, 'She could not give you what she lacked. And you can't give to another generation what you don't have.' It seemed clear that God wanted to connect me to myself." Part of that reconciliation was emotional and spiritual, and part of it was physical. Natalie realized she'd been unable to embrace her womanhood, and specifically her womb, because of the misogyny her mother had passed on to her. "This experience began the context for healing my self-hatred. It was very powerful."

Accepting ourselves and each other as complex, complicated people with strengths and weaknesses who repeatedly fail should allow us to grow in empathy.

Pastor Anyabwile became more empathetic after he willingly listened to Beth Moore's painful experiences, acknowledged his apathy, and confessed his complicity. In an email exchange, Anyabwile explained, "It was the sincerity and truthfulness of her post that helped me see this dynamic from her side. What she wrote made sense of my experiences in meeting rooms and conference planning rooms where

* It's fairly common for those who have a deep relationship with God to sense an unspoken but very real back-and-forth.

her name has been spoken. I think following her on [X] and getting a sense of who she is as a person also made me more open and ready to hear her experience and the truth in it. Those personal interactions made her human to me."[29]

As Pastor Anyabwile's experience demonstrates, if men hope to see women aright and love them fully, they'll need to stop dismissing or reacting defensively to women's pain and instead choose to empathize with them.

Healing also allows women to move away from victimhood into a greater sense of agency and empowerment. This helps us gain insight about when it may be time to walk away from spaces or relationships that routinely harm us. Knowing when to quit or move on can be complicated for several reasons. American culture favors empirical knowledge and devalues the more intuitive ways of knowing. Because of this bias, we're discouraged from trusting our instincts. Women also carry the responsibility to address or fix broken relational dynamics, even if we lack the authority to do so. And as discussed in the workplace chapter, troubling the waters might make it more difficult to get another job. All these factors may incline us to keep quiet and stay put.

Author and acquisitions editor Katelyn Beaty knows this territory. After serving as the youngest and first female managing editor at a prominent Christian publication for five years, she chose to leave, partially because of toxic workplace dynamics. In a conversation with me, Beaty noted that "knowing when to leave is both an intuitive and embodied decision for each person" and added that "learning to distinguish the myriads of voices that are pulling us in different directions is crucial."[30] Beaty took time to be still and listen to the Holy Spirit. She sensed God saying, "You don't have to stay to be a good Christian. You don't have to stay just because you believe in the mission when it's negatively affecting you." Beaty also met with a life coach who knew her and had some understanding of what she was going through.

The combination of discerning God's voice, receiving good counsel, and paying attention to shifting circumstances ultimately allowed her to walk away from what was initially a dream job. Beaty encourages women to "pay attention to what and how much you are sacrificing for the sake of the mission, especially if the feedback you're receiving is that you're not doing enough. No woman should sacrifice her mental and spiritual well-being trying to win a game that's rigged against them from the outset." Leaving is infinitely more complicated if the disabuse is connected to one's livelihood or one's marriage.[31]

The healing process can feel incredibly slow and at times not worth the effort. We may feel like the finish line keeps moving or that we're going backward. If we come to understand deep transformation as an essential component of ending misogyny and something we will continue to do until we draw our final breath, it should help us to be patient and stay the course. The freedom and wholeness we're moving toward will allow us to walk in greater integrity and authority, which we need if we hope to transform our families and our culture.

CHAPTER 9

IMAGINE IF . . .

Writing Misogyny Out of the Narrative

Sometimes healing comes when we least expect it.

In the first chapter, I relayed a story about what happened after I had been invited to ~~preach~~ share at a church on Mother's Day. That same week, I spoke at the men's prison where my husband and I volunteer. My talk focused on the Old Testament character Joseph and how God never stops working to redeem our suffering, even when we feel alone or forgotten.

I'll offer a quick recap for anyone not familiar with the story. A Hebrew teenager named Joseph is sold into slavery by his jealous older brothers. Years later, things take a dark turn when he's falsely accused of sexual assault by Pharaoh's wife and then imprisoned. While there's no record of Joseph's inner life, I imagine he experienced confusion and anger—and perhaps even doubted he would be vindicated. After an epic series of twists and turns, he is freed from jail, placed in a position of great authority, and later reunited with his brothers, who initially fail to recognize him (possibly because at that point, he looked like an Egyptian). After his siblings bow down to him and fulfill Joseph's prophetic childhood dream, he weeps so loudly the entire palace can hear him. In that holy moment, Joseph realizes his pain has not been wasted. God prevented his family and his people from perishing through the suffering and injustice Joseph endured.

This is one of the most powerful and beautiful stories in all of Scripture. I knew this message would resonate with the incarcerated men. And it did. When I concluded my talk, they clapped and cheered. Not for me, but because God's truth and hope transcended their circumstances.

What these beloved brothers didn't know was that their enthusiastic response was healing for me. It affirmed my voice and silenced the lie that as a woman, I had no right to authoritatively teach men biblical truths.

From time to time, many of us may feel stuck in discouragement, pain, or destructive patterns. Though we faithfully do our work, nothing seems to change. We may wait for months or years or, like Joseph, decades. Then suddenly, inexplicably, the clouds break, the sun streams in, and change happens. That night in the men's prison was a "suddenly" for me. I was simply doing what I felt called to do, and layers of doubt and heartache lifted.

God's kingdom has been interrupting injustice and transforming pain throughout history. These breakthroughs may be supernatural, but they don't happen via divine edict. God works through us. When slavery was outlawed, when women gained the right to vote, when apartheid fell in South Africa, committed Christians like William Wilberforce, Harriet Tubman, Sojourner Truth, Frances Willard, Martin Luther King Jr., and Bishop Desmond Tutu were actively resisting forces of oppression through prayer and protest. Every time we pray, "Let your kingdom come, let your will be done, on earth as it is in heaven," we proclaim our desire for justice, shalom, and love to triumph over evil and declare our intention to do whatever it takes to make that happen.

Imagine If . . .

Transformed Hearts

I believe that one of the reasons misogyny persists in the US is that we—individually and collectively—have failed to faithfully love women. If that's true, then love is the ultimate antidote to misogyny and foundational to the work of repair and restoration.

Every human being is created with the capacity and desire to give and receive love. That doesn't mean loving is easy. By the time we become adults, we've been wounded and have wounded others, which compromises our ability to love well. We have to learn—or relearn—how to love and then keep practicing. In a broken world like ours, this is a radical choice. Contemporary culture doesn't encourage us to love others sacrificially, particularly those who aren't like us. Instead, we're encouraged to pursue individual happiness and personal gain and to push aside (or even hate) anyone who gets in our way or disagrees with us.

As broken human beings living in a broken world, we must repeatedly choose love over ambivalence and hate. Though we can experience the emotions associated with love and hate in proximity—even in the same hour—ultimately, we cannot orient our internal compass toward both love and hate because they pull us in opposite directions. We must decide who we want to become. (One of the reasons I find Jesus so compelling is that he clarifies this choice.) Loving women leads to flourishing, healing, justice, beauty, and life—for everyone. Misogyny leads to languishing, sickness, injustice, ugliness, and death—for everyone.

If we hope to eradicate misogyny, we need a robust understanding of love. In his letter to the early Corinthian church, the apostle Paul left us one of the most poetic, insightful renderings on love ever written. First and foremost, his description should help us understand how God loves us. God's love is patient, kind, humble, long-suffering, and quick to forgive. This love is not sentimental, unpredictable, or fragile. It's a steady, dependable love that never abuses power and never gives up on us.

Applying this to relationships between men and women, men cannot diminish, oppress, threaten, control, or in any way harm women and claim they're acting under the banner of love. And women cannot dismiss or malign men, seek revenge,* or use deception to manipulate men while claiming to love.† On a bad day, any of us might resort to such behaviors. When we do, it's imperative that we quickly course correct and make amends.

The harm misogyny has done to women and the resultant fear we carry in our bodies can make it challenging for us to fully love *anyone*. As Natalie's story from the previous chapter revealed, before we can direct our love outward, we need to love ourselves. To live into that space, we cannot allow the patriarchal measuring tape to find us lacking. We bear God's image, and no one can take that from us. Because our misogyny-shaped scars may never totally disappear, we will need to continue stretching and massaging them (in other words, validating, grieving, and forgiving) so they do not inhibit us from receiving and giving God's love. When women have a secure sense of self and are treated as equals, our capacity to love is staggeringly beautiful.

Men also face barriers to loving themselves, each other, and women. They will need to relinquish control along with their perceived right to power. This means learning how to trust. In a culture that eschews or even derides male vulnerability, this is no small ask. I truly believe once men have experienced the kind of redemptive, mutual love that Paul described, their eyes will be opened and they will no longer be satisfied with what misogyny offers them.

Transformed Minds

Another reason why we remain mired in misogyny is because it's so pervasive and deeply entrenched that it has warped our understanding

* Revenge and justice are not the same. We can and should seek justice.
† Unless they're in physical danger. Then one does what one needs to do.

of what's normal and what's possible. If we want to loosen misogyny's grip, we must change how we think and the stories we tell.

The Christian faith refers to the former as the renewing of our minds. Scripture puts it this way: "Do not conform to the pattern of this world, but be transformed by the renewing of your mind. Then you will be able to test and approve what God's will is—his good, pleasing and perfect will" (Romans 12:2 NIV). As the passage implies, renewing our minds involves recognizing and then rejecting the patterns of this world that oppose God's work.

Renewing our minds is slow and multilayered, particularly as it pertains to how we think about and respond to systemic injustice. Author and scholar Karen Swallow Prior helps to explain why: "We live with a communal pool of stories, expectations, beliefs, and myths. Because we've inherited them and they're precognitive, they become underlying assumptions. We need to first recognize these assumptions and then examine them to see if they are true or helpful."[1]

I spoke with David Swanson, lead pastor at New Community Covenant Church on the south side of Chicago, about what it has looked like for him to recognize any underlying assumptions that might foster misogyny. He was raised as a missionary kid in South America and came into adulthood carrying more of a global perspective that was less influenced by American evangelicalism or misogyny. "It was clear to me growing up that my parents were equal partners. Though my dad was a pilot with a missionary organization, they were doing the work together. Nevertheless, when I came to the States as a fourteen-year-old, there was no way of growing up in contemporary society and not being formed by misogynistic assumptions. I breathed the same air that everyone else did."[2] One of his limiting assumptions was that women could not be senior pastors, not because he believed women lacked the intelligence or ability, but because he'd never witnessed this.

While Swanson was in grad school, his aunt was invited to be the lead pastor of a church in Iowa. She was their first female senior pastor.

Swanson recounts seeing a church full of men and women flourish under her leadership: "I had a front row seat to witness the good fruit of her ministry and the importance of a more egalitarian theology. Watching her ministry filled in the gaps in my imagination from never having seen women in senior pastoral roles."

Swanson now pastors alongside several women, including Professor Michelle Dodson. "Michelle and I have worked closely since 2010. We have a great deal of admiration for each other. I allow myself to be formed by her. This partnership makes our theological commitment visible to others." Swanson continues, "When a prominent woman becomes a visible leader, and we hear 'It's so important for our girls to see what they can become,' I've got two boys. I'm also thinking, it's really good for them too!" Swanson's sons will most likely not carry the same doubts he did about women in senior leadership roles because they have witnessed women succeed in such positions.

Transforming our minds involves learning to interrogate our stories and discern which beliefs have been corrupted by bias and brokenness. Swanson did this when he realized he held a false narrative about women's leadership capabilities. Thabiti Anyabwile also allowed himself to feel disturbed by his passive participation in Beth Moore's mistreatment.

The process of interrogating our narratives and dismantling lies about ourselves or others requires courage, unflinching honesty, and an unwavering commitment to get well. Whether we have been harmed by misogyny or perpetuated it, we will face unique challenges to renewing our minds. Those on the receiving side know misogyny is real but may feel so beaten down, discouraged, and disempowered that they conclude the issue is simply too massive to address. Those guilty of practicing misogyny may dismiss or minimize it because they don't want to forsake the benefits or share power. Entitlement and worldly power operate as default settings in our culture. Because of this reality, men can become so focused on the potential losses of power and privilege they fail to recognize that by clinging to them, they lose something much more valuable: mutual partnerships and reciprocal love.

Two practices are essential if we hope to align ourselves with God's plan for humanity and weaken misogyny: learning from people whose experiences and narratives differ from our own and cultivating our imaginations.

Regarding the former, Karen Swallow Prior believes, "If we haven't personally experienced racism or misogyny, it's harder for us to understand what it's like. That's why it's so important to listen to those who have a different social imaginary and draw from them." Reading from a diverse pool of authors moves us in this direction.

Forging relationships with people whose lives have been different from our own broadens our minds and enlarges our capacity to care. The gaps between women and men (or any other diverse groups) get smaller when we become curious and empathetic. Compassion, which is empathy in action, naturally flows out of such relationships. The combination of proximity, curiosity, empathy, and compassion can move us toward love. Genuine love will motivate a desire to make things right. We tend to repair what we care about. Conversely, misogyny and other abuses of power result, at least in part, from an inability or unwillingness to imagine the experiences of those being harmed.

Because God is a creator and we are made in his image, we all have the capacity to imagine and create. Creativity manifests uniquely but always starts as an idea—by asking some version of *what if?* The direction *what if?* takes us depends on what and whom we love.

Humans have the capacity to imagine for good—and for ill. Many acts of misogyny result from men employing their imaginations for immoral, unethical ends. A tech company recently launched an app that can show you what someone looks like naked simply by uploading a photograph of them fully clothed. An employee sat in their office cubicle, thought this would be a good idea, and then wrote the code for it. Similarly, those in the pornography industry imagine the degrading scenes they will film before the camera starts rolling. This is the opposite of how we want to cultivate our imaginations so that we might eradicate misogyny.

It may seem far-fetched to propose that an essential component of eradicating misogyny begins with an idea. Yet most reforms—both individual and societal—share this humble beginning. Author Scott Russell Sanders refers to the imagination as "a shaping force at work in the universe."[3] Those who fought to end slavery in Europe and North America first imagined a world where kidnapped men and women could live in freedom. Mother Teresa was so moved by the needs of the poor in India that she imagined and then founded the Missionaries of Charity to feed, clothe, support, and care for people who were unwanted and unloved.

In *The Evangelical Imagination*, Karen Swallow Prior writes, "The imagination shapes us and our world more than any other human power or ability. Communities, societies, movements, and yes, religions are formed and fueled by the power of the imagination."[4]

Assuming the imagination is indeed that powerful, it's essential for us to intentionally develop our imaginations toward having a moral, ethical vision for humanity. Asking questions such as *What does this woman or this group of women need so they can thrive?* and *How can I use my influence to change the status quo and alleviate women's suffering?* is a great place to start. Setting the trajectory of our imaginations toward what is moral and ethical should help us craft a clear, practical vision of who we want to become and how we want to spend our lives.

When our hearts are open to receiving and then giving God's love, and when our minds are focused on what is true, noble, right, pure, lovely, admirable, excellent, and praiseworthy (Philippians 4:8), we'll be able to imagine something new, something we may not have experienced or that may not even exist yet. If, as Prior believes, there is "no limit to our imagination,"[5] then it's not beyond us to imagine how to treat women as equals and curtail misogynistic practices in every sphere of life. And if we can't imagine heaven including gender-based hierarchies, pornography, rape, and so on, then we should work to eradicate those manifestations of misogyny here and now. That's what "your kingdom come" is referring to.

As I've been writing this book, I've wondered how my story—how our stories—might change if women were *consistently* seen, heard, believed, respected, cared for, honored, and loved from the cradle to the grave.

I have imagined all of the following . . .

A world where women can go for a walk or run alone without any fear of being harmed.

A world where male executives and senior pastors regularly seek input from female leaders. Where these same men act quickly and decisively to make amends and bring justice when men in their organizations disadvantage or harm women or children.

A world where men refuse to sexualize or objectify women and always respect a woman's autonomy.

A world where there's no demand for sex workers because men find the practice abhorrent and have learned to care more about women's welfare than having an orgasm.

A world where the government and corporations value mothers' contributions by supporting them structurally and financially.

A world where churches embrace and encourage women to bring the whole of who they are and all their gifting into the community.

A world where all healthcare professionals are trained in the art of empathy, genuinely seek to understand the unique challenges women face, and respect their female patients' self-knowledge.

A world where all of us can freely talk about our emotions and pain without being ridiculed, shamed, or punished.

A world where men share their power and use it to benefit everyone.

A world where single women are seen, valued, and supported rather than overlooked and diminished.

A world where elderly women are treated with dignity and respect and finish out their days receiving the same generous care they gave to others throughout their lives.

Imagining all of this is one thing. Making it happen is quite another.

Transformed World

Transforming our hearts and minds should result in a desire to transform our relationships, families, churches, communities, and the larger culture. Four components of this external transformation include identifying and dismantling unbiblical gender norms, increasing male engagement, resisting misogyny's pull, and doing the work of repair.

Dismantling Unbiblical Gender Norms

Cultures and subcultures create and uphold specific expectations for what men and women can and can't do and how they should relate to one another. These gender norms tend to protect those in power and funnel down into calcified gender roles that govern male-female relationships. Many of the gender roles that shape our day-to-day existence emerge out of cultural mores, personal expectations, and biases, not the New Testament.

When misogyny is woven throughout a culture, women receive clear messages about what they can and cannot do and should or shouldn't feel.[6] Cultural critic and author bell hooks explains, "Patriarchal gender roles are assigned to us as children and we are given continual guidance about the ways we can best fulfill these roles."[7] When people started calling me a tomboy at age five, they were communicating I'd strayed from the girls' lane and needed to reform my behavior if I wanted to fit in. Similarly, when my husband's family called him a crybaby, they reinforced the message that feeling and expressing sadness wasn't acceptable for boys.

Creating and enforcing rigid, hierarchal gender roles becomes yet another way to perpetuate misogyny. The bias that men are more logical and therefore make better leaders is inherently misogynistic because it wrongly assumes women can't be logical and predetermines that logic is the most important criterion for leadership. This belief persists despite the growing body of evidence suggesting skilled leaders need to value and demonstrate emotional intelligence. Some Christians claim the Bible mandates that women should limit their productivity to raising children and caring for their homes. This disadvantages single women, reflects economic privilege, and contradicts Scripture. The Proverbs 31 woman, often held up by conservative Christians as an example of the perfect housewife (which she may have been), was also a successful entrepreneur in the marketplace.

Gender bias and rigid gender norms have prohibited or limited women from occupying positions of authority in government, corporations, and churches. That translates to women having a diminished voice in shaping the rules, laws, and cultural practices that affect them. By including more women in top positions within law enforcement, we could shift how rape and domestic violence cases are handled. By promoting more women to leadership positions in the academy, we could help the educational system to become more grounded and more fully human. If more women were elevated to key leadership and governing roles within religious institutions, it's more likely that sexual abuse would be called out and stopped.

We must examine our own biases if we hope to dismantle misogynistic gender norms in our relationships. Australian pastor Mandy Smith likens these broken, biased narratives as "bad scripts that manipulate us like puppets."[8] Biases come into play for both men and women. The prevailing cultural bias is that men are out of touch with their emotions and less competent relationally. When men lean into this, they may default to women regarding child-rearing and carrying the emotional load in romantic relationships. While this might make their lives easier and less conflictual in the short term, it's damaging and counterproductive in the long term.

When women function as if men are either incapable or less

capable emotionally and relationally, we perpetuate gender bias. Assuming we know better or are more skilled relationally can be self-serving by giving us more authority and autonomy in certain realms, but it can encourage men to disengage, which results in endless conflict and asymmetrical divisions of responsibilities. Men are neither incapable nor inept. They have the capacity to see an issue, assess how to fix it, and then do so. (They are logical, after all.) These are the requisite skills necessary to parent and keep homes running smoothly. It makes no sense for families to order their lives around the assumption that women should be assigned or limited to parenting and caregiving work while men focus all their creative energies outside the home. We need each other to make life work.

Allies, Advocates, and Interrupters

While recognizing and dismantling any unhelpful, unbiblical gender roles will certainly help diminish misogyny, we won't make substantial progress until more men engage. Women cannot do this work alone. One practical way to frame male engagement is for men to become allies, advocates, and interrupters. Allies, advocates, and interrupters refuse to look away, be apathetic, or see misogyny as someone else's problem. They refuse to create or uphold hierarchies or abuse power, and they intentionally work to change the system regardless of the personal cost. When men engage in these ways, they break misogyny's hold.

An ally is someone who seeks to understand and support a demographic that is discriminated against and/or mistreated while not being a member of that group. When applied to misogyny, an ally is a safe man who esteems women, refuses to take advantage of them, looks out for their welfare, and promotes gender equality in his own life when no one else is watching.[9] Writing to men, professors W. Brad Johnson and David G. Smith believe "authentic allyship starts with humility and vulnerability to accept our complicit role in systemic inequities and then have the courage to change those practices."[10]

Those who choose to be allies understand it's a lifelong commitment requiring them to continually learn and grow.

Advocates take allyship to the next level. They're action oriented when it comes to supporting women. Male advocates consistently vindicate and defend women whenever they're being threatened or mistreated. They cite women's work in their books or sermons. They commend and recommend women in public spaces. My husband has regularly done this throughout his career. He makes opportunities for women to walk in their gifts. When there's pushback, he intercepts it. During the years I worked as a photographer with a news agency, one of my editors (they were all male back then) made sure I got prime assignments even though some of the men protested. Advocates care more about justice than personal gain.

An interrupter points out, stops, or even prevents harm to women caused by other men, sometimes risking his reputation or comfort in the process. Pastor Anyabwile did this when he apologized to Beth Moore. He first interrupted himself and then went public with his apology. Male seminary professors who recognize the animosity that female divinity students face and go out of their way to both challenge male bias and create safe spaces for their students are interrupters.

By paying attention and doing something simple, you can disrupt misogyny. Multiple friends recounted stories of men they didn't even know who stepped into dangerous situations to protect them from harm. One friend remembered the night she was getting gas in a notoriously unsafe part of town:

> I went inside to prepay, and behind me were a couple of White guys leering, laughing, and making it clear how vulnerable I was. An older man wearing overalls was there too. As I walked out, the older man followed me to the door and quietly said, "I got you. They won't mess with you." He stood there, making sure the guys left me alone. That was more than thirty years ago. I can still see him just standing in the doorway, with his hands in his overall pockets.

Men, I want to clarify something here. Women definitely need to be protected when we're in danger, but we're hoping and longing for much more. We want you to see all of who we are—not just our bodies—and value the ways we're beautifully different but equal. We want you to leverage your power and influence to ensure that we can function in our gifts and work alongside you to make the world a better place. That will mean making sacrificial, countercultural choices to relinquish your entitlement and share your power. Make no mistake—you will experience discomfort and loss. But this is not a zero-sum game. When you choose to live as allies, advocates, and interrupters, it benefits everyone.

David Swanson believes that men need to have a paradigm shift to function as allies, advocates, and interrupters. He explains, "For men to really help diminish misogyny, we've got to be convinced that treating each other as equals is better. Yes, it's righteous, it's just, but also, your life is going to be quantifiably better. As Christians you will get to experience more of God's character, more of the fruit of the Spirit, more of the in-breaking kingdom of God."

In *Half the Church*, theologian Carolyn Custis James observes, "The notion that things work better and human beings become their best selves when men and women work together is found on page 1 of the Bible. When God was launching the most ambitious enterprise the world has ever known, the team He put together to do the job was male and female."[11] According to Scripture, that team was very good. When men and women partner together as equals, there's little we cannot do—including eradicating misogyny.

Resist and Repair

Misogyny is thousands of years old, and the principles behind it are deeply embedded in our psyches and our systems. We're not going to fix this in one generation. Each of us will need to discern what it means to faithfully show up, resist misogyny's pull, and do the work of repair. This needs to happen individually and systemically.

If you're a man in a position of influence in the workplace or within an organization, consider putting yourself under the leadership of a woman for a time. Make it clear to your employees or coworkers that crude or sexist jokes will not be tolerated. Sit down with female employees or parishioners and ask them what you could do to make the workplace or church safer and more equitable. Hire, promote, and support a diverse pool of employees. If you're married, ask your spouse if she's ever experienced any forms of misogyny in the marriage, including sexual coercion, entitlement, abdication of household or parenting responsibilities, or indifference to her dreams. And do read books written by women, especially Women of Color.

Women can resist and repair by recognizing any of the ways we may have participated in or colluded with misogyny. That could be choosing to be compliant rather than telling the truth. For example, muting ourselves or pretending we're content to tuck in when our calling requires us to speak up. We will need to forsake any power gained by disadvantaging other women. If you're married, try to discern if you carry any unrealistic, potentially harmful gender-based expectations for your spouse.

If you're a parent, raise your sons to value and respect girls and women. Encourage them to identify and express all their emotions. Help them to understand and remedy inequitable power dynamics. Curb male entitlement (which they start to learn as children), and teach them to respect a girl's "no"—the first time. Train them to do housework and communicate that these jobs should not be relegated to women.

Raise your daughters to respect themselves and their bodies, understand their innate worth, and refuse to believe they're second-class citizens. Teach them to recognize red flags in dating relationships and to believe that their dignity is worth much more than a boy's sexual pleasure. Attend a church that values women's contributions so your daughters can believe the promises of the gospel.

Englewood Christian Church in Indianapolis stands out as an example of a church that esteems women and actively resists misogyny on many fronts. They have created a community development corporation that offers affordable housing through new builds and renovation projects, developed a garden that serves the community, and run a childcare center that serves 170 children. Englewood also breaks the mold by having a man (Mike Bowling) and woman (Dr. Katy Drage Lines) who aren't married to each other serve as lead copastors for the last seven years.

The church's willingness to recognize and meet the practical needs of their neighborhood is directly connected to fostering a robust social imaginary and valuing everyone, including women and those typically marginalized. Lines and Bowling desire to cultivate a community of people who live and love "consistent with the ways of Jesus." Lines believes Bowling's commitments to dismantle hierarchies within the church before she arrived (he was in this position for twenty years prior to Lines), to amplify women's voices, and to decenter himself all contribute to the church's unique DNA.

In an interview with me, Lines explained, "When Mike and I are out and someone talks to him but ignores me, he brings me back into the conversation. Even though he's older, he defers to me in public and elevates me as his copastor." Bowling's actions remind others of his partnership with Lines, and they have also brought healing and stability to her: "In previous ministry settings, if I felt anxious, my body would confirm that. As I do this work knowing he's my teammate and knowing I'm part of a community that is gracious and trusting, it alleviates any anxiety." Lines concluded, "I've experienced a fair bit of misogyny over thirty years of ministry. Englewood is a breath of fresh air, and I'm so thankful to be part of the life here."[12]

Envisioning and creating a space where women and men are seen as equals is rarely frictionless. In fact, any type of institution or organization that intentionally values diverse leadership will encounter tension and conflict, in part because taking others' needs and beliefs into consideration slows things down and requires us to genuinely care about them and their experiences.

Lisa Rodriguez-Watson is both a pastor at Christ City Church in Washington, DC, and the current national director of Missio Alliance, an organization that places a high value on women and men partnering together to create theologically robust, missionally oriented, and culturally attuned content for today's church. Rodriguez-Watson is open about the complexities and challenges she's faced while partnering with men at Missio: "I remember a time when I was in a conversation with one of my male colleagues and there was some tension in the relationship. He asked, 'Do you want to run an all-female organization?'"[13] She recalls laughing and admitting that she'd thought about this option. "But then I said very clearly, 'I don't want that.' I will always have a higher value for men and women on this team because it models what we're talking about. In some ways, it could be easier to run an all-female team, but the trade-off of greater ease for a more embodied and more faithful witness isn't worth it for me."

According to Rodriguez-Watson, partnering with men creates "a well-rounded team dynamic and offers the opportunity for balanced perspectives." She believes that when women and men partner together, they model the biblical narrative of God's creative design: "God intended for men and women to work alongside one another for mutual flourishing for that specific relationship and for the rest of the ecosystems that they operate in. Some of the most meaningful, satisfying seasons have been those when women and men are shoulder to shoulder, doing the work of reconciliation and repair. I'm excited that we get to live into all the messy and beautiful parts of this."

Eschatology of Hope

When I wrote about developing our imaginations a few pages back, I omitted one key component: hope. Without hope, our imaginations will be fettered. To imagine and then work toward eradicating misogyny, we need to believe that change is possible. We need an eschatology of hope.

What we put our hope in matters. It would be misguided if I encouraged you to hope in our government, corporate America, religious organizations, or powerful individuals. Our hope must be firmly rooted in something fail-safe that has a consistent record of opposing misogyny. That points to God's kingdom and, specifically, the work Jesus accomplished while he was here on earth. It's because of Jesus that we can forge an eschatology of hope. His love liberated women. It freed them to embrace the fullness of who they were created to be and then to move boldly through the world. If enough men decide to be like Jesus, misogyny will fall.

Though the church has had and continues to have many deplorable failures throughout history, the arc of Christianity—and therefore the arc of the Christian—is toward healing, reconciliation, and justice. That includes learning how to love God, love ourselves, and love others with all of who we are so that we can forgive debts, fight injustice, and set captives free. Our goal, or telos, is to bring God's kingdom to the here and now—to finish the work Jesus initiated. Our eschatology of hope will need to foreshadow what is to come and simultaneously guide us in the present tense as we rewrite narratives that have been broken by misogyny.

If God, in partnership with women and men, is making *all things* new, that includes eradicating misogyny in cultures, systems, governments, corporations, churches, and relationships. It means women will be consistently seen as equals, gender hierarchies will be dismantled, and everyone will have the opportunity to thrive.

When I started this book, I felt angry and discouraged. I'd witnessed and personally experienced six decades of misogyny, far too much of it within religious settings. I questioned if we as culture would ever find the will, let alone the capacity, to change.

But as I bring this project to a close, something has shifted.

Though my heart has repeatedly been broken over the past

twenty-four months, I've also had incredibly encouraging conversations with smart, resilient women who are pursuing their callings with conviction while doing their part to eradicate misogyny. I've witnessed dignified older women who have forgiven much and continue to love even after decades of mistreatment. I've learned how many "good and safe men"[14] are working to dismantle misogyny in their lives, their families, and their spheres of influence. I've discovered religious and secular organizations that are prioritizing equality and demonstrating how deeply they value women. All these data points allow me to hope that change is truly coming. Given my age, I don't know if I'll see it in my lifetime, but I'm confident my daughters-in-law and hoped-for granddaughters will.

Psychologist and Holocaust survivor Viktor Frankl ends his searing memoir *Man's Search for Meaning* with this thought: "The world is in a bad state, but everything will become still worse unless each of us does [our] best."[15]

Go do your best. For the love of women.

APPENDIX

Resources

To learn more about trauma, search for the ACE (Adverse Childhood Experiences) test.

If you need help and support or are in danger at home, reach out to the National Domestic Violence Hotline, https://www.thehotline.org/. Consider accessing this on your library's computer.

Recommended Resources

Chapter 1: The Air We Breathe: Misogyny's Persistence and Prevalence

Half the Sky: Turning Oppression into Opportunity for Women Worldwide, Nicholas D. Kristof and Sheryl WuDunn

What's a Woman Worth? Quina Aragon, https://www.youtube.com/watch?v=GrS9zDsgr_o

Chapter 2: It's All in Your Head (or Maybe Your Uterus): Misogyny in Healthcare

The Connection Cure: The Prescriptive Power of Movement, Nature, Art, Service, and Belonging, Julia Hotz

Doing Harm: The Truth About How Bad Medicine and Lazy Science Leave Women Dismissed, Misdiagnosed, and Sick, Maya Dusenbery

Happy Pills in America: From Miltown to Prozac, David Herzberg
The Lady's Handbook for Her Mysterious Illness: A Memoir, Sarah Ramey
"Period," Quina Aragon, https://quinaaragon.com/period-poem/
This Here Flesh: Spirituality, Liberation, and the Stories That Make Us, Cole Arthur Riley
Unwell Women: Misdiagnosis and Myth in a Man-Made World, Elinor Cleghorn
For those dealing with endometriosis, check out Citizen Endo, https://citizenendo.org/.

Chapter 3: Unseen, Unappreciated, and Underpaid: Misogyny in the Workplace

Brotopia: Breaking Up the Boys' Club of Silicon Valley, Emily Chang
Career and Family: Women's Century-Long Journey Toward Equity, Claudia Goldin
Invisible Women: Data Bias in a World Designed for Men, Caroline Criado Perez
A Woman's Place: A Christian Vision for Your Calling in the Office, the Home, and the World, Katelyn Beaty

Chapter 4: Making It Legal: Misogyny in the Government

The Price of Motherhood, Ann Crittenden
Speaking Truth to Power, Anita Hill

Chapter 5: Behind the Screens: Misogyny in Media and Entertainment

The Anxious Generation: How the Great Rewiring of Childhood Is Causing an Epidemic of Mental Illness, Jonathan Haidt
Girls on the Brink: Helping Our Daughters Thrive in an Era of Increased Anxiety, Depression, and Social Media, Donna Jackson Nakazawa

Over the Influence: Why Social Media Is Toxic for Women and Girls—and How We Can Take It Back, Kara Alaimo
What Is a Girl Worth?, Rachael Denhollander

Chapter 6: In the Flesh: Misogyny in Sexual Relationships

All About Love: New Visions, bell hooks
Divine Sex: A Compelling Vision for Christian Relationships in a Hypersexualized Age, Jonathan Grant
The Great Sex Rescue: The Lies You've Been Taught and How to Recover What God Intended, Sheila Wray Gregoire
*How Not to Be an *ss: Essays on Becoming a Good and Safe Man*, Andrew J. Bauman
Making Marriage Beautiful: Lifelong Love, Joy, and Intimacy Start with You, Dorothy Littell Greco
Not Marked: Finding Hope and Healing After Sexual Abuse, Mary DeMuth
Unwanted: How Sexual Brokenness Reveals Our Way to Healing, Jay Stringer

Chapter 7: Baptizing Sin: Misogyny in the Church

The Bible vs. Biblical Womanhood: How God's Word Consistently Affirms Gender Equality, Philip B. Payne
Confronting Sexism in the Church: How We Got Here and What We Can Do About It, Heather Matthews
Gender Roles and the People of God: Rethinking What We Were Taught About Men and Women in the Church, Alice Mathews
Half the Church: Recapturing God's Global Vision for Women, Carolyn Custis James
Jesus and John Wayne: How White Evangelicals Corrupted a Faith and Fractured a Nation, Kristin Kobes Du Mez
The Making of Biblical Womanhood: How the Subjugation of Women Became Gospel Truth, Beth Allison Barr

Reckoning with Power: Why the Church Fails When It's on the Wrong Side of Power, David E. Fitch

Recovering from Biblical Manhood and Womanhood: How the Church Needs to Rediscover Her Purpose, Aimee Byrd

Redeeming Power: Understanding Authority and Abuse in the Church, Diane Langberg

Safe Church: How to Guard Against Sexism and Abuse in Christian Communities, Andrew J. Bauman

The Very Good Gospel: How Everything Wrong Can Be Made Right, Lisa Sharon Harper

Women and the Gender of God, Amy Peeler

Chapter 8: Naming Our Needs and Broken Places: Healing Misogyny's Wounds

The Body Keeps the Score: Brain, Mind, and Body in the Healing of Trauma, Bessel van der Kolk

Four Gifts: Seeking Self-Care for Heart, Soul, Mind, and Strength, April Yamasaki

Healing Leadership Trauma: Finding Emotional Health and Helping Others Flourish, Nicholas Rowe and Sheila Wise Rowe

Healing Racial Trauma: The Road to Resilience, Sheila Wise Rowe

I Forgive You: Finding Peace and Moving Forward When Life Really Hurts, Wendy Alsup

The Louder Song: Listening for Hope in the Midst of Lament, Aubrey Sampson

Malestrom: How Jesus Dismantles Patriarchy and Redefines Manhood, Carolyn Custis James

My Grandmother's Hands: Racialized Trauma and the Pathway to Mending Our Hearts and Bodies, Resmaa Menakem

Prophetic Lament: A Call for Justice in Troubled Times, Soong-Chan Rah

Raise Your Voice: Why We Stay Silent and How to Speak Up, Kathy Khang

To Be Made Well: An Invitation to Wholeness, Healing, and Hope, Amy Julia Becker

Trauma and Recovery: The Aftermath of Violence—from Domestic Abuse to Political Terror, Judith L. Herman, MD

Try Softer: A Fresh Approach to Move Us Out of Anxiety, Stress, and Survival Mode—and into a Life of Connection and Joy, Aundi Kolber

What Happened to You? Conversations on Trauma, Resilience, and Healing, Bruce D. Perry, MD, PhD, and Oprah Winfrey

The Will to Change: Men, Masculinity, and Love, bell hooks

Chapter 9: Imagine If . . . : Writing Misogyny Out of the Narrative

Art and Faith: A Theology of Making, Makoto Fujimura

The Evangelical Imagination: How Stories, Images, and Metaphors Created a Culture in Crisis, Karen Swallow Prior

Made for More: An Invitation to Live in God's Image, Hannah Anderson

Strong Girls, Strong World: A Practical Guide to Helping Them Soar—and Creating a Better Future for Us All, Dale Hanson Bourke

Truth's Table: Black Women's Musings on Life, Love, and Liberation, Ekemini Uwan, Christina Edmondson, and Michelle Higgins

ACKNOWLEDGMENTS

Thanks to my agent Keely Boeving for finding a home for this project and your ongoing support; Kyle Rohane for seeing the value of this book, being patient with my slow process, and believing in me; Serena DeKryger and team for your marketing expertise; and Kim Tanner for your careful reading during the copyediting phase. Special thanks to Jeff Miller for bringing my cover idea to life.

Hannah, I can't thank you enough for encouraging me to trust my voice and for helping me find my way through this minefield. PS: You are *always* a light.

I am deeply grateful to Beth Alison Barr for her generous foreword and for those who wrote endorsements for me.

Special thanks to all the women and men who shared their stories with me.

To my patrons and prayer team:

Chelsea and Peter Vessenes, Stephanie and Peter Choo, Dan and Kathy Szatkowski, Jeff and Sharon Bjorck, Danny and Deidre Tao, John and Lila Tocci, Gary and Kathy MacDonald, Larry and Susan James, Mary and Stephen Vono, Lisa Calderon, Pascha and Paul Griffiths, Linda MacKillop, Jeannine Hodge, Kara Wetzel, Ann Armstrong, Dorena Williamson, Kristie Anyabwile, Cliff Chaung, Erica Illanes, Kristin Wensel, Nick and Sheila Rowe, Richard and Amanda Wang, Laura and Sean Richmond, Tim and Sarah Yoon, Mark and Susan Buckner, Marla Chaneta, Megan and AJ Lease, Alistair and Rebecca Bell, Karen Stevenson, Jessica Finch, Barbara Brescia, Carole Duff,

Ilona Maki, Colleen McEwen, Terry and Dave Landon, Val and Tom Andrews, Michelle Van Loon, Faith Ann Polanski, Eli and Felix Wehrli, Jane and Hans Huber, Sophia and Albert Ma, Rich and Carolyn Farrell, Bobby Sargent, Kelly Chiu, "Emma," Amy Chaney, Annika and William Thompson, Bekah Mason, Jonathan Tetrault, Ebube Iheme, Joanne Turner, Pucinellagawain, Joe O'Connor, Rachel Wilson, and Jason and Sandy Smith. Extra-special thanks to Amanda Ilg for the many ways you came alongside me in this process.

Early readers, interviewees, and experts in their fields:

Christopher Greco; Paul and Ruth Goodwin-Groen; Linda MacKillop; Trey Skinner; Brian Marchionni; Lara Newman; Jeff Bell; Jeff Bass; Jeff Bjorck, PhD; Pierce VanDunk; Greg Comiskey, Esq.; Molly Richmond Otey, Esq.; Mardi Dolfo-Smith; Karen Swallow Prior; Carolyn Custis James; Dr. Andrew Bauman; Rev. Dana Miller Baker; Carlene Hill; Dorena and Chris Williamson; Carmen Johnson; Christine Parter; Derek and Amanda Ilg; Dr. Valerie Andrews; Dr. Marlena Fez; Marlena Graves; Rev. Liz Walker; "Emma"; Natalie Larson; Pastor Thabiti and Kristie Anyabwile; Dr. Almi Abeyta; Jennifer Reilly; Brigit Helms; Heather Matthews; Cara Kennedy; Elizabeth Glass-Turner; Charly Haversat; Marie Griffith; Mandy Smith; Annika and William Thompson; Geoff Freeman; Aaron Kook; Ellen Mandeville; Liza Cagua-MacAllister; Jane Huber; Lisa Rodriguez-Watson; Bernice Sim; Marika Siewert; Woody Romelus; Mimi Haddad; Dr. John Peteet; David Swanson; Katelyn Beaty; Gina Dafonzo; Marybeth Baggett; "Miriam"; Julie Roys; Sheila Wise Rowe and Nicholas Rowe; Margot Starbuck; Rebecca Masterson, RN; Annalaura Montgomery; Byron Borger; Quantrilla Ard, PhD, Black Maternal and Infant Health Advocate; Rebecca Ray, CNM; Kate Jaggard Tyo, Certified Doula; Margie and Ray Kollbocker; Dr. Katy Drage Lines; Michele Sterlace-Accorsi; Nicole Doyley; Lashunta Edwards Hoover; Kelley Mathews; Ashley Diane Worsham; Sara Easterly; Kathy Khang; Leslie Littell; Ron Lusk; Claudine Wright; Cheryl Berto; Rachael Berglund; Rebecca Bell; Wendy

Tanahasi-Works; Jane Huber; and Natalie Nyquist. If you read and gave me feedback or helped me create this project and I've not listed your name, I'm so sorry!

I am indebted to many female theologians who do the difficult work of discerning and explaining Scripture: Beth Felker Jones, Kristie Anyabwile, Quina Aragon, Dr. Christina Edmondson, Carolyn Custis James, Marg Mowczko, Gail Wallace, Mimi Haddad, Wendy Alsup, Lisa Sharon Harper, Marlena Graves, April Yamasaki, Sandra Glahn, Amy Peeler, and Kelley Mathews.

To the amazing women of Redbud Writers' Guild, Pelican Project, and The Clutch: Thank you for always responding to my questions and supporting me in this endeavor.

Thanks to my three friends who researched and checked many details for me: Rachel Bicha, Carlene Hill, and Gretchen Saalbach.

I owe a debt of gratitude to my coaches, who taught me how to push myself and trust my body: John and Joyce Scott, Gretta Sencevicky, John Danko, Jeannette Weiner, Paula Wachter, Kathleen Parker, and Sally Starr.

Finally, a huge thanks to those members of my family who supported and loved me in this process: Jane and Leslie; Mom and Charles; Laurie and Linda; Annika and William; our three sons and their wives: Anthony and Kate, GianCarlo and Charlotte, Matthew and Alina. Finally, Christopher, thank you for helping me to find the words, for always encouraging me to follow God's lead, and for wanting me as your *ezer*. After thirty-four years, I wouldn't choose anyone else.

NOTES

Foreword

1. "The Bone Crypt at Holy Trinity Church, Rothwell, Northamptonshire," Holy Trinity Rothwell, https://www.rothwellholytrinity.org.uk/the building.htm.
2. Elizabeth Marvel, "Hunting the 'Henchmen of Satan': Episcopal Registers as a Source for the Pastoral Care of Women Religious," *Magistra* 29, no. 2 (Winter 2023): 11, https://www.proquest.com/scholarly-journals/hunting-henchmen-satan-episcopal-registers-as/docview/2925640577/se-2. See also A. Hamilton Thompson, ed., *Visitations of Religious Houses in the Diocese of Lincoln, Injunctions and Other Documents from the Registers of Richard Flemyng and William Gray, Bishops of Lincoln, A.D. 1420–1436*, 3 vols. (London: Canterbury and York Society, 1914) 1:107–9.
3. Marvel, "Hunting the 'Henchmen of Satan,'" 12.
4. Jason DeRose, "Jennifer Lyell, Southern Baptist Sexual Abuse Whistle-Blower, Dies at 47," NPR, June 11, 2025, https://www.npr.org/2025/06/11/nx-s1-5430485/jennifer-lyell-southern-baptist-sexual-abuse-whistle-blower-dies-at-47.
5. "Final Guidepost Solutions Independent Investigation Report: Report of the Independent Investigation, The Southern Baptist Convention Executive Committee's Response to Sexual Abuse Allegations and an Audit of the Procedures and Actions of the Credentials Committee," *Guidepost*, May 15, 2022, https://www.documentcloud.org/documents/22031737-final-guidepost-solutions-independent-investigation-report/

Introduction

1. This continued until the Equal Credit Opportunity Act was passed in October 1974.
2. This continued until 1978, when Congress passed the Pregnancy Discrimination Act.
3. Aaron O'Neill, "Number of Events for Male and Female Athletes at the Summer Olympics from 1896 to 2020," Statista, July 4, 2024, https://

www.statista.com/statistics/1090670/olympics-number-events-by-gender-since-1896/.

4. "#MeToo, #TakeAKnee and #Covfefe: Hashtags That Dominated in 2017," BBC, December 26, 2017, https://www.bbc.com/news/world-42251490. Some men did contribute to these posts, but it was overwhelmingly women.
5. Hannah Fingerhut, "In both parties, men and women differ over whether women still face obstacles to progress," Pew Research Center, August 16, 2016, https://www.pewresearch.org/short-reads/2016/08/16/in-both-parties-men-and-women-differ-over-whether-women-still-face-obstacles-to-progress/.
6. Madelyn Snodgrass, "Women's Perspectives on Gender Discrimination and Society Today," PRRI, August 26, 2023, https://www.prri.org/spotlight/womens-perspectives-on-gender-discrimination-and-society-today/.
7. Carolyn Custis James, *Half the Church: Recapturing God's Global Vision for Women* (Zondervan, 2010), 23.

Chapter 1: The Air We Breathe

1. Ben Zimmer, "Misogyny: Does It Mean Hate or Bias?" *Wall Street Journal*, May 30, 2014, https://www.wsj.com/articles/misogyny-has-its-meaning-shifted-1401490009. Accessed January 11, 2025.
2. Andrew Tate is a kickboxer turned influencer with an enormous following. His TikTok and YouTube posts include descriptions of how to control and rape women. As of January 2025, he is waiting the outcome of a criminal investigation charging him with trafficking minors and having sex with minors.
3. Kate Manne, *Down Girl: The Logic of Misogyny* (Oxford University Press, 2018), 33.
4. In the original poem, Pandora was given a jar. Erasmus apparently mistranslated *jar* as *box* in the sixteenth century.
5. Jack Holland, *Misogyny: The World's Oldest Prejudice* (Carroll & Graf Publishers, 2006), 12.
6. Foot binding was outlawed in 1912. Though attitudes toward FGM are changing, this barbaric procedure, often done without any form of anesthesia, still takes place.
7. There are, or have been, exceptions where people groups are matrilineal, such as for Iroquois Nation tribes, the Umoja in Kenya, or the Bribri in Costa Rica. And in these spaces, misogyny is typically less of a factor. It's also true that in some cultures, only men were permitted to rule/govern, but they did not hold absolute power. Women held positions of influence in the home and other venues. See Carol L. Meyers, "Was Ancient Israel a Patriarchal Society?" *Journal of Biblical Literature* 133, no. 1 (April 2014), 8–27, https://

scholarlypublishingcollective.org/sblpress/jbl/article/133/1/8/179125/Was-Ancient-Israel-a-Patriarchal-Society?.

8. Alice Mathews, *Gender Roles and the People of God: Rethinking What We Were Taught About Men and Women in the Church* (Zondervan, 2017), 35.
9. Cited in Beth Allison Barr, *The Making of Biblical Womanhood: How the Subjugation of Women Became Gospel Truth* (Brazos Press, 2021), 13.
10. "The Nobel economist Amartya Sen estimated there were about 100 million missing women, women that were never born or killed or aborted across Asia." Quote taken from "How China's One-Child Policy Led to Forced Abortions, 30 Million Bachelors," NPR, February 1, 2016, https://www.npr.org/2016/02/01/465124337/how-chinas-one-child-policy-led-to-forced-abortions-30-million-bachelors.
11. Yousafzai was shot in 2012, in Pakistan, for refusing to submit to the Taliban's prohibition of education for girls.
12. Nicolas Garriga and John Leicester, "Gisèle Pelicot's Ex-Husband, Imprisoned for Rape and Drugging Her, Now Caught Up in Other Cases," Associated Press, January 30, 2025, https://apnews.com/article/france-pelicot-crime-police-sexual-violence-murder-8e5fa0e1b0dcfbacb0255b807aa7998f.
13. Philip B. Payne, *The Bible vs. Biblical Womanhood: How God's Word Consistently Affirms Gender Equality* (Zondervan, 2023), 3.
14. The same Hebrew word for "helper" is used to describe God in various places, including in the book of Psalms.
15. Marg Mowczko, "A Suitable Helper (in Hebrew)," author's website, March 8, 2010, https://margmowczko.com/a-suitable-helper/. Accessed August 5, 2024.
16. Carolyn Custis James, *Malestrom: Manhood Swept into the Currents of a Changing World* (Zondervan, 2015), 52.
17. Conversation with Carolyn Custis James recorded on April 17, 2024.
18. Payne, *Bible vs. Biblical Womanhood*, 13.
19. Payne, *Bible vs. Biblical Womanhood*, 23.
20. Inspired by a conversation with Dr. Lisa Lamb.
21. N. T. Wright, *Surprised by Scripture: Engaging Contemporary Issues* (New York: HarperOne, 2014), 115.
22. Veera Korhonen, "Number of Murder Victims in the United States in 2023, by Gender," Statista, November 7, 2024, https://www.statista.com/statistics/1388777/murder-victims-in-the-us-by-gender/; and UN Women, "Facts and Figures: Ending Violence Against Women," November 25, 2004, https://www.unwomen.org/en/what-we-do/ending-violence-against-women/facts-and-figures. Accessed June 17, 2024.
23. "Violence Against Women," World Health Organization, March 25, 2024, https://www.who.int/news-room/fact-sheets/detail/violence-against-women. Accessed June 17, 2024.

24. Lundy Bancroft, "Men's Angry Messages to Me," author's website, October 19, 2022, https://lundybancroft.com/mens-angry-messages-to-me/.
25. Quoted in Sean Illing, "What We Get Wrong About Misogyny," Vox, March 7, 2020, https://www.vox.com/identities/2017/12/5/16705284/elizabeth-warren-loss-2020-sexism-misogyny-kate-manne. Accessed June 17, 2024.
26. For example, Iran (2022) and Venezuela (during the early 2000s).
27. Nadine Nyhus, "Trauma," chapter 8 in *Christianity and Psychiatry*, ed. John R. Peteet and H. Steven Moffic (Springer Publishing, 2021), chapter 8, Nadine Nyhus, "Trauma," 84–85: "Examples include combat experiences, natural disasters, severe accidents, assault, birth complications, illness, and surgery as well as physical, emotional, and sexual abuse."
28. Aundi Kolber, *Try Softer: A Fresh Approach to Move Us Out of Anxiety, Stress, and Survival Mode—and into a Life of Connection and Joy* (Tyndale, 2020), 34.
29. Judith Herman, MD, *Trauma and Recovery: The Aftermath of Violence—from Domestic Abuse to Political Terror* (Perseus Books, 1992, 1997), 33.
30. "Top 20 Most Destructive Wildfires," Consumer Watchdog, April 3, 2025, https://consumerwatchdog.org/wp-content/uploads/2025/04/IRH-SFG-164-2025-02-07-Top-20-Most-Destructive-California-Wildfires-CAL-FIRE.pdf.
31. Joel W. Berry on X, January 14, 2025, https://x.com/JoelWBerry/status/1879168707613831346.
32. Frederick Joseph, *Patriarchy Blues: Reflections on Manhood* (Harper Perennial, 2022), 30.
33. bell hooks, *The Will to Change: Men, Masculinity, and Love* (Washington Square Press, 2004), 12.
34. Custis James, *Malestrom*, 135.
35. Barbara Plett Usher and Natasha Booty, "One-Year-Olds Among Those Raped During Sudan Civil War, UN Says," March 4, 2025, https://www.bbc.com/news/articles/cvgpdxk853jo; Carlotta Gall and Oleksandr Chubko, "Slowly, Ukrainian Women Are Beginning to Talk About Sexual Assault in the War," *New York Times*, March 15, 2025, https://www.nytimes.com/2025/03/15/world/europe/ukraine-women-sexual-violence-war.html.
36. Custis James, *Malestrom*, 134.
37. Custis James, *Malestrom*, chapter 6.
38. Email exchange with Brian Marchionni on June 3, 2024.

Chapter 2: It's All in Your Head (or Maybe Your Uterus)

1. Email exchange with "Melissa" on December 17, 2024.
2. Christine Ro, "The Overlooked Condition That Can Trigger Extreme Behaviour," BBC, December 15, 2019, https://www.bbc.com/future/article

/20191213-pmdd-a-little-understood-and-often-misdiagnosed-condition. Accessed December 17, 2024. PMDD was included in the *Diagnostic and Statistical Manual of Mental Disorders* (DSM) in 2013.

3. "Treating Premenstrual Dysphoric Disorder," Harvard Health Publishing, January 19, 2022, https://www.health.harvard.edu/womens-health/treating-premenstrual-dysphoric-disorder. Accessed December 2024. David Danish, "Yaz For PMDD: An Overview," Philadelphia Integrative Psychiatry, August 28, 2024, https://phillyintegrative.com/blog/yaz-for-pmdd.
4. Each oral contraceptive has a different formulation and works differently with the body's hormones.
5. Divya Prasad, Bianca Wollenhaupt-Aguiar, et al., "Suicidal Risk in Women with Premenstrual Syndrome and Premenstrual Dysphoric Disorder: A Systematic Review and Meta-Analysis," Journal of Women's Health 30, no. 12 (December 16, 2021), https://pmc.ncbi.nlm.nih.gov/articles/PMC8721500/.
6. Joshua Chaffin and Julie Wernau, "Doctors Say Dealing with Health Insurers Is Only Getting Worse," *Wall Street Journal*, December 12, 2024, https://www.wsj.com/health/healthcare/doctor-physician-health-insurance-companies-anger-6f23b470. Accessed January 14, 2025.
7. Karen Tang, MD, MPH, *It's Not Hysteria: Everything You Need to Know About Your Reproductive Health (But Were Never Told)* (Flatiron Books, 2024), 10.
8. Elinor Cleghorn, *Unwell Women: Misdiagnosis and Myth in a Man-Made World* (Penguin Random House, 2022), 21.
9. Cleghorn, *Unwell Women*, 21. This would include Hippocratic physicians.
10. Helena Trindade Lopes and Ronaldo G. Gurgel Pereira, "The Gynaecological Papyrus Kahun," IntechOpen, October 13, 2021, https://doi.org/10.5772/intechopen.98039.
11. Cleghorn, *Unwell Women*, 21.
12. Cleghorn, *Unwell Women*, 2.
13. Cleghorn, *Unwell Women*, 22, referring to Hippocrates' *Diseases of Women*.
14. "How Victorian Women Were Oppressed Through the Use of Psychiatry," *Atlantic*, https://www.theatlantic.com/sponsored/netflix-2017/how-victorian-women-were-oppressed-through-the-use-of-psychiatry/1607/. Accessed September 23, 2024. (Original quote ". . . ought to behave," she says. "There were . . .").
15. "How Victorian Women Were Oppressed."
16. Kate Moore, *The Woman They Could Not Silence* (Sourcebooks, 2022).
17. Andrea Tone and Mary Koziol, "Failing Women in Psychiatry: Lessons from a Painful Past," *Canadian Medical Association Journal*, May 22, 2018: "A comprehensive survey of US psychiatric facilities between 1949 and 1951 found that most patients lobotomized by doctors were women. At a

time when women were expected to be calm, cooperative, and attentive to domestic affairs, definitions of mental illness were as culturally bound as their treatments."

18. Erick Trickey, "Inside the Story of America's 19th-Century Opiate Addiction," *Smithsonian Magazine*, January 4, 2018, https://www.smithsonianmag.com/history/inside-story-americas-19th-century-opiate-addiction-180967673/.
19. Kellie Schmitt, "A Brief History of Opioids in the U.S.," *Hopkins Bloomberg Public Health*, Fall/Winter 2023, https://magazine.publichealth.jhu.edu/2023/brief-history-opioids-us.
20. Taylor Prewitt, "Take Some Pills for Your Hysteria, Lady: America's Long History of Drugging Women Up," *Vice*, April 28, 2015, http://www.vice.com/en/article/gqmx9j/here-lady-take-some-pills-for-your-hysteria-253. Accessed September 23, 2024. Charlotte Perkins Gilman wrote the novel *Yellow Wallpaper*, describing her experience of navigating postpartum depression and the dangers of rest cures. It was published in 1892.
21. These jobs included mechanics, pilots, and NASA engineers.
22. "From the 1950s there has been an epidemic of psychological illness in women. Others maintain that women are simply more likely to seek medical advice and that doctors have tended to 'code' psychological disorders as female problems." In a study done in Great Britain, "17.1 per cent of prescriptions were for women and 8 per cent were for men." Both quotes: Ali Haggett, "Why are twice as many women as men prescribed psychotropic drugs? A historical perspective," Centre for Male Psychology, https://www.centreformalepsychology.com/male-psychology-magazine-listings/why-are-twice-as-many-women-as-men-prescribed-psychotropic-drugs-a-historical-perspective. Accessed June 25, 2025.
23. Trickey, "America's 19th-Century Opiate Addiction."
24. David Herzberg, *Happy Pills in America: From Miltown to Prozac* (Johns Hopkins University Press, 2010), 56.
25. Herzberg, *Happy Pills*, 80.
26. Leila K. Asadi and Asim A. Shah, "Gender bias in antidepressant direct-to-consumer pharmaceutical advertising," *Comprehensive Psychiatry* 123 (May 2023), https://www.sciencedirect.com/science/article/pii/S0010440X23000214; C. Lee Ventola, "Direct-to-Consumer Pharmaceutical Advertising: Therapeutic or Toxic?," *P&T*, 36, no. 10 (October 2011), https://pmc.ncbi.nlm.nih.gov/articles/PMC3278148/.
27. As of 2023, of the top ten moneymaking companies, only one had a woman CEO: "Sick and Tired: How the Lack of Women CEOs in Big Pharm Impacts Women's Health," *StoryMD*, March 7, 2023, https://storymd.com

/story/8dnXrlauZA-sick-and-tired-how-the-lack-of-women-ceos-in-big-pharm-impacts-women-s-health.

28. Suzanne White Junod, PhD, "FDA and Clinical Drug Trials: A Short History," 2008, https://www.fda.gov/media/110437/download: "In 1938, a newly enacted U.S. Food, Drug, and Cosmetic Act subjected new drugs to pre-market safety evaluation for the first time. This required FDA regulators to review both pre-clinical and clinical test results for new drugs."
29. White Junod, "FDA and Clinical Drug Trials."
30. Veronica Geng, "Thalidomide: The American Experience," *New York Times*, April 29, 1973, https://www.nytimes.com/1973/04/29/archives/thalidomide-the-american-experience.html. Accessed January 15, 2025.
31. Katie Thomas, "The Unseen Survivors of Thalidomide Want to Be Heard," *New York Times*, March 23, 2020, https://www.nytimes.com/2020/03/23/health/thalidomide-survivors-usa.html.
32. Katie Thomas, "The Story of Thalidomide in the U.S., Told Through Documents," *New York Times*, March 23, 2020, https://www.nytimes.com/2020/03/23/health/thalidomide-fda-documents.html. Accessed December 2024: In a 1964 trial, the Department of Justice "concluded that 'criminal prosecution is neither warranted nor desirable.'"
33. Thomas, "Story of Thalidomide."
34. Thomas, "Story of Thalidomide."
35. The Kefauver-Harris Amendments of 1962 "strengthened the rules for drug safety and required manufacturers to prove their drugs' effectiveness"; "Laws Enforced by FDA," FDA, updated April 19, 2021, https://www.fda.gov/regulatory-information/laws-enforced-fda. It also required informed consent.
36. Pamela Verma Liao and Janet Dollin, "Half a Century of the Oral Contraceptive Pill," *Canadian Family Physician* 58, no. 12 (December 2012), https://pmc.ncbi.nlm.nih.gov/articles/PMC3520685/. Jonathan Eig, *The Birth of the Pill: How Four Crusaders Reinvented Sex and Launched a Revolution* (W. W. Norton, 2014), chapter 25.
37. Drew C. Pendergrass and Michelle Y. Raji, "The Bitter Pill: Harvard and the Dark History of Birth Control," *Harvard Crimson*, September 28, 2017, https://www.thecrimson.com/article/2017/9/28/the-bitter-pill/. Accessed January 14, 2025.
38. Eig, *Birth of the Pill*, 253.
39. Eig, *Birth of the Pill*, 256. G. D. Searle applied for FDA approval of the drug not as a contraceptive but as a "treatment for menstrual disorders."
40. "G.D. Searle Develops the Pill," PBS, https://www.pbs.org/wgbh/americanexperience/features/pill-g-d-searle-develops-pill/. Accessed June 25, 2025.

41. Multiple studies, including one done in 2023 by UCLA, state "increased risk for chronically elevated inflammation, which carries the long-term risk of developing illnesses such as cancer, cardiovascular disease, osteoporosis, and autoimmune disorders, as well as potential mood disorders including depression": Will Houston, "Study shows how birth control pills affect women's psychological and biological responses to stress," *UCLA Health*, December 6, 2023, https://www.uclahealth.org/news/release/study-shows-how-birth-control-pills-affect-womens. Summer Mengelkoch, Jeffrey Gassen, George M. Slavich, and Sarah E. Hill, "Hormonal contraceptive use is associated with differences in women's inflammatory and psychological reactivity to an acute social stressor," *Brain, Behavior, and Immunity* 115 (January 2024): 747–57, https://doi.org/10.1016/j.bbi.2023.10.033.
42. Alexandra Z. Sosinsky, Janet W. Rich-Edwards, et al., "Enrollment of female participants in United States drug and device phase 1–3 clinical trials between 2016 and 2019," *Contemporary Clinical Trials* 115 (April 2022), https://www.sciencedirect.com/science/article/abs/pii/S1551714422000441?via%3Dihub.
43. "Questions and answers: Risk of next-morning impairment after use of insomnia drugs; FDA requires lower recommended doses for certain drugs containing zolpidem (Ambien, Ambien CR, Edluar, and Zolpimist)," FDA, updated February 13, 2018, https://www.fda.gov/drugs/drug-safety-and-availability/questions-and-answers-risk-next-morning-impairment-after-use-insomnia-drugs-fda-requires-lower. Accessed December 19, 2024.
44. Caroline Criado Perez, *Invisible Women: Data Bias in a World Designed for Men* (Harry N. Abrams, 2021), 229.
45. Kristen P. Mark, Kat Arenella, Abby Girard, et al., "Erectile dysfunction prevalence in the United States: Report from the 2021 National Survey of Sexual Wellbeing," *Journal of Sexual Medicine* 21, no. 4 (April 26, 2024), https://academic.oup.com/jsm/article-abstract/21/4/296/7614307.
46. "Estimates of Funding for Various Research, Condition, and Disease Categories (RCDC)," National Institutes of Health, March 31, 2023, https://report.nih.gov/funding/categorical-spending#/. NIH does set aside large amounts of money to study maternal mortality and morbidity as well as pregnancy.
47. Sharon Malone and Jennifer Weiss-Wolf, "A Menopause Research Bill Reaches Congress," Oprah Daily, December 14, 2023, https://www.oprahdaily.com/life/health/a45549121/menopause-research-congressional-bill/.
48. "DoD Commits $500 Million for Women's Health Research, Supports Better Care for All Women," U.S. Department of Defense, September 23, 2024, https://www.defense.gov/News/Releases/Release/Article/3913913

/dod-commits-500-million-for-womens-health-research-supports-better-care-for-all/.

49. This idea is often reinforced because of the passages in the Old Testament that refer to menstruating women as unclean. See Leviticus 12.
50. "New Study by U by Kotex Shows 35% Increase in Period Poverty Since 2018," PR Newswire, May 24, 2021, https://www.prnewswire.com/news-releases/new-study-by-u-by-kotex-shows-35-increase-in-period-poverty-since-2018-301297210.html: "Over one-third (38%) of low-income women report missing work, school or similar events due to lack of access to period supplies." Robin Bleiweis, Diana Boesch, and Alexandra Cawthorne Gaines, "The Basic Facts About Women in Poverty," Center for American Progress, August 3, 2020, https://www.americanprogress.org/article/basic-facts-women-poverty/.
51. Deb Gordon, "20% of Female College Students Can't Afford Period Products, New Survey Shows," *Forbes*, October 10, 2023, https://www.forbes.com/sites/debgordon/2023/10/10/20-of-female-college-students-cant-afford-period-products-new-survey-shows/. Accessed June 21, 2024.
52. Maggie O'Neill, "Even Oprah Couldn't Get Her Doctors to Take Her Menopause Symptoms Seriously," *Self*, April 6, 2023, https://www.self.com/story/oprah-winfrey-menopause-heart-palpatations. Accessed June 21, 2024.
53. "Menopause Hormone Therapy: Is It Right for You?" Mayo Clinic, April 18, 2025, https://www.mayoclinic.org/diseases-conditions/menopause/in-depth/hormone-therapy/art-20046372. Susan Dominus, "Women Have Been Misled About Menopause," *New York Times*, updated June 15, 2023, https://www.nytimes.com/2023/02/01/magazine/menopause-hot-flashes-hormone-therapy.html. Every medication has a potential side effect. Risks and benefits should be discussed with a sympathetic doctor. Some of the side effects were more evident if women started taking estrogen therapy after age sixty.
54. Chris Stubbs, Lisa Mattingly, et al., "Do SSRIs and SNRIs reduce the frequency and/or severity of hot flashes in menopausal women?," *Journal of Oklahoma State Medical Association* 110, no. 5 (May 2017): 272–74, https://pmc.ncbi.nlm.nih.gov/articles/PMC5482277/.
55. Max Roser and Hannah Ritchie, "Maternal Mortality," Our World in Data, February 2024, https://ourworldindata.org/how-many-women-die-in-childbirth. Accessed June 21, 2024.
56. Donna L. Hoyert, "Maternal Mortality Rates in the United States, 2021," CDC, https://www.cdc.gov/nchs/data/hestat/maternal-mortality/2021/maternal-mortality-rates-2021.htm. Accessed December 12, 2024.
57. "Preventing Pregnancy-Related Deaths," CDC, September 25, 2024, https://www.cdc.gov/maternal-mortality/preventing-pregnancy-related-deaths/.

Accessed June 21, 2024. Munira Z. Gunja, Evan D. Gumas, Relebohile Masitha, and Laurie C. Zephyrin, "Insights into the U.S. Maternal Mortality Crisis: An International Comparison," Commonwealth Fund, June 4, 2024, https://www.commonwealthfund.org/publications/issue-briefs/2024/jun/insights-us-maternal-mortality-crisis-international-comparison. Accessed December 19, 2024.

58. Donna L. Hoyert, "Maternity Mortality Rates in the United States, 2020," CDC, https://www.cdc.gov/nchs/data/hestat/maternal-mortality/2020/maternal-mortality-rates-2020.htm.
59. "Four in 5 pregnancy-related deaths in the U.S. are preventable," CDC, September 19, 2022, https://archive.cdc.gov/www_cdc_gov/media/releases/2022/p0919-pregnancy-related-deaths.html. Accessed December 19, 2024.
60. Carly Mallenbaum and Kavya Beheraj, "1 in 3 Births: C-Section Rate Increases, Again," Axios, April 29, 2024, https://www.axios.com/2024/04/29/c-section-rate-high-why-risks.
61. "Caesarean Section Rates Continue to Rise, amid Growing Inequalities in Access," World Health Organization, June 16, 2021, https://www.who.int/news/item/16-06-2021-caesarean-section-rates-continue-to-rise-amid-growing-inequalities-in-access. Accessed December 19, 2024.
62. Emily Oster and Nathan Fox, MD, *The Unexpected: Navigating Pregnancy During and After Complications* (Penguin Press, 2024), chapter 11.
63. Quoted in Holly P. Kennedy, Eleanor Doig, et al., "Perspectives on promoting hospital primary vaginal birth; A qualitative study," *Birth* 43, no. 4 (August 2016): 7.
64. Gunja et al., "Insights into the U.S. Maternal Mortality Crisis."
65. "Midwives: Information on Births, Workforce, and Midwifery Education," U.S. Government Accountability Office, April 26, 2023, https://www.gao.gov/products/gao-23-105861.
66. Hannah Steffen, "Does Insurance Cover Midwife Services?" SuperDial, May 12, 2023, https://www.thesuperdial.com/blog/does-insurance-cover-midwife-services.
67. Liz Szabo, "Medical mistakes are more likely in women and minorities," NBC News, January 15, 2024, https://www.nbcnews.com/health/health-news/medical-mistakes-are-likely-women-minorities-rcna133726. Also see David E. Newman-Toker, Najilla Nassery, et al., "Burden of serious harms from diagnostic error in the USA," *BMJ Quality and Safety* 33, no. 2 (2024), https://qualitysafety.bmj.com/content/33/2/109. Accessed December 30, 2024. Andrew D. Auerbach, Tiffany M. Lee, et al., "Diagnostic errors in hospitalized adults who died or were transferred to intensive care," *JAMA Internal Medicine* 184, no. 2 (2024), https://jamanetwork.com/journals/jamainternalmedicine/article-abstract/2813854.

68. Atul Gawande, *Being Mortal: Medicine and What Matters in the End* (Metropolitan Books, 2014), 4.
69. "Endometriosis," World Health Organization, March 24, 2023, https://www.who.int/news-room/fact-sheets/detail/endometriosis. Accessed December 30, 2024.
70. Katherine Ellis, Deborah Munro, and Jennifer Clarke, "Endometriosis Is Undervalued: A Call to Action," *Frontiers in Global Women's Health*, May 10, 2022, https://pmc.ncbi.nlm.nih.gov/articles/PMC9127440/.
71. Tracey Lindeman, *Bleed: Destroying Myths and Misogyny in Endometriosis Care* (ECW Press, 2023), 9.
72. Tracy Jarrett, "Endometriosis Increases Risk of Heart Disease in Young Women," NBC News, March 29, 2016, https://www.nbcnews.com/health/womens-health/endometriosis-increases-risk-heart-disease-young-women-n547381. Accessed December 31, 2024.
73. Heather C. Guidone, "The Womb Wanders Not: Enhancing Endometriosis Education in a Culture of Menstrual Misinformation," chapter 22 in *The Palgrave Handbook of Critical Menstruation Studies*, ed. Chris Bobel, Inga T. Winkler, et al. (Palgrave Macmillan, 2020), https://www.ncbi.nlm.nih.gov/books/NBK565622/.
74. Bobel, Winkler, et al., *Palgrave Handbook*, 271. For the cost of endo, see T. D'Hooghe, C. D. Dirksen, et al., "The costs of endometriosis: It's the economy, stupid," *Fertility and Sterility* 98, no. 3, Supplement (September 2012), https://www.fertstert.org/article/S0015-0282(12)01525-7/fulltext.
75. "Endometriosis," World Health Organization. Guidone, "Womb Wanders Not."
76. Interview with "Carolyn" on May 31, 2023.
77. Elinor Cleghorn, "Medical Myths About Gender Roles Go Back to Ancient Greece. Women Are Still Paying the Price Today," *Time*, June 17, 2021, https://time.com/6074224/gender-medicine-history/.
78. Criado Perez, *Invisible Women*, chapter 11.
79. Mika Guzikevits, Tom Gordon-Hecker, et al., "Sex Bias in Pain Management Decisions," *PNAS* 121, no. 33 (August 5, 2024), https://doi.org/10.1073/pnas.2401331121. Kelly M. Hoffman, Sophie Trawalter, et al., "Racial Bias in Pain Assessment and Treatment Recommendations, and False Beliefs About Biological Differences Between Blacks and Whites," *PNAS*, 113, no. 16 (April 4, 2016): 4296–301, https://doi.org/10.1073/pnas.1516047113.
80. Quotes from email exchanges with "Kayla" in December 2024.
81. Amanda Seitz, "Dozens of Pregnant Women, Some Bleeding or in Labor, Are Turned Away from ERs Despite Federal Law," Associated Press, August

14, 2024, https://apnews.com/article/pregnant-women-emergency-room-ectopic-er-edd66276d2f6c412c988051b618fb8f9.

82. This would include health challenges that either only or primarily affect women, such as fibromyalgia, endometriosis, Polycystic Ovary Syndrome (PCOS), ectopic pregnancy, and Premenstrual Dysphoric Disorder (PDD).
83. Ellis et al., "Endometriosis Is Undervalued": "The combined effect of these phenomena is that over time non-painful stimuli can produce incredibly painful signals in sensitized patients."
84. Camran Nezhat, Farr Nezhat, and Ceana Nezhat, "Endometriosis: ancient disease, ancient treatments," *Journal of Fertility and Sterility* 98, no. 6, Supplement (December 2012), https://www.fertstert.org/article/S0015-0282%2812%2901955-3/fulltext. Accessed September 23, 2024.
85. See Mark 5:25–34.
86. Notable exceptions did occur, and some people groups were more open to women serving as doctors and healers, including the ancient Egyptians, Native Peoples in North America, and those in Italy's Salerno region during the eleventh and twelfth centuries.
87. *Physician Specialty Data Report*, Association of American Medical Colleges, 2022, https://www.aamc.org/data-reports/workforce/report/physician-specialty-data-report.
88. "Women of Color Initiative," AAMC, 2019, https://www.aamc.org/data-reports/workforce/data/women-physician-workforce-select-race/ethnicity. According to this study White women make up 54 percent of the physician workforce, Asians comprise 21 percent, and Black or African American 7 percent. This article—Simar Singh Bajaj, Lucy Tu, and Fatima Cody Stanford, "Superhuman, but Never Enough: Black Women in Medicine," *Lancet* 398 (October 16, 2021): 1398–99, https://pmc.ncbi.nlm.nih.gov/articles/PMC9908326/—lists the percentage of Black women as physicians at less than 3 percent.
89. J. Howick, L. Steinkopf, et al., "How empathic is your healthcare practitioner?" *BMC Medical Education* 17, no. 1 (August 21, 2017), https://doi.org/10.1186/s12909-017-0967-3. Accessed June 21, 2024.
90. Sosinsky et al., "Enrollment of female participants." Women do make up almost 50 percent of NIH trials: Sergey Feldman, Waleed Ammar, et al., "Quantifying Sex Bias in Clinical Studies at Scale with Automated Data Extraction," *JAMA Network Open* 2, no. 7 (2019), https://doi.org/10.1001/jamanetworkopen.2019.6700.
91. Check out Citizen Endo online and you can find several different bras with heart monitors built in: Rina Raphael, *The Gospel of Wellness: Gyms, Gurus, Goop, and the False Promise of Self-Care* (Henry Holt, 2022), 165.

92. Julia Hotz, *The Connection Cure: The Prescriptive Power of Movement, Nature, Art, Service, and Belonging* (Simon & Schuster, 2024).
93. Large-scale crises such as 9/11 and the 2020 pandemic tend to cause usage spikes: Sophia Frangou, Yael Travis-Lumer, et al., "Increased Incident Rates of Antidepressant Use During the Covid-19 Pandemic: Interrupted Time-Series Analysis of a Nationally Representative Sample," *Psychological Medicine* 53, no. 11 (August 2023): 4943–51, https://pmc.ncbi.nlm.nih.gov/articles/PMC9273730/.
94. "New York State Paid Prenatal Leave," The State of New York, accessed March 20, 2025, https://www.ny.gov/programs/new-york-state-paid-prenatal-leave.

Chapter 3: Unseen, Unappreciated, and Underpaid

1. Caroline Criado Perez, *Invisible Women: Data Bias in a World Designed for Men* (Abrams Press, 2019), 142.
2. All quotes from an interview with "Ana" in June 2024.
3. "The diversity of the top 50 Fortune 500 CEOs over time," Qualtrics, August 4, 2023, https://www.qualtrics.com/blog/fortune-500-ceo-diversity/. This article reveals that in 2023, of the top fifty CEOs, thirty-seven were White men. According to Malcolm Gladwell in *Blink*, "In the U.S. population, about 14.5 percent of all men are six feet or taller. Among CEOs of Fortune 500 companies, that number is 58 percent" (Back Bay Books, 2005), 86–87.
4. Alan Benson, Danielle Li, and Kelly Shue, "'Potential' and the Gender Promotions Gap," MIT Sloan Business School, updated March 4, 2004, https://ssrn.com/sol3/abstract=4747175.
5. Criado Perez, *Invisible Women*, 4.
6. Boris Kingma and Wouter van Marken Lichtenbelt, "Energy Consumption in Buildings and Female Thermal Demand," *Nature Climate Change*, August 3, 2015, https://www.nature.com/articles/nclimate2741.
7. Criado Perez, *Invisible Women*, 157–58.
8. "Fit for Women: Making PPE Safe and Dignified for Women Health Workers," *The BMJ*, April 8, 2022, https://www.bmj.com/content/377/bmj.o940.long (found in Karen Korellis Reuther, "Shrink It and Pink It: Gender Bias in Product Design," Harvard Advanced Leadership Initiative Social Impact Review, https://www.sir.advancedleadership.harvard.edu/articles/shrink-it-and-pink-it-gender-bias-product-design).
9. Men are more likely driving trucks and larger vehicles, which factors in. Cars manufactured after 2020 that include both front and side airbags have significantly reduced female fatalities: "Female Crash Fatality Risk Relative to Males for Similar Physical Impacts," NHTSA, August 2022,

https://crashstats.nhtsa.dot.gov/Api/Public/ViewPublication/813358. "NHTSA's Crash Test Dummies," NHTSA, https://www.nhtsa.gov/nhtsas-crash-test-dummies. According to one study, "The odds of a belt-restrained female driver sustaining serious injuries was 47% higher than that of a belt-restrained male driver when both were involved in comparable crashes": Jason Forman, Gerald S. Poplin, et al., "Automobile injury trends in the contemporary fleet: Belted occupants in frontal collisions," Traffic Injury Prevention 20, no. 6 (2019), 607–12, https://doi.org/10.1080/15389588.2019.1630825.

10. Gabriela Ramos, "Why we must act now to close the gender gap in AI," *World Economic Forum*, August 22, 2022, https://www.weforum.org/stories/2022/08/why-we-must-act-now-to-close-the-gender-gap-in-ai/. According to the World Economic Forum, only 22 percent of AI professionals are female. Common sources for Large Language Models (LLMs) include Wikipedia, Reddit, and Twitter, which reinforce racial and gender prejudices.
11. Ryan Daws, "Joy Buolamwini: Fighting algorithmic bias needs to be 'a priority,'" AI News, January 24, 2019, https://www.artificialintelligence-news.com/2019/01/24/joy-buolamwini-algorithmic-bias-priority/. Facial recognition software relies on statistical machine learning.
12. Kashmir Hill, "Eight Months Pregnant and Arrested After False Facial Recognition Match," *New York Times*, August 6, 2023, https://www.nytimes.com/2023/08/06/business/facial-recognition-false-arrest.html. Accessed June 24, 2024.
13. Lorena O'Neil, "These Women Tried to Warn Us About AI," *Rolling Stone*, August 12, 2023, https://www.rollingstone.com/culture/culture-features/women-warnings-ai-danger-risk-before-chatgpt-1234804367/. Emily M. Bender, Timnit Gebru, et al., "On the Dangers of Stochastic Parrots: Can Language Models Be Too Big?" Conference on Fairness, Accountability, and Transparency, March 3–10, 2021, https://dl.acm.org/doi/pdf/10.1145/3442188.3445922.
14. Claudia Goldin, *Career and Family: Women's Century-Long Journey Toward Equity* (Princeton University Press, 2021), chapter 5.
15. In 2024, women made up 2 percent of electricians and 3.5 percent of carpenters: "Occupations with the Smallest Share of Women Workers," U.S. Department of Labor, updated April 2024, https://www.dol.gov/agencies/wb/data/occupations/occupations-smallest-share-women-workers.
16. "Historical Women CEOs of the Fortune Lists: 1972–2023," Catalyst, June 22, 2023, https://www.catalyst.org/insights/2023/historical-list-of-women-ceos-of-the-fortune-lists-1972-2023.
17. Female designers: Korellis Reuther, "Shrink It and Pink It"; Architects: "Architect Demographics and Statistics in the US," Zippia, https://www

.zippia.com/architect-jobs/demographics/; Surgical specialties: "Active Physicians by Sex and Specialty, 2021," AAMC, archived May 22, 2024 at https://web.archive.org/web/20240522043615/https://www.aamc.org/data-reports/workforce/data/active-physicians-sex-specialty-2021; Law: Raphael Bohne, "Share of Lawyers in the United States from 2020 to 2023, by Gender," Statista, February 21, 2024, https://www.statista.com/statistics/1086790/share-lawyers-united-states-gender/; Pilots: "Airline Pilot Demographics and Statistics in the US," Zippia, https://www.zippia.com/airplane-pilot-jobs/demographics/; Software engineers: "Software Engineer Demographics and Statistics in the Us," Zippia, https://www.zippia.com/software-engineer-jobs/demographics/; Politics: "Women in Elective Office 2024," CAWP, https://cawp.rutgers.edu/facts/current-numbers/women-elective-office-2024.

18. Goldin, *Career and Family*, 159: Study data from the U.S. Census Bureau, appendix 248–49 (.83 cents to the male dollar for White women, .93 cents for Asian women, .64 cents for Black women, and .54 cents for Latinas). Goldin, *Career and Family*, 153, 158: "Occupational Employment and Wage Statistics," U.S. Bureau of Labor Statistics, May 2022, https://www.bls.gov/oes/current/oes_nat.htm#00-0000. Incomes are lower for those without college degrees and for Black and Brown wage earners. Rakesh Kochhar, "The Enduring Grip of the Gender Pay Gap," Pew Research Center, March 1, 2023, https://www.pewresearch.org/social-trends/2023/03/01/the-enduring-grip-of-the-gender-pay-gap/.
19. William Lutz, "Women Earn Less Than Men in All Occupations, Even Ones Commonly Held by Women," Institute for Women's Policy Research, March 7, 2024, https://iwpr.org/new-report-women-earn-less-than-men-in-all-occupations-even-ones-commonly-held-by-women/. Accessed January 2, 2025. Latina women earn 59.2 cents on the dollar and Black women earn 65.8 cents.
20. Ariane Hegewisch and Hannah Gartner, "Women Earn Less Than Men Whether They Work in the Same or Different Occupations," Institute for Women's Policy Research Fact Sheet #C521, March 2024, https://iwpr.org/wp-content/uploads/2024/03/Occupational-Wage-Gap-2024-Fact-Sheet-1.pdf.
21. Katie Spoon, Nicholas Laberge, et al., "Gender and Retention Patterns Among U.S. Faculty," *Science Advances* 9, no. 42 (October 20, 2023), https://www.science.org/doi/10.1126/sciadv.adi2205.
22. Beth Wang, "Google Must Pay Female Executive $1 Million for Gender Bias," Bloomberg Law, October 20, 2023, https://news.bloomberglaw.com/litigation/google-must-pay-female-executive-1-million-for-gender-bias.
23. Women venture capitalists tend to receive one quarter of the funding they request, while men tend to receive approximately half: "Advancing Gender

Equality in Venture Capital," Harvard Kennedy School, October 2019, https://www.hks.harvard.edu/sites/default/files/2023-09/gender_and_culture_in_vc_literature_review_final.pdf.

24. Emily Chang, *Brotopia: Breaking Up the Boys' Club of Silicon Valley* (Portfolio/Penguin, 2018), 154.
25. Evan D. Gumas, Munira Z. Gunja, "The Unequal Weight of Caregiving: Women Shoulder the Responsibility in 10 Countries," The Commonwealth Fund, March 19, 2024, https://www.commonwealthfund.org/blog/2024/unequal-weight-caregiving-women-shoulder-responsibility-10-countries.
26. Susan C. Reinhard, Lynn Friss Feinberg, et al., "Valuing the Invaluable: 2015 Update," AARP Public Policy Institute, July 2015, https://www.aarp.org/content/dam/aarp/ppi/2015/valuing-the-invaluable-2015-update-new.pdf. The Canadian government estimated that the value of unpaid work would amount to 30.6 to 41.4 percent of their GDP: Katrine Marçal, *Who Cooked Adam Smith's Dinner?: A Story of Women and Economics* (Pegasus Books, 2016), 61.
27. Damla Onder, "Women's Unpaid Work and the American Economy," *Economics Review*, September 1, 2022, https://theeconreview.com/2022/09/01/womens-unpaid-work-and-the-american-economy/. Accessed September 27, 2024.
28. Onder, "Women's Unpaid Work."
29. Arlie Hochschild, *The Second Shift: Working Parents and the Revolution at Home* (Penguin Books, 1980).
30. Marçal, *Who Cooked Adam Smith's Dinner?*, 60. In developing countries or areas largely dependent on agriculture, the statistic is even higher: Taylor Hanna, Collin Meisel, et al., "Forecasting Time Spent in Unpaid Care and Domestic Work," UNWomen, accessed March 25, 2025, https://www.unwomen.org/sites/default/files/2023-10/technical-brief-forecasting-time-spent-in-unpaid-care-and-domestic-work-en.pdf.
31. Marçal, *Who Cooked Adam Smith's Dinner?*, 30.
32. The gross domestic product is supposed to measure the aggregate or overall economic well-being of a country. The GDP reflects the priorities of capitalism (making money), not the intrinsic value of work, the well-being of the country, or individuals' overall satisfaction with their lives. This is one of the reasons some economists believe that the GDP is outdated and somewhat irrelevant.
33. Egill Bjarnason, "Women across Iceland, including the prime minister, go on strike for equal pay and no more violence," Associated Press, October 24, 2023, https://apnews.com/article/iceland-women-strike-equal-pay-970669466116a2b1a5673a8737089d46.
34. Marçal, *Who Cooked Adam Smith's Dinner?*, 17.

35. Ann Crittenden, *The Price of Motherhood: Why the Most Important Job in the World Is Still the Least Valued* (Henry Holt, 2001, 2010), 68.
36. The highest-paid football coach was the Patriots' Bill Belichick, who made $25 million a year, down to the paltry sum of $8 million paid to many other pro coaches: "50 Highest-Paid Coaches in U.S. Sports," Sportico, https://www.sportico.com/feature/highest-paid-coaches-american-sports-1234747983/. "Preschool Teacher Salary," *US News & World Report*, https://money.usnews.com/careers/best-jobs/preschool-teacher/salary. Accessed June 26, 2025.
37. Crittenden, *Price of Motherhood*, 73–74.
38. Marçal, *Who Cooked Adam Smith's Dinner?*, 194.
39. Marçal, *Who Cooked Adam Smith's Dinner?*, 192.
40. Crittenden, *Price of Motherhood*, 6.
41. Interview with "Michelle" on January 4, 2024.
42. All quotes in this section from an interview with "Dr. R." on May 18, 2024.
43. "Life and Leadership After HBS—Pervasive and Pernicious: Sexual Harassment at Work," Harvard Business School, 2018, https://www.hbs.edu/race-gender-equity/projects/life-and-leadership-after-hbs/Pages/sexual-harassment.aspx. This study survey focused on women from Asia, Latin American, Europe, and the US/Canada.
44. Kimberly Hamlin, "A primer on the history of sexual harassment—and why it deserves a place in diversity training," Fast Company, March 8, 2021, https://www.fastcompany.com/90611160/a-primer-on-the-history-of-sexual-harassment-and-why-it-deserves-a-place-in-diversity-training. Accessed December 30, 2024.
45. "Migrant women are especially vulnerable to violence and harassment at work," LR Foundation World Risk Poll, January 23, 2023, https://wrp.lrfoundation.org.uk/safe-at-work-global-experiences-of-violence-and-harassment/migrant-women-more-likely-to-experience-violence-and-harassment-at-work/. The top three areas for violence against migrant women are Australia/New Zealand, Southern Europe, and North America.
46. Diplomatic immunity is granted to foreign diplomats and to some extent their families and support teams. *Diplomatic and Consular Immunity*, U.S. Department of State, August 2018, https://www.state.gov/wp-content/uploads/2019/07/2018-DipConImm_v5_Web.pdf.
47. Quoted in Claire Cain Miller, "It's Not Just Fox: Why Women Don't Report Sexual Harassment," *New York Times*, April 10, 2017, https://www.nytimes.com/2017/04/10/upshot/its-not-just-fox-why-women-dont-report-sexual-harassment.html.
48. Obviously, not all companies' HR departments disregard women or People of Color's bona fide complaints. Many do their job and protect vulnerable

employees. However, there are stories where HR departments collude with abusive bosses or misuse NDAs to silence those who seek justice. See Daniel Silliman, "Sexual Harassment Went Unchecked at Christianity Today," *Christianity Today*, March 15, 2022, https://www.christianitytoday.com/news/2022/march/sexual-harassment-ct-guidepost-assessment-galli-olawoye.html.

49. Based on a conversation I had with a cashier at a Whole Foods store in December 2023.
50. Jodi Kantor, "Working Anything but 9 to 5," *New York Times*, August 13, 2014, https://www.nytimes.com/interactive/2014/08/13/us/starbucks-workers-scheduling-hours.html. Accessed July 9, 2024.
51. Ryan Mac, "Tech's Hottest Lunch Spot? A Strip Club," *Forbes*, July 14, 2015, https://www.forbes.com/sites/ryanmac/2015/07/14/gold-club-tech-lunch-spot-strip-club-yelp-san-francicso/.
52. Michael Kimmel, "Why Gender Equality Is Good for Everyone—Men Included," TED, October 6, 2015, https://www.youtube.com/watch?v=7n9IOH0NvyY.
53. Marcus Noland, Tyler Moran, and Barbara R. Kotschwar, "Is Gender Diversity Profitable? Evidence from a Global Survey," Peterson Institute for International Economics Working Paper No. 16-3, February 2016, https://papers.ssrn.com/sol3/papers.cfm?abstract_id=2729348.
54. Lone Engbo Christiansen, Huidan Huidan Lin, et al., "Gender Diversity in Senior Positions and Firm Performance: Evidence from Europe," International Monetary Fund, March 7, 2016, https://www.imf.org/en/Publications/WP/Issues/2016/12/31/Gender-Diversity-in-Senior-Positions-and-Firm-Performance-Evidence-from-Europe-43771 (found in Chang, *Brotopia*, 251).
55. Chang, *Brotopia*, 251.
56. Phone conversation with Brigit Helms on February 6, 2024.
57. Phone conversation with Brigit Helms on February 6, 2024.
58. Chang, *Brotopia*, 254.
59. Chang, *Brotopia*, 255.
60. David Curry, "Slack Revenue and Usage Statistics (2024)," Business of Apps, January 22, 2024, https://www.businessofapps.com/data/slack-statistics. Denise Dresser was appointed CEO of Slack in 2023.
61. According to Patagonia's 2023–2024 annual report, in 2022, Patagonia made the bold decision to transfer ownership to trusts, LLCs, and charitable groups with the goal of protecting the environment and fighting adverse effects of climate change. "We're in business to save our home planet"; https://www.patagonia.com/on/demandware.static/-/Library-Sites

-PatagoniaShared/default/dw2f8292a3/PDF-US/Patagonia-2023-2024-BCorp-Report.pdf.

62. Katelyn Beaty, *A Woman's Place: A Christian Vision for Your Calling in the Office, the Home, and the World* (Howard Books, 2016), 10–11.

Chapter 4: Making It Legal

1. As of 2022, the US census estimated there were 168 million females living in the United States: "Women's History Month: March 2024," US Census Bureau, March 6, 2024, https://www.census.gov/newsroom/facts-for-features/2024/womens-history-month.html.
2. All quotes from C-SPAN's recorded testimony from the Senate subcommittee hearing on October 11, 1991, https://www.youtube.com/watch?v=-QbVKSvm274. Accessed December 29, 2024.
3. Quoted in Katelyn Fossett, "30 Years After Her Testimony, Anita Hill Still Wants Something from Joe Biden," *Politico*, October 1, 2021, https://www.politico.com/news/magazine/2021/10/01/30-years-after-her-testimony-anita-hill-still-wants-something-from-joe-biden-514884. Accessed September 25, 2024.
4. Interview between Dr. Anita Hill and Jessica Bennett at the New Rules Summit on Women and Power, hosted by *New York Times*, "How History Changed Anita Hill," June 17, 2019, https://www.nytimes.com/2019/06/17/us/anita-hill-women-power.html.
5. An interview between Dr. Anita Hill and Jessica Bennett at the New Rules Summit on Women and Power.
6. When Biden became president, he apologized to Dr. Hill.
7. See Carol L. Meyers, "Was Ancient Israel a Patriarchal Society?" *Journal of Biblical Literature* 133, no. 1 (April 1, 2014): 17–20, https://www.researchgate.net/publication/308043183_Was_Ancient_Israel_a_Patriarchal_Society. There were exceptions like the women from Sparta and those who served as philosophers, poets, priestesses, and even healers/doctors.
8. During the Middle Ages, the power differential was more along class lines. A royal woman had more influence than an underclass man. Convents and religious orders gave women the ability to govern. The Reformation disrupted this and reestablished gender-based hierarchies.
9. Before women could vote, they contributed to the betterment of culture by improving the sewing machine, creating fire escapes in train cars, designing commercial barrels, innovating in healthcare and farming, etc. "Inventive Women: American Women in Innovation and Invention," National Women's History Museum, April 18, 2018, https://www.womenshistory.org/exhibits/inventive-women.

10. Marina Koren, "Why Men Thought Women Weren't Made to Vote," *Atlantic*, July 11, 2019, https://www.theatlantic.com/science/archive/2019/07/womens-suffrage-nineteenth-amendment-pseudoscience/593710/.
11. Letter from Abigail Adams to John Adams, March 31, 1776, Massachusetts Historical Society, https://www.masshist.org/digitaladams/archive/doc?id=L17760331aa.
12. Granted, their definition of pluralism was deficient. By knowingly incorporating slavery, committing genocide against the Native Peoples, and denying women basic rights, they were mainly protecting White men.
13. George MacAdam, "Feminist Revolutionary Principle Is Biological Bosh; Prof. William. T. Sedgwick, Noted Biologist, Riddles the Pretensions of Supporters of the New Doctrine for Women and Says If the Movement Succeeds It Will Throw the World Back a Thousand Years," *New York Times*, January 18, 1914, https://www.nytimes.com/1914/01/18/archives/feminist-revolutionary-principle-is-biological-bosh-prof-william-t.html. Italics mine.
14. This includes self-proclaimed pastors Doug Wilson and Joel Webbon and John McEntee, advisor for the Heritage Foundation's Project 2025. Steve Rabey, "Doug Wilson's Disciples Question Women's Right to Vote," *Roys Report*, November 15, 2022, https://julieroys.com/doug-wilson-disciples-advocate-taking-away-womens-right-vote/.
15. Title IX, passed in 1972, along with the Public Health Service Act of 1975, forced universities to reevaluate their admission policies and give equal access to women.
16. Sir William Blackstone's *Commentaries of the Laws of England*, Book the First: Chapter the Fifteenth: Of Husband and Wife (Oxford: Clarendon, 1765). Accessed through National Constitution Center, "Commentaries on the Laws of England, vol. 1 The Rights of Persons (1765) and vol. 2 The Rights of Things (1766)," https://constitutioncenter.org/the-constitution/historic-document-library/detail/sir-william-blackstone-commentaries-on-the-laws-of-england-vol-1-the-rights-of-persons-1765-and-vol-2-the-rights-of-things-1766.
17. Examples include *Martin v. The Commonwealth of Massachusetts*, 1805, and *Furey v. Furey*, 1952.
18. Julie Carr Smyth and Steve Karnowski, "Some States Seek to Close Loopholes in Marital Rape Laws," Associated Press, May 4, 2019, https://apnews.com/article/3a11fee6d0e449ce81f6c8a50601c687. Shockingly, some states still offer legal exemptions to protect husbands from rape prosecution. In 2019, Minnesota governor Tim Walz signed a law that eliminated a loophole protecting partners from being prosecuted for rape in his state.
19. Recall the story in chapter 2: Elizabeth Packard was sent to an asylum for disagreeing with her husband.

20. "About Intimate Partner Violence," CDC, https://www.cdc.gov/intimate-partner-violence/about/. Accessed September 25, 2024.
21. This happened in the court case *Kirchberg v. Feenstra*, which struck down Louisiana law that upheld Head and Master law. The Married Women's Property Acts struck down coverture doctrines on a state-by-state basis.
22. In 1968 Mississippi became the last state to permit women to sit on juries. Not until 1994 in *J.E.B. v. Alabama* did the Court rule that, due to the Equal Protection Clause of the Fourteenth Amendment, gender can't be used to exclude jurors from a trial.
23. As of 2023, women make up 30 percent of state court judges nationwide. This varies from state to state. Tracey E. George and Albert H. Yoon, "Gavel Gap," American Constitution Society, April 9, 2018, https://www.acslaw.org/analysis/reports/gavel-gap/. The first woman to serve on a federal bench was appointed by President Calvin Coolidge in 1928. Justice Sandra Day O'Connor became the first female member of the Supreme Court in 1981.
24. Vivian N. Rotenstein and Valerie P. Hans, "Gentlewomen of the Jury," *Michigan Journal of Gender and Law* 29, no. 2 (2022): 264, https://repository.law.umich.edu/cgi/viewcontent.cgi?article=1302&context=mjgl.
25. Quoted in Ruth Bader Ginsburg, *My Own Words* (Simon & Schuster, 2016), 106. Bradford directly contradicted an earlier dissent in the Slaughterhouse Case.
26. *Reed v. Reed* fully overturned *Bradwell v. Illinois* and affirmed that the Equal Protection Clause of the Fourteenth Amendment prohibited gender-based discrimination. U.S. Supreme Court, "Bradwell v. The State, 83 U.S. 130 (1872)," Justia, https://supreme.justia.com/cases/federal/us/83/130/.
27. Quote from L. H. Schafran, "Overwhelming Evidence: Reports on Gender Bias in the Courts," *Trial* 26, no. 2 (February 1990): 28–30, 32–35, https://www.ojp.gov/ncjrs/virtual-library/abstracts/overwhelming-evidence-reports-gender-bias-courts. Also see the 2020 gender study "New York State Judicial Committee on Women in the Courts," https://www.nycourts.gov/LegacyPDFS/ip/womeninthecourts/Gender-Survey-2020.pdf.
28. Deborah Epstein and Lisa A. Goodman, "Discounting Women: Doubting Domestic Violence Survivors' Credibility and Dismissing Their Experiences," *University of Pennsylvania Law Review* 167 (2019): 402, https://scholarship.law.upenn.edu/cgi/viewcontent.cgi?article=9644&context=penn_law_review. Accessed December 26, 2024.
29. There is one notable exception to this: "Innocent Black people are almost eight times more likely than white people to be falsely convicted of rape." "Race and Wrongful Convictions in the United States, 2022," National Registry of Exonerations, September 2022, https://exonerationregistry.org

/sites/exonerationregistry.org/files/documents/Updated%20CP%20-%20 Race%20Report%20Preview.pdf.

30. The crime against Taylor and the subsequent trials became catalysts in the civil rights movement. In 2011, the Alabama legislature apologized to Recy Taylor for their failure to protect her.
31. Jeannie Suk Gersen, "Revisiting the Brock Turner Case," *New Yorker*, March 29, 2023, https://www.newyorker.com/news/our-columnists /revisiting-the-brock-turner-case.
32. Amna Nawaz and Matt Loffman, "Breaking Down the Verdict as Jury Finds Trump Liable for Sexual Assault and Defamation," *PBS News Hour*, May 9, 2023, https://www.pbs.org/newshour/show/breaking-down-the-verdict-as -jury-finds-trump-liable-for-sexual-assault-and-defamation. Accessed December 29, 2024. Trump claimed he could do whatever he wanted to women, including "grab 'em by the pussy," while recorded on a hot mic in 2005. This became public in a 2016 *Washington Post* article and has since been referred to as the Access Hollywood tape.
33. "Quick Facts: Sexual Abuse Offenders," United States Sentencing Commission, fiscal year 2021, https://www.ussc.gov/sites/default/files/pdf /research-and-publications/quick-facts/Sexual_Abuse_FY21.pdf. "Victims of Sexual Violence: Statistics," RAINN, https://rainn.org/statistics/victims -sexual-violence.
34. The National Sexual Violence Resource Center puts the false report rate at 2 to 10 percent.
35. Blake Stilwell, "The Tailhook Scandal: How a 'Top Gun Mentality' Led to a Disastrous Navy Conference," Military.com, August 11, 2022, https:// www.military.com/history/tailhook-scandal-how-top-gun-mentality-led -disastrous-navy-conference.html. Derek J. Vander Schaaf, "Report of Investigation: Tailhook 91—Part 1, Review of the Navy Investigations," 1992, https://ncisahistory.org/wp-content/uploads/2017/07/DoDIG-Report-of -Investigation-Tailhook-91-Review-of-the-Navy-Investigations.pdf.
36. "The Criminal Justice System: Statistics," RAINN, https://www.rainn.org /statistics/criminal-justice-system: The National Crime Victimization Survey found a higher rate of nonreporting: 75.1 percent. Rachel E. Morgan and Barbara A. Oudekerk, "Criminal Victimization, 2018," U.S. Department of Justice Office of Justice Programs, Bureau of Justice Statistics, September 2019, NCJ 253043, 1: In a 2019 annual report, the Pentagon estimated that in one year, more than twenty thousand sexual assaults happened in the military but only 30 percent of those attacked reported the crime. Per the *2018 Department of Defense Annual Report of Sexual Assault in the Military*, the DoD took disciplinary action in 65 percent of the cases.https://www.sapr.mil/sites

/default/files/FY18_DOD_Annual_Report_on_Sexual_Assault_in_the _Military.pdf (site discontinued).

37. Quoted in Kate Harding, *Asking for It: The Alarming Rise of Rape Culture—and What We Can Do About It* (Balance Press, 2015), 88.
38. Barbara Bradley Hagerty, "An Epidemic of Disbelief," *Atlantic*, August 2019, https://www.theatlantic.com/magazine/archive/2019/08/an-epidemic-of-disbelief/592807/. More than 11,000 kits were discovered in a warehouse in the Detroit area and 7,000 in Cleveland. In Memphis more than 12,000 were found. New York City admitted to having more than 17,000 untested kits.
39. Hagerty, "An Epidemic of Disbelief."
40. Cora Peterson, Sarah DeGue, Curtis Florence, et al., "The Economic Burden of Rape Among U.S. Adults," NIH, National Library of Medicine (June 2017), https://pubmed.ncbi.nlm.nih.gov/28153649/.
41. "Fact Check: Termination of Pregnancy Can Be Necessary to Save a Woman's Life, Experts Say," Reuters, December 27, 2021, https://www.reuters.com/article/fact-check/termination-of-pregnancy-can-be-necessary-to-save-a-womans-life-experts-say-idUSL1N2TC0VD/.
42. Majority decision in *Roe v. Wade*, written by Justice Blackmun, https://caselaw.findlaw.com/court/us-supreme-court/19–1392.html.
43. In *Planned Parenthood v. Casey*, 1992, the Supreme Court upheld that an abortion restriction is unconstitutional when it imposes burdens that outweigh the benefits. The undue burden standard protecting the right to an abortion was overturned in *Dobbs*. Undue burden essentially means excessive burden.
44. Planned Parenthood v. Casey. Majority opinion written by Justice Harry Blackmun, https://www.law.cornell.edu/supct/html/91–744.ZX2.html.
45. Cited in Julie Suk, *After Misogyny: How the Law Fails Women and What to Do About It* (University of California Press, 2023), 91.
46. The 1977 Hyde Amendment forbade the use of federal funds to pay for abortion (through Medicaid) except for when the mother's life was in danger or in the case of rape or incest. Edward C. Liu and Wen W. Shen, "The Hyde Amendment: An Overview," *Congressional Research Service*, July 20, 2022, https://crsreports.congress.gov/product/pdf/IF/IF12167.
47. Erika Bachiochi, "Embodied Equality: Debunking Equal Protection Arguments for Abortion Rights," *Harvard Journal of Law and Public Policy* 34 (June 27, 2011): 893.
48. "44 percent of Custodial Parents Receive the Full Amount of Child Support," US Census Bureau, January 30, 2018, https://www.census.gov/newsroom/press-releases/2018/cb18-tps03.html.
49. Blake Ellis and Melanie Hicken, "These male politicians are pushing for women who receive abortions to be punished with prison time," CNN,

September 21, 2022, https://www.cnn.com/2022/09/20/politics/abortion-bans-murder-charges-invs/index.html.

50. The Affordable Care Act (ACA) mandates that insurance companies provide free birth control for women but requires a prescription. Male contraception is not included under the ACA. One study done by Kaiser Permanente included more than 1.5 million participants and took place over eleven years. It found that since the ACA was implemented, rates of unintended pregnancy and abortion declined. Sue Rochman, "Free contraception under ACA increased use, reduced pregnancy and abortion," Kaiser Permanente, October 31, 2024, https://divisionofresearch.kaiserpermanente.org/contraception-aca/.
51. The effectiveness rate is reported to be 98 percent when used properly. "Condoms," World Health Organization, February 14, 2025, https://www.who.int/news-room/fact-sheets/detail/condoms.
52. Eda Algur, Elin Wang, et al., "A Systemic Global Review of Condom Availability Programs in High Schools," Journal of Adolescent Health 64 (2019), 292–304, https://www.jahonline.org/article/S1054-139X(18)30798-5/pdf. Gina M. Secura, Tiffany Adams, et al., "Change in Sexual Behavior with Provision of No-Cost Contraception," Obstetrics and Gynecology 123, no. 4 (April 2014): 771–76, https://pmc.ncbi.nlm.nih.gov/articles/PMC4009508/. It seems to me that education typically results in better, wiser choices.
53. The Federal Employee Paid Leave Act (FEPLA, for birth, adoption, or foster care placement) offers up to twelve weeks for civilian, federal employees who qualify under the Family and Medical Leave Act (FMLA).
54. The average annual cost for infant-based childcare in rural areas is approximately $7,500 per child and can go up to $15,000 in a metro area. The fees diminish as the child gets older but tend to take up 8 to 19 percent of the median family income. Christin Landivar, "New Childcare Data Shows Prices Are Untenable for Families," U.S. Department of Labor, January 24, 2023, https://blog.dol.gov/2023/01/24/new-childcare-data-shows-prices-are-untenable-for-families.
55. Maggie Davis, "It Costs an Additional $297674 to Raise a child over 18 years, Up 25.3%," LendingTree, March 31, 2025, https://www.lendingtree.com/debt-consolidation/raising-a-child-study/. This does not factor in the cost of a college education.
56. This amount may be reduced by 50 percent in 2026. Congress is currently debating this possibility.
57. Under pressure from the medical establishment, this bill also attempted to regulate pregnant women and discourage them from relying on midwives

and instead turn to medical "professionals." This had negative repercussions on those who had less financial means.

58. Claire Cain Miller, "Women Actually Do Govern Differently," *New York Times*, November 10, 2016, https://www.nytimes.com/2016/11/10/upshot/women-actually-do-govern-differently.html.
59. The Equal Rights Amendment, written in 1923 and updated in 1972, reads, "Equality of rights under the law shall not be denied or abridged by the United States or by any state on account of sex. The Congress shall have the power to enforce, by appropriate legislation, the provisions of this article."
60. Anita Hill, *Speaking Truth to Power: A Memoir* (Knopf Doubleday, 1998), 343.

Chapter 5: Behind the Screens

1. The games were postponed a year due to COVID-19 and took place without fans.
2. Alex Cooper, host, *Call Her Daddy*, interview with Simone Biles, April 17, 2024, https://www.youtube.com/watch?v=uHVVCXojhQk. Accessed September 17, 2024.
3. Jordan Moreau, "Michael Che Wipes Instagram Account After Backlash to Simone Biles Jokes," *Variety*, July 30, 2021, https://variety.com/2021/tv/news/michael-che-simone-biles-instagram-1235031377/.
4. Benjamin Wermund, "Texas Deputy Ag Apologizes After Slamming Simone Biles' Olympic Exit," *Houston Chronicle*, July 29, 2021, https://www.houstonchronicle.com/politics/texas/article/Childish-national-embarrassment-Some-Texas-16346260.php.
5. *Simone Biles Rising*, directed by Katie Walsh, Netflix (2024), https://www.netflix.com/title/81700902.
6. Ella Alexander, "10 Famous Women Who Were Brutally Destroyed by the Press," *Harper's Bazaar*, February 16, 2021, https://www.harpersbazaar.com/uk/culture/g35489023/10-famous-women-who-were-brutally-destroyed-by-the-press/.
7. Directors: Laura Carollo, "Distribution of Movie Directors in the United States from 2011 to 2023, by Gender," Statista, May 24, 2024, https://www.statista.com/statistics/696871/movie-director-gender/. Writers: Laura Carollo, "Distribution of Movie Writers in the United States from 2011 to 2023, by Gender," Statista, May 24, 2024, https://www.statista.com/statistics/696898/movie-writer-gender/. Video game designers: "Video Game Designer Demographics and Statistics in the US," Zippia, accessed July 8, 2024, https://www.zippia.com/video-game-designer-jobs/demographics/. Software developers: Lionel Sujay Vailshery, "Software Developer Gender Distribution

Worldwide as of 2022," Statistica, May 23, 2024, https://www.statista.com/statistics/1126823/worldwide-developer-gender/.

8. "100 Women: How Hollywood Fails Women on Screen," BBC, March 2, 2018, https://www.bbc.com/news/world-43197774.
9. Certain writers, actors, and producers do use their influence to tell stories that reveal injustice and champion strong women. Several films or TV series that come to mind include *The Six Triple Eight*, *She Said*, *The Iron Lady*, *The Crown*, and *Hidden Figures*.
10. "Body Measurements," CDC, National Center for Health Statistics, September 10, 2021, https://www.cdc.gov/nchs/fastats/body-measurements.htm. "Vital and Health Statistics," CDC, National Center for Health Statistics, January 2021, https://www.cdc.gov/nchs/data/series/sr_03/sr03-046-508.pdf.
11. "How to Get into Modeling," Best Agency, https://www.best-agencies.com/models/how-to-get-into-modeling/.
12. "Modeling," UCLA Statistics and Data Science, http://www.stat.ucla.edu/~vlew/stat10/archival/FA02/handouts/modeling.pdf.
13. Claudia Rankine, "The Meaning of Serena Williams," *New York Times*, August 25, 2015, https://www.nytimes.com/2015/08/30/magazine/the-meaning-of-serena-williams.html.
14. All quotes from an interview with Rev. Liz Walker on March 12, 2024. She worked as the co-anchor on Boston's WBZ-TV nightly news for almost twenty years.
15. Madeleine Aggeler, "Gen Z has had work done—and they'll tell you all about it," *Washington Post*, June 13, 2023, https://www.washingtonpost.com/lifestyle/2023/06/13/gen-z-plastic-surgery-tiktok/.
16. "2022 Cosmetic Surgery Age Distribution (19 And Under)," American Society of Plastic Surgeons, https://www.plasticsurgery.org/documents/News/Statistics/2022/cosmetic-procedures-ages-13-19-2022.pdf. This is the most recent year that stats are available. The figure may include a small percentage of trans youth who have this procedure, but it's overwhelmingly biological women who elect to have breast augmentation.
17. Diana Zuckerman, "Teenagers and Cosmetic Surgery," *AMA Journal of Ethics*, March 2005, https://journalofethics.ama-assn.org/article/teenagers-and-cosmetic-surgery/2005-03. Zuckerman serves as the president of the National Center for Health Research.
18. TikTok influencer Alix Earle, January 5, 2023, https://www.tiktok.com/@alixearle/video/7185355951661206827?_r=1&_t=8YnB9lcV2Fv.
19. Jonathan Rothwell, "Teens Spend Average of 4.8 Hours on Social Media Per Day," Gallup, October 13, 2023, https://news.gallup.com/poll/512576/teens-spend-average-hours-social-media-per-day.aspx.

20. Mia Taylor, "'Sephora Kids' and the Booming Business of Beauty Products for Children," BBC, January 22, 2024, https://www.bbc.com/worklife/article/20240119-sephora-kids-and-the-booming-business-of-beauty-products-for-children. Regarding damage to girls' skin, see Jocelyn Gecker, "Young girls are using anti-aging products they see on social media. The harm is more than skin deep," Associated Press, August 31, 2024, https://apnews.com/article/influenced-skincare-routine-mental-health-f59bb09114ab93323e3a47197a1ad914.
21. Kara Alaimo, *Over the Influence: Why Social Media Is Toxic for Women and Girls—and How We Can Take It Back* (Alcove Press, 2024), 14, quoting Sarah J. Durkin and Susan J. Paxton, "Predictors of Vulnerability to Reduced Body Image Satisfaction and Psychological Wellbeing in Response to Exposure to Idealized Female Media Images in Adolescent Girls," *Journal of Psychosomatic Research* 53, no. 5 (2002): 995–1005, https://doi.org/10.1016/S0022-3999(02)00489-0.
22. Frances Haugen, *The Power of One: How I Found the Strength to Tell the Truth and Why I Blew the Whistle on Facebook* (Little, Brown and Co., 2023), 290.
23. Barbara Jiotsa, Benjamin Naccache, et al., "Social Media Use and Body Image Disorders: Association Between Frequency of Comparing One's Own Physical Appearance to That of People Being Followed on Social Media and Body Dissatisfaction and Drive for Thinness," *International Journal of Environmental Research and Public Health* 18, no. 6 (March 11, 2021), https://www.ncbi.nlm.nih.gov/pmc/articles/PMC8001450/. Sheera Frenkel et al., "Whistleblower Discusses How Instagram May Lead Teenagers to Eating Disorders," *New York Times*, October 5, 2021, updated June 6, 2024, https://www.nytimes.com/live/2021/10/05/technology/facebook-whistleblower-frances-haugen?partner=IFTTin-hearing-haugen-discusses-how-instagram-may-lead-teenagers-to-eating-disorders.
24. "Youth Risk Behavior Survey Data Summary and Trends Report 2013–2023," CDC, https://www.cdc.gov/yrbs/?CDC_AAref_Val=https://www.cdc.gov/healthyyouth/data/yrbs/pdf/YRBS_Data-Summary-Trends_Report2023_508.pdf. "QuickStats: Suicide Rates for Teens Aged 15–19 Years, by Sex—United States, 1975–2015," *Morbidity and Mortality Weekly Report* 66, no. 30 (August 4, 2017), https://www.cdc.gov/mmwr/volumes/66/wr/mm6630a6.htm.
25. Donna Jackson Nakazawa, *Girls on the Brink: Helping Our Daughters Thrive in an Era of Increased Anxiety, Depression, and Social Media* (Harmony Books, 2022), 10.
26. Jonathan Haidt, *The Anxious Generation: How the Great Rewiring of Childhood Is Causing an Epidemic of Mental Illness* (Penguin Random House, 2024), 146–47.

27. Haidt, *Anxious Generation*, 153.
28. Marcie Bianco, "Feminism's Greatest Obstacle in the Digital Age Is the Commodification of Women's Bodies," *Quartz*, April 17, 2016, https://qz.com/658036/feminisms-greatest-obstacle-in-the-digital-age.
29. Kayleigh Dray, "These Shocking 21st-Century Adverts Are a Grim Reminder That Sexism Is Alive and Well," *Stylist*, 2018, https://www.stylist.co.uk/life/ridiculously-sexist-misogyny-anti-feminist-adverts-posters-billboards-present-modern-day/69598. Accessed July 5, 2024.
30. Alan Duke, "Vodka ad draws anti-rape controversy," CNN, March 25, 2012, https://edition.cnn.com/2012/03/25/showbiz/vodka-ad-controversy/. Kashmir Hill, "Social Media Idiocy of the Day: Belvedere Vodka's Rape Joke," *Forbes*, March 23, 2012, https://www.forbes.com/sites/kashmirhill/2012/03/23/social-media-idiocy-of-the-day-belevedere-vodkas-rape-joke/.
31. All quotes in this paragraph from Jennifer Valentino-DeVries and Michael H. Keller, "A Marketplace of Girl Influencers Managed by Moms and Stalked by Men," *New York Times*, February 22, 2024, https://www.nytimes.com/2024/02/22/us/instagram-child-influencers.html?smid=em-share. Some accounts feature boys, but the overwhelming majority focus on girls.
32. OnlyFans is a website that allows users to sell adult content to paying subscribers. It is primarily used by sex workers.
33. Valentino-DeVries and Keller, "A Marketplace of Girl Influencers."
34. Valentino-DeVries and Keller, "A Marketplace of Girl Influencers."
35. Valentino-DeVries and Keller, "A Marketplace of Girl Influencers."
36. C. Ramsey Fahs, "2012 Harvard Men's Soccer Team Produced Sexually Explicit 'Scouting Report' on Female Recruits," *Harvard Crimson*, October 25, 2016, https://www.thecrimson.com/article/2016/10/25/harvard-mens-soccer-2012-report/. Accessed July 6, 2024. Harvard's administration swiftly canceled the remainder of their season.
37. Katharine A. Kaplan, "Facemash Creator Survives Ad Board," *Harvard Crimson*, November 19, 2003, https://www.thecrimson.com/article/2003/11/19/facemash-creator-survives-ad-board-the/.
38. Nancy Jo Sales, *American Girls: Social Media and the Secret Lives of Teenagers* (Alfred A. Knopf, 2016), 75.
39. "A 2020 meta-analysis of 50 studies found that over 47 percent of young people engage in reciprocal sexting, sharing nude or practically nude images of themselves." Alaimo, *Over the Influence*, Kindle loc. 515 of 760.
40. Quoted in Alaimo, *Over the Influence*, 29.
41. Holly Patrick, "Fox Guest Describes Kamala Harris as 'Original Hawk Tuah Girl,'" Independent TV, July 25, 2024, https://www.independent.co.uk/tv/news/kamala-harris-hawk-tuah-fox-b2585954.html. This article refers to

guest Alec Lace who appeared on Fox Business News on July 5, 2024, and made this comment.

42. Roxane Gay, "Dave Chappelle's Brittle Ego," *New York Times*, October 13, 2021, https://www.nytimes.com/2021/10/13/opinion/dave-chappelle-netflix-trans.html. Accessed July 7, 2024.
43. Melena Ryzik, Cara Buckley, and Jodi Kantor, "Louis C.K. Is Accused by 5 Women of Sexual Misconduct," *New York Times*, November 9, 2017, https://www.nytimes.com/2017/11/09/arts/television/louis-ck-sexual-misconduct.html.
44. *Sorry/Not Sorry*, directed by Cara Mones and Caroline Suh, documentary produced by *New York Times* (2023), https://www.imdb.com/title/tt28642260/.
45. Chloe Melas, "Louis C.K.: 'These stories are true,'" CNN, November 10, 2017, https://www.cnn.com/2017/11/10/entertainment/louis-ck-apology/index.html. Full statement: https://www.cnn.com/2017/11/10/entertainment/louis-ck-full-statement/index.html.
46. *Sorry/Not Sorry*.
47. *Sorry/Not Sorry*.
48. Matt Fernandez, "'Parks and Recreation' Creator Mike Schur Apologizes for Casting Louis C.K.," *Variety*, November 9, 2017, https://variety.com/2017/tv/news/louis-c-k-sexual-misconduct-parks-and-recreation-creator-apologizes-1202611493/.
49. *Louis C.K.: Oh My God*, directed by Lous C.K., HBO Comedy special (2013), quoted in "Louis CK—On Dating—Men the Number One Threat to Women," posted by NeoLegolasSkywalkerStark, July 19, 2016, 3:52, https://www.youtube.com/watch?v=yRzs7v0do_Q.
50. It was reported that Chappelle pocketed approximately $20 million for his recent Netflix show, *The Closer*: Matthew Thomas, "How Much Dave Chappelle Really Makes on His Netflix Specials After Taxes and Expenses," TheThings, January 3, 2024, https://www.thethings.com/how-much-dave-chappelle-makes-netflix-specials-after-taxes-expenses/.
51. Email exchange with Hannah Anderson on March 10, 2024.
52. Anuradha Bhagwati, *Unbecoming: A Memoir of Disobedience* (Simon & Schuster, 2020), 300.
53. Emily Chang, *Brotopia: Breaking Up the Boys' Club of Silicon Valley* (Portfolio/Penguin, 2018), 233.
54. "Toxic Twitter—A Toxic Place for Women," Amnesty International, March 21, 2018, https://www.amnesty.org/en/latest/research/2018/03/online-violence-against-women-chapter-1-1/. Published before Twitter was sold to Elon Musk and renamed X.

55. Isabella Kwai, "What to Know About the Accusations Against Andrew Tate," *New York Times*, March 12, 2024, https://www.nytimes.com/article/andrew-tate-arrests-explained.html. Accessed August 20, 2024.
56. Brandon Sparks, Alexandra M. Zidenberg, and Mark E. Olver, "Involuntary Celibacy: A Review of Incel Ideology and Experiences with Dating, Rejection, and Associated Mental Health and Emotional Sequelae," *Current Psychiatry Reports* 24, no. 12 (November 17, 2022): 731–40, https://doi.org/10.1007/s11920-022-01382-9.
57. Amanda Taub, "On Social Media's Fringes, Growing Extremism Targets Women," *New York Times*, May 9, 2018, https://www.nytimes.com/2018/05/09/world/americas/incels-toronto-attack.html.
58. The following statistic is quoted from Sparks, Zidenberg, and Olver, "Involuntary Celibacy": "In a recent survey, the prevalence rate of depression and anxiety among incels was 95% and 93%, respectively, trumping national figures (gathered by the Centers for Disease Control and Prevention) of 28% and 36%, respectively." See Sophia Moskalenko, Juncal Fernández-Garayzábal González, Naamal Kates, and Jesse Morton, "Incel Ideology, Radicalization and Mental Health: A Survey Study," *Journal of Intelligence, Conflict, and Warfare* 4, no. 3 (2022): 1–29, https://doi.org/10.21810/jicw.v4i3.3817.
59. Alyssa K. Davis, "16 Movies & TV Shows That Are Excessively Violent Toward Women," SheKnows, May 16, 2025, https://www.sheknows.com/entertainment/slideshow/2617581/movies-tv-shows-violent-toward-women/.
60. Fiona Sturges, "Cattleprods! Severed tongues! Torture porn! Why I've stopped watching the Handmaid's Tale," *The Guardian*, June 16, 2018, https://www.theguardian.com/tv-and-radio/2018/jun/16/handmaids-tale-season-2-elisabeth-moss-margaret-atwood.
61. In 1999, comic book writer Gail Simone coined the term "fridging," but killing off women as a plot device to motivate men can be traced all the way back to *The Iliad*.
62. "Screen violence: A real threat to mental health in children and adolescents," *Lancet Regional Health–Americas* 19 (March 9, 2023), https://www.ncbi.nlm.nih.gov/pmc/articles/PMC10025407/. Rebecca L. Collins, Victor C. Strasburger, et al., "Sexual Media and Childhood Well-Being and Health," *Pediatrics* 140, Supplement_2 (November 2017): S162–S166, https://doi.org/10.1542/peds.2016-1758X.
63. Kelly-Leigh Cooper, "Bianca Devins: The Teenager Whose Murder Was Exploited for Clicks," BBC News, July 20, 2019, https://www.bbc.com/news/world-us-canada-49002486. EJ Dickson, "A 17-Year-Old Girl Was Murdered. How Did Photos of Her Death Go Viral?" *Rolling Stone,* July 15, 2019, https://www.rollingstone.com/culture/culture-news/bianca-devins-murder-brandon-andrew-clark-858874/.

64. Holly Baxter, "Footage of Her Daughter's Murder Went Viral. Now Bianca Devins' Mother Wants to Change the Internet," *The Independent*, March 1, 2023, https://www.independent.co.uk/news/world/americas/bianca-devins-murder-brandon-clark-kimberly-b2291549.html. Accessed June 26, 2024.
65. Juliet Macur and Nate Schweber, "Rape Case Unfolds on Web and Splits City," *New York Times*, December 16, 2012, https://www.nytimes.com/2012/12/17/sports/high-school-football-rape-case-unfolds-online-and-divides-steubenville-ohio.html.
66. Macur and Schweber, "Rape Case Unfolds on Web and Splits City."
67. *Little Women* was written by Alcott in 1868–1869. In the original version, Jo March did not marry. Alcott's editor convinced her that no one would be interested in the book if March remained single. Alcott, a feminist and an abolitionist, never married. The quote "paddle my own canoe" is from *The Journals of Louis May Alcott*, ed. Joel Myerson and Daniel Shealy (University of Georgia Press, 1997), 99.
68. *Barbie*, directed and cowritten by Greta Gerwig (Warner Brothers, 2023), YouTube, https://www.youtube.com/watch?v=CBqlDWHkdHk.
69. "Simone Biles Complete Opening Statement," C-Span, September 15, 2021, https://www.c-span.org/video/?c4977178/simone-biles-complete-opening-statement. Camonghne Felix, "Simone Biles Chose Herself," The Cut, September 27, 2021, https://www.thecut.com/article/simone-biles-olympics-2021.html.
70. "Justice Department Reaches Civil Settlement with Victims Abused by Lawrence Nassar," U.S. Department of Justice, April 23, 2024, https://www.justice.gov/opa/pr/justice-department-reaches-civil-settlement-victims-abused-lawrence-nassar.

Chapter 6: In the Flesh

1. Details and quotes from "Nick and Amy" from several interviews and email exchanges during 2024.
2. Email exchange with Lisa Lamb on April 8, 2025.
3. Dorothy Littell Greco, *Marriage in the Middle: Embracing Midlife Surprises, Challenges, and Joys* (InterVarsity Press, 2020), 19.
4. "Porn in the Digital Age: New Research Reveals 10 Trends," Barna, April 6, 2016, https://www.barna.com/research/porn-in-the-digital-age-new-research-reveals-10-trends/.
5. Numbers vary depending on the source. PornHub reported more than one hundred million visits per day in 2023. More Americans visited the site than any other nationality: PornHub, https://www.pornhub.com/insights/2024-year-in-review#traffic.
6. This happened to pop icon Taylor Swift in 2024.

7. When a disgruntled ex or someone with an ax to grind posts naked photos or sexual videos without permission.
8. According to ZipRecruiter, the average wage for pornography actors and actresses in the US is $22.00/hour, https://www.ziprecruiter.com/Salaries/Porn-Star-Salary.
9. Alex Riggins, "62 women sue PornHub in latest San Diego case involving GirlsDoPorn videos," *San Diego Union Tribune*, October 6, 2023, https://www.sandiegouniontribune.com/news/courts/story/2023-10-04/pornhub-lawsuit-san-diego-federal-court-girlsdoporn-new.
10. It's impossible to have an accurate figure for how common this is. Reported percentages vary, but it's clear that it happens: Maddy Savage, "Why People Watch Pornography at Work," BBC, July 18, 2022, https://www.bbc.com/worklife/article/20220714-why-people-watch-pornography-at-work. British MP Neil Parish resigned from his job after getting caught watching porn in the House of Commons: Rina Torchinsky, "British lawmaker Neil Parish resigning after watching porn in the House of Commons," NPR, April 30, 2022, https://www.npr.org/2022/04/30/1095759573/british-mp-porn-house-of-commons-neil-parish-resigns.
11. Michael Castleman, "How Much Time Does the World Spend Watching Porn?" *Psychology Today*, October 31, 2020, https://www.psychologytoday.com/us/blog/all-about-sex/202010/how-much-time-does-the-world-spend-watching-porn.
12. The age of exposure to pornography continues to drop and is now around ten or eleven for both boys and girls. Caroline Giroux, "Early exposure to pornography: A form of sexual trauma," *Journal of Psychiatry Reform* 10, no. 15 (December 7, 2021), https://journalofpsychiatryreform.com/2021/12/07/early-exposure-to-pornography-a-form-of-sexual-trauma/. "Protection of Children from the Harmful Impacts of Pornography," UNICEF, https://www.unicef.org/harmful-content-online.
13. Emily F. Rothman, Jonathon J. Beckmeyer, et al., "The Prevalence of Using Pornography for Information About How to Have Sex: Findings from a Nationally Representative Survey of U.S. Adolescents and Young Adults," *Archives of Sexual Behavior* 50, no. 2 (February 2021), https://pubmed.ncbi.nlm.nih.gov/33398696/. Accessed August 24, 2022.
14. Samuel L. Perry and Cyrus Schleifer, "Till Porn Do Us Part? A Longitudinal Examination of Pornography Use and Divorce," *Journal of Sex Research* 55, no. 3 (2017): 284–96, https://doi.org/10.1080/00224499.2017.1317709.
15. Men do pay other men for sex, and women may also pay for sex, but overwhelmingly, it's men paying women.
16. This varies greatly depending on geography: Ju Nyeong Park, Charlotte A. Gaydos, et al., "Incidence and Predictors of Chlamydia . . ." *Sexually*

Transmitted Diseases 46, no. 12 (December 2019): 788–94, https://doi.org/10.1097/OLQ.0000000000001085.

17. Sheila Jeffreys, "Globalizing Sexual Exploitation: Sex Tourism and the Traffic in Women," *Leisure Studies* 18, no. 3 (1999): 179–96, https://doi.org/10.1080/026143699374916.
18. Rachel Moran, *Paid For: My Journey Through Prostitution* (W. W. Norton, 2015), 112.
19. Some female sex workers and dancers claim their work is empowering. After reading several books by such women, I believe they are indeed experiencing power or a sense of control over men, which is markedly different from when a woman gets in touch with her body and sexual preferences. This is not to invalidate these women, but to add context.
20. Moran, *Paid For,* 151–52.
21. A study published by Harvard Law School revealed that legalized prostitution results in an increase in trafficked women and children: "Does Legalized Prostitution Increase Human Trafficking?" Harvard Law School, June 12, 2014, https://orgs.law.harvard.edu/lids/2014/06/12/.
22. Across the globe, more than forty million women and girls are engaged in prostitution: Gus Lubin, "There Are 42 Million Prostitutes in the World, and Here's Where They Live," Business Insider, January 17, 2012, https://www.businessinsider.com/there-are-42-million-prostitutes-in-the-world-and-heres-where-they-live-2012-1. Jay Stringer, *Unwanted: How Sexual Brokenness Reveals Our Way to Healing* (NavPress, 2018), xvii: "The average age of initial involvement in prostitution is estimated between fourteen and eighteen years of age." Catherine Goldmann, "Current Assessment of the State of Prostitution," Fondation Scelles, https://www.fondationscelles.org/pdf/current-assessment-of-the-state-of-prostitution-2013.pdf: "In Southeast Asia, between 30–35% of prostitutes are between twelve and seventeen years old."
23. Matthew Birkhold, "Patriarchy: A Primer for Men," *The Nation*, July 19, 2007, https://www.thenation.com/article/archive/patriarchy-primer-men/. Accessed August 24, 2024.
24. Peggy Orenstein, "The Troubling Trend in Teenage Sex," *New York Times*, April 12, 2024, https://www.nytimes.com/2024/04/12/opinion/choking-teen-sex-brain-damage.html.
25. Lucy Cocoran, "Women Are Finding Themselves Being Strangled During Sex—The Consequences Can Be Deadly," *Elle*, April 26, 2022, https://www.elle.com.au/culture/sexual-choking-strangulation-dangers-26953. See Debby Herbenick, Tsung-Chieh Fu, et al., "Prevalence and characteristics of choking/strangulation during sex: Findings from a probability survey of undergraduate students," *Journal of American College Health* 71, no. 4

(2023): 1059–73, https://pubmed.ncbi.nlm.nih.gov/34242530/: "A 2021 study of more than 4,000 university students in the United States found that more than a quarter of women (26.5%) and more than one-fifth of trans and non-binary students (22.3%) had been choked during their most recent sexual encounter."

26. K. C. Basile, S. G. Smith, et al., "The National Intimate Partner and Sexual Violence Survey: 2016/2017 Report on Sexual Violence," CDC: National Center for Injury Prevention and Control, June 2022, https://www.cdc.gov/nisvs/documentation/nisvsReportonSexualViolence.pdf. "Preventing Sexual Violence," CDC, archived July 14, 2020, at https://web.archive.org/web/20200714023903/https://www.cdc.gov/violenceprevention/sexualviolence/fastfact.html.
27. Sheila Wray Gregoire, *The Great Sex Rescue: The Lies You've Been Taught and How to Recover What God Intended* (Baker Books, 2021), 186.
28. Gregoire, *The Great Sex Rescue*, chapter 10.
29. Clinton had been charged with sexual harassment in a civil lawsuit brought by Paula Jones in 1994. During the pretrial hearing, he lied under oath by denying that he had sexual relations with a White House intern. Impeachment charges against him were perjury and obstruction of justice, not abusing his power and authority. He was later acquitted and settled the Jones lawsuit in 1998.
30. "Larry Nassar case: The 156 women who confronted a predator," BBC, January 15, 2018, https://www.bbc.com/news/world-us-canada-42725339. Juliet Macur, "Nassar Abuse Survivors Reach a $380 Million Settlement," *New York Times*, December 13, 2021, https://www.nytimes.com/2021/12/13/sports/olympics/nassar-abuse-gymnasts-settlement.html.
31. "Victims of Sexual Violence: Statistics," RAINN, accessed April 17, 2025, https://www.rainn.org/statistics/victims-sexual-violence.
32. I am referring to nonmedical, nonreconstructive plastic surgery here.
33. Jonathan Grant, *Divine Sex: A Compelling Vision for Christian Relationships in a Hypersexualized Age* (Brazos Press, 2015), 24.
34. Grant, *Divine Sex,* 17.
35. Amy Peeler, *Women and the Gender of God* (Eerdmans, 2022), 4.

Chapter 7: Baptizing Sin

1. All details and quotes from a conversation with "Emma" on March 5, 2024.
2. Mark Driscoll, "Passive Men and Controlling Women," March 10, 2023, YouTube, https://www.youtube.com/watch?v=7EAc1dZ3hUw. As of 2025, Driscoll is the head pastor of Trinity Church in Scottsdale, Arizona.
3. Warren Throckmorton, "Twenty-One Former Mars Hill Church Pastors Bring Formal Charges Against Mark Driscoll," author's website, August 21, 2014, https://wthrockmorton.com/2014/08/21/former-mars-hill-church

-pastors-bring-formal-charges-against-mark-driscoll/. "Statement of Formal Charges and Issues—Mark Driscoll," https://wthrockmorton.com/wp-content/uploads/2014/08/FormalCharges-Driscoll-814.pdf. Also see *Christianity Today*'s podcast series on Mars Hill, "The Rise and Fall of Mars Hill," hosted by Mike Cosper, June–August 2021, https://podcasts.apple.com/us/podcast/the-rise-and-fall-of-mars-hill/id1569401963.

4. Emma learned this detail via someone who attended the meeting.
5. Perhaps the only thing women were not invited to do was to become one of the twelve disciples. Some biblical scholars believe that was due to social mores of the time and the way that the twelve apostles represented the original twelve tribes of Israel.
6. Marg Mowczko, "A List of the 29 People in Romans 16:1–16," author's website, May 18, 2019, https://margmowczko.com/list-of-people-in-romans-16_1-16. Accessed July 17, 2024.
7. Tertullian, from *De Cultu Feminarium (On the Apparel of Women)*, chapter 1; accessed at Marg Mowczko, "Misogynistic Quotations from Church Fathers and Reformers," January 24, 2013, https://margmowczko.com/misogynist-quotes-from-church-fathers/.
8. Augustine, from *De Genesi ad literam* (*The Literal Meaning of Genesis*), 9.5.9; accessed at Marg Mowczko, "Misogynistic Quotations from Church Fathers and Reformers," January 24, 2013, https://margmowczko.com/misogynist-quotes-from-church-fathers/.
9. David E. Fitch, *Reckoning with Power: Why the Church Fails When It's on the Wrong Side of Power* (Brazos Press, 2024), 77.
10. There were notable exceptions here, such as the Hagia Sophia in Istanbul, Turkey.
11. Sandra Glahn, *Nobody's Mother: Artemis of the Ephesians in Antiquity and the New Testament* (InterVarsity Press, 2023), 24–25.
12. For more information on female spiritual leaders during the Middle Ages and Age of Reformation, please turn to the scholarship of Beth Allison Barr, Katharine Bushnell, Alice Mathews, Lucy Peppiatt, Carolyn Custis James, Sandra Glahn, and Marg Mowczko.
13. The Danvers Statement, The Council on Biblical Manhood and Womanhood, CBMW.org, https://cbmw.org/about/danvers-statement.
14. The Council on Biblical Manhood and Womanhood used the KJV for their work and based their interpretations on several key passages in Scripture, including the household codes. These include Ephesians 5–6 and Colossians 3–4. Other key passages include Genesis 3 and 1 Timothy 2:11–15.
15. Many people seem to think that the concepts complementarian and egalitarian are mutually exclusive. Someone can hold to complementarianism and equality. And vice versa. It's beyond the scope of this book to explore

all the relevant Scriptures, historic contexts, and exegesis necessary for one to make informed conclusions regarding this issue. I personally believe that men and women complement each other by design and are equal, and I disagree with CBMW's positions and the Danvers Statement.

16. January 30, 2025
17. Aimee Byrd, *Recovering form Biblical Manhood and Womanhood: How the Church Needs to Rediscover Her Purpose* (Zondervan, 2020), 111.
18. Fitch, *Reckoning with Power,* 11–12.
19. Terry Gross, host, "How the Southern Baptist Convention Covered Up Its Widespread Sexual Abuse Scandal," NPR, June 2, 2022, https://www.npr.org/2022/06/02/1102621352/how-the-southern-baptist-convention-covered-up-its-widespread-sexual-abuse-scand.
20. Diane Langberg, *Redeeming Power: Understanding Authority and Abuse in the Church* (Brazos Press, 2020), 54.
21. Michael J. Kruger, *Bully Pulpit: Confronting the Problem of Spiritual Abuse in the Church* (Zondervan, 2023), 24.
22. All quotes from an interview with "Miriam" on March 21, 2025.
23. I have heard multiple men describe female worship leaders in this sexualized way.
24. Carolyn Custis James, "Dismantling Patriarchy to Recover the Blessed Alliance," *Missio Alliance,* May 21, 2024, https://www.missioalliance.org/dismantling-patriarchy-to-recover-the-blessed-alliance-part-1/.
25. Heather Matthews, *Confronting Sexism in the Church: How We Got Here and What We Can Do About It* (InterVarsity Press, 2024), 42.
26. Tia Levings, *A Well-Trained Wife: My Escape from Christian Patriarchy* (St. Martin's Press, 2024), 146.
27. Beth Moore, "A Letter to My Brothers," The LPM Blog, May 3, 2018, https://blog.lproof.org/2018/05/a-letter-to-my-brothers.html.
28. Jesse T. Jackson, "Two Years Later, Beth Moore Addresses John MacArthur Telling Her to 'Go Home,'" ChurchLeaders, February 4, 2022, https://churchleaders.com/news/416530-two-years-later-beth-moore-addresses-john-macarthur-telling-her-to-go-home.html. Also see Maywood Church, YouTube, https://www.youtube.com/watch?v=tO9JWqJJmdo. Accessed August 24, 2024.
29. In 2023, Reuters reported that more than two hundred thousand children had been abused by Catholic clergy in France over a seventy-year period: Tangi Salaün and Ingrid Melander, "French clergy sexually abused over 200,000 children since 1950, report finds," Reuters, October 5, 2021, https://www.reuters.com/world/europe/report-finds-216000-children-were-victims-french-clergy-sex-abuse-since-1950-2021-10-05/. The US has never compiled such a comprehensive report, and therefore the total number of abuses in this country is not known. Matt Ford, "America Still

Hasn't Reckoned with Its Own Catholic Child Abuse Scandal," New Republic, October 7, 2021, https://newrepublic.com/article/163905/france-catholic-church-abuse-scandal-american-reckoning.

30. "The Sexual Abuse of Children in the Roman Catholic Archdiocese of Boston: A Report by the Attorney General," Commonwealth of Massachusetts, July 23, 2003, https://www.mass.gov/doc/the-sexual-abuse-of-children-in-the-roman-catholic-archdiocese-of-boston/download.
31. Matt Carroll, Sacha Pfeiffer, and Michael Rezendes, "Church allowed abuse by priest for years," *Boston Globe*, January 6, 2002, http://www.bostonglobe.com/news/special-reports/2002/01/06/church-allowed-abuse-priest-for-years/cSHfGkTlrAt25qKGvBuDNM/story.html.
32. Robert Downen, Lise Olsen, and John Tedesco, "20 Years, 700 Victims: Southern Baptist Sexual Abuse Spreads as Leaders Resist Reforms," *Houston Chronicle*, February 10, 2019, updated January 31, 2022, https://www.houstonchronicle.com/news/investigations/abuse-of-faith/.
33. Downen et al., "20 Years, 700 Victims."
34. Downen et al., "20 Years, 700 Victims."
35. "Southern Baptist leaders release a previously secret list of accused sexual abusers," NPR, May 27, 2022, https://www.npr.org/2022/05/27/1101734793/southern-baptist-sexual-abuse-list-released. Accessed April 15, 2024. Most but not all of those on the list were affiliated with SBC churches.
36. SBC is not a denomination but rather a loosely affiliated group of churches. Statistically, only a small percentage of these churches provided a home for abusers. Assuming that they agree to church polity and pay their annual dues, they are free to hire, fire, and offer platforms to whomever they wish—including known pedophiles and abusers.
37. Gross, "How the Southern Baptist Convention Covered Up."
38. Elizabeth Dias and Ruth Graham, "Southern Baptists Move to Purge Churches with Female Pastors," *New York Times*, June 13, 2023, https://www.nytimes.com/2023/06/13/us/southern-baptist-movement-women-pastors.html.
39. Isaac Chotiner, interview with Kate Shellnut, "Decades of Sexual-Abuse Coverups in the Southern Baptist Convention," *New Yorker*, May 26, 2022, https://www.newyorker.com/news/q-and-a/decades-of-sexual-abuse-coverups-in-the-southern-baptist-convention.
40. Christa Brown, *Baptistland: A Memoir of Abuse, Betrayal, and Transformation* (Lake Drive Books, 2024), 238. Gross, "How the Southern Baptist Convention Covered up Its Widespread Sexual Abuse Scandal."
41. Quoted in Chotiner, "Decades of Sexual-Abuse Coverups."
42. This 2023 article claims that a 2010 study showed men pastored 88 percent of Protestant churches in the US: Andrew S. Denney, "Child Sex Abusers

in Protestant Christian Churches: An Offender Typology," QC, January 2, 2023, https://www.qualitativecriminology.com/pub/osa148h6/release/2.

43. Liz Lykins, "Liberty University Hit with Record $14 Million Fine for Clery Act Violations," *Roys Report*, March 5, 2024, https://julieroys.com/liberty-university-hit-with-record-14-million-fine-for-clery-act-violations/.
44. Lisa Desjardins, "Congress passes law banning non-disclosure agreements in sexual harassment cases," PBS, November 23, 2022, https://www.pbs.org/newshour/show/congress-passes-law-banning-non-disclosure-agreements-in-sexual-harassment-cases; https://www.congress.gov/bill/117th-congress/senate-bill/4524.
45. Interview with Hannah Anderson, March 2024. It's not uncommon for pastors to advise abused wives not to talk about their abuse and to "stay and pray" rather than helping them do whatever it takes to protect themselves and their children.
46. Langberg, *Redeeming Power*, 83.
47. Matthews, *Confronting Sexism in the Church*, 47.

Chapter 8: Naming Our Needs and Broken Places

1. Unless otherwise noted, all quotes from Andrew Bauman are from a May 2024 interview.
2. Andrew Bauman, *How Not to Be an *ss: Essays on Becoming a Good and Safe Man* (independently published, 2021), 5.
3. For example, belittling, shaming, diminishment, verbal threats, and controlling behaviors.
4. Judith Lewis Herman, *Trauma and Recovery: The Aftermath of Violence—from Domestic Abuse to Political Terror* (Basic Books, 1997), 28.
5. Aundi Kolber, *Try Softer: A Fresh Approach to Move Us Out of Anxiety, Stress, and Survival Mode—and into a Life of Connection and Joy* (Tyndale, 2020), 34–35.
6. Interview with "Mindy," May 2023.
7. Historian and college professor Kristin Kobes Du Mez details this in her book *Jesus and John Wayne.*
8. Unless otherwise noted, all quotes from Andrew Bauman are from a May 2024 interview.
9. For example, in his book *The Care and Feeding of Children*, well-known pediatrician Dr. Luther Holt advocated that young babies should never be played with and should be sleep trained and that mothers should adhere to strict feeding and training practices with their babies. Dr. William Sears started writing about and advocating for attachment parenting in the 1980s.
10. James J. Gross and Oliver P. John, "Individual differences in two emotion regulation processes: implications for affect, relationships, and well-being,"

Journal of Personality and Social Psychology 85, no. 2 (2003): 348–62, https://citeseerx.ist.psu.edu/document?repid=rep1&type=pdf&doi=1e1b482036d74c00258b912568ac6c98f0b6d450. Benjamin P Chapman, Kevin Fiscella, et al., "Emotion Suppression and Mortality Risk over a 12-Year Follow-Up," *Journal of Psychosomatic Research* 75, no. 4 (October 2013): 381–85, https://doi.org/10.1016/j.jpsychores.2013.07.014.

11. *Mansplaining* is a term coined by Rebecca Solnit. She writes about it here: "Men Explain Things to Me," *Guernica*, August 20, 2012, https://www.guernicamag.com/rebecca-solnit-men-explain-things-to-me/.
12. All quotes with Kathy Khang taken from emails exchanges, January 24 through February 3, 2025.
13. Kolber, *Try Softer*, 15.
14. See Mark 2:17.
15. Obviously, not all the areas of brokenness and need we experience are directly connected to misogyny. Many of us will need the help of a trained therapist to do this work.
16. All quotes from an interview with Sheila Wise Rowe on June 11, 2024.
17. Soong-Chan Rah, *Prophetic Lament: A Call for Justice in Troubled Times* (IVP, 2015), 44.
18. Brenda Salter McNeil, *Empowered to Repair: Becoming People Who Mend Broken Systems and Heal Our Communities* (Brazos Press, 2024), 47–48.
19. Aubrey Sampson, *The Louder Song: Listening for Hope in the Midst of Lament* (NavPress, 2019), 12–13.
20. For example, Psalms 6, 10, 13, 38, and 88.
21. Dorothy Littell Greco, *Making Marriage Beautiful: Lifelong Love, Joy, and Intimacy Start with You* (David C Cook, 2017), 25.
22. Rah, *Prophetic Lament*, 131.
23. Thabiti Anyabwile, "An Apology to Beth Moore and My Sisters," *The Gospel Coalition* (blog), May 3, 2018, https://www.thegospelcoalition.org/blogs/thabiti-anyabwile/apology-beth-moore-sisters/.
24. Rah, *Prophetic Lament*, 123, 131.
25. Greco, *Making Marriage Beautiful*, 148.
26. Everett Worthington, *Five Steps to Forgiveness: The Art and Science of Forgiving* (Crown, 2001).
27. Dorothy Littell Greco, "Is the Gospel the Antidote to Misogyny?" CBE International, August 14, 2018, https://www.cbeinternational.org/resource/gospel-antidote-misogyny/. Accessed July 9, 2024.
28. All quotes from an interview with Natalie on April 19, 2024.
29. Email exchange with Pastor Thabiti Anyabwile, June 2024.
30. All quotes from an interview with Katelyn Beaty on July 9, 2024.
31. It's also incredibly complicated if one's marriage is abusive. It's beyond the

scope of this book to address this issue. If you find yourself in an abusive marriage, please seek help. Information is listed in the appendix.

Chapter 9: Imagine If . . .

1. All quotes from an interview with Karen Swallow Prior on May 31, 2024.
2. All quotes from an interview with David Swanson on August 19, 2024.
3. Scott Russell Sanders, *The Way of Imagination: Essays* (Counterpoint, 2020), 33.
4. Karen Swallow Prior, *The Evangelical Imagination: How Stories, Images and Metaphors Created a Culture in Crisis* (Brazos Press, 2023), 7.
5. Prior, *The Evangelical Imagination*, 5.
6. "Factbox: Which are the world's 10 most dangerous countries for women?" Reuters, June 25, 2018, https://www.reuters.com/article/world/factbox-which-are-the-worlds-10-most-dangerous-countries-for-women-idUSKBN1JM01Z/. The US is listed 10th after Yemen, Saudi Arabia, and other Islamic countries.
7. bell hooks, *The Will to Change: Men, Masculinity, and Love* (Washington Square Press, 2002), 18.
8. Interview with author and pastor Mandy Smith on July 9, 2024.
9. W. Brad Johnson and David G. Smith, "Men, Stop Calling Yourselves Allies," *Harvard Business Review*, August 5, 2022, https://hbr.org/2022/08/men-stop-calling-yourselves-allies-act-like-one.
10. Johnson and Smith, "Men, Stop Calling Yourselves Allies. Act Like One."
11. Carolyn Custis James, *Half the Church: Recapturing God's Global Vision for Women* (Zondervan, 2015), excerpted in "The Blessed Alliance," September 18, 2012, https://carolyncustisjames.com/2012/09/18/the-blessed-alliance/.
12. All quotes from an interview with Dr. Kathy Drage Lines on August 14, 2024.
13. All quotes from an interview with Lisa Rodriguez-Watson on August 15, 2024.
14. Referencing Dr. Andrew Bauman's terminology here.
15. Viktor E. Frankl, *Man's Search for Meaning: An Introduction to Logotherapy* (Simon & Schuster, 1984 edition), 154.